AF224929

Lighting the Lamp

CEDAR RAPIDS RACOONS

LASAIRIONA MCMASTER

DRUMA LLAMA PUBLISHING

Dedication

In memory of

Adam Johnson
1994 – 2023
Rest in Peace

32. de la Peña

2. de la Peña

91. Raine (a)

71. Shaw

26. Ashe (c)

17. de la Peña

CEDAR RAPIDS
RACCOONS

CHAPTER 1
Victoria
THREE YEARS AGO

"Victoria Barnett?"

"Yeah?"

"Ma'am, you're under arrest." The cop towers over me, hands planted on his hips, lips in a grim line, brow wrinkled with a scowl. His starched, navy-blue shirt pulls over his broad shoulders, and a pair of shiny chrome handcuffs dangle from his index finger.

He doesn't move. His expression doesn't change. There's a challenging glint in those dark, almost black eyes.

Some of my classmates shift in their seats. Someone—I bet it's my best friend—is giggling so hard I wouldn't be surprised if she pisses her pants. Bet she paid for my warrant in this whole charade.

The early afternoon sun shines off the cars in the parking lot, making me squint. There's no use fighting it. I can't even say I have classes to attend. After this one, my afternoon is wide open. And from the bemused smirk on my teacher's face, he's in cahoots with my best friend.

Instead of arguing, I offer my wrists to the law enforcement officer with a heavy sigh.

"You have the right to remain silent."

Someone snorts behind me, and it takes all my strength not to flip him off. I guess this is my punishment for coming home. Or perhaps for leaving in the first place.

I'm not sure what I was thinking. Moving out of state for college wasn't everything it was cracked up to be. I mean, it was, until my no good, piece of shit, jock boyfriend banged his resident adviser. Repeatedly. In the quad for all to see.

Combined with the worst homesickness I bet anyone has ever felt in the history of the world... Well, let's just say, I'm glad the University of Cedar Rapids let me come home.

When I pull myself to my feet, the police officer cuffs my hands behind my back. Someone whispers something I can't quite make out. I let my head drop forward, then the cop's enormous hand grips right above my elbow as he starts to half-walk half-drag my ass out the door.

I should have known.

I should have invested in the "get out of jail free" card that was dangled in my face this morning. But I took the risk. Do the crime, do the time—isn't that what they say?

I was arrogant to think I'd get away with it, that my friends would let me just slide back into the space I created when I left them for a hot-shot hockey player.

But here we are. It's all in good humor and for a good cause, so I shouldn't be *too* upset about it. Even if it's mildly inconvenient.

After he folds me unceremoniously into the back of a squad car, the officer settles in the front seat and hits a button. An ear-piercing siren fractures the air around me, swallowing my groan.

This can't be happening.

Heat consumes my body as we do a couple laps of the university at a snail's pace. It's almost like the cop wants my peers to point and stare. A couple guys wave their "get out of jail free" cards at me through the window, and despite my hands being cuffed, I most definitely flip them off.

When we pull up to the doors of jail, my stomach grumbles. I skipped lunch. Playing catch up on college work plus the whole life I "abandoned" hasn't been fun, but I'm nothing if not determined.

There's a granola bar in my backpack, back at my desk, but that's not helpful to me right now. And I bet Officer Scowly didn't bring snacks on this adventure.

At the front desk, there's a "mugshot" of me sitting next to some paperwork. My whole body cringes. I don't know where they got the photo, but it's a doozy. Could have sworn I deleted it from all my socials. I hope Mom doesn't see it—she'd never let me outside again. Her darling daughter doesn't do such crass things as drink liquor or leave the house scantily clad.

The mean-muggin' receptionist offers me a pen, and I shrug. I'm good, but I'm not write-with-my-hands-cuffed-behind-my-back good. Keys jingle behind me, and my arms are freed from their cold, hard prison.

I rub at my wrists, because isn't that what everyone does when they get released from metal handcuffs? Sue me. I'm leaning into the cliché.

I fill in the paperwork, accept the wholly unflattering bright orange jumpsuit and the list of phone numbers with another sigh, and turn to face my gated fate. There's about a dozen pretty lifelike looking prison cells in a horse-shoe-shape around the space that could be a gymnasium or an event space depending on the decor.

Today, it's a prison. With an intake desk, a receptionist, and metal rail cells lining the room.

Thankfully, my cell is otherwise unoccupied. It's just me. Will my luck hold out? I'm not taking my clothes off in front of these people, so I jerk the onesie over my clothes before reviewing the list. My best friend's name is printed in tidy black letters across the top of the page next to her number.

Should I even bother making my phone call?

Would anyone come to my rescue?

My best friend, Jazz, howls with laughter when the call connects.

Bitch.

If this whole debacle wasn't for a charity, I'd give her a piece of my mind right about now.

"What's the slammer like, Vic? Has anyone made you their bitch yet?"

My lips twitch. And I don't fight the eye roll this time. "Just pay my damn bail."

She snorts. "Nope."

"The fuck you mean, nope?"

As soon as the cop appeared at my desk in class, I suspected she'd been the one to pay for my warrant. The cackling behind me in class only partly gave it away. At only ten bucks a pop to get someone arrested, she'll probably have half the school thrown into fake jail before the day's done.

She laughs again. "You're stuck, Vic. There's no way out. No one is coming to save you." She sniffs, and something brushes against the speaker like she might be wiping away tears of utter hilarity from her cheeks. "It doesn't matter who you call, I've made sure you can't get out." The crack of hands slapping together with glee meets my ears through the phone speaker.

Groaning, I drag a hand over my face. "You paid to keep me here the whole time?"

"And then some." Her voice is laced with delight. "It's all for a good cause."

"Yeah, yeah." It is. But that doesn't mean I want to spend an hour of study time in a cage looking like an exotic bird in this damn orange suit.

"Get comfy. You never know. Maybe your Prince Charming will get sent to prison too, and you'll live happily ever after." Her voice breaks on the last line as she dissolves into even more frenzied laughter.

I suppose it could be worse. She could have not given a shit that I left Iowa at all. If sending my ass to prison for a fundraiser is as much punishment as I'm going to get, I guess I should shut up and do my time.

"Fine." I huff out a puff of air. "But no princes. No more men."

"They aren't all like that enormous dickwad you ran away to Colorado with."

Prickles of pain radiate through my chest like each of her words lands a direct hit as a fresh wave of heat sears the back of my neck. I've known Jazz since we were awkward teens at band camp, but I'll never get used to her being so...on the nose.

"No more men." I'm resolved. Really. I am. No dick is worth a broken heart.

"How about no more hockey players."

"Fine. No more hockey players," I repeat with a firm nod.

And I mean it.

Movement to my right pulls my attention outside my fake cell. Fresh prisoner meat approaches the check-in desk. If the light didn't catch his super dark hair I'd say it was black, but it's got hints of red in it. Is he a redhead too?

His lopsided smile with a glimmer of mischief doesn't work on the woman at reception—she still processes him into fake-jail—but I bet he gets his way more often than not.

"Vic?" Jazz is on the other end of the phone. I'm glad she can't see me drooling over whoever the guy walking toward my cell right now is. I'm already retracting my "no more men" manifesto for this one. I can put my man hating in temporary time out.

His smile lights up the room, which considering it's

January in Iowa is pretty hard to do. And he's not even smiling directly at me.

"Vic?"

"Gotta go." Hanging up, I attempt to smooth out my unruly auburn curls with my palms. I should have washed it this morning, dammit. Matted pre-wash-day curls are the worst.

Actually, a bright orange jumpsuit on a redhead is the worst.

There's no fixing this.

My phone buzzes on my thigh.

> Jazz: Did Prince Charming show up?

> Victoria: No. But I do have a cellmate.

> Jazz: Is he cute?

The air in the makeshift cell changes as he plops down on the bench about a foot to my left.

"No hockey players, eh? Someone do you dirty? I know some people. We could make sure they never find his body." He crosses his long, muscular legs at his ankles, and stretches back, tucking both hands behind his head as he leans against the wall.

> Jazz: He's cute, isn't he?

The weight of his stare on my face makes me turn to look at him. His blue eyes dance with delight and appraisal. My dude must have hit his head if he thinks his Prison Chic look is going to get him anywhere.

> Victoria: No.

Jazz: Maybe your time together in the big
house will change your mind.

My stomach growls so loudly the woman at the desk glances over the top of her purple-rimmed glasses, and no amount of silent praying makes the ground open up and swallow me.

The guy beside me pats his stomach. "I could go for some food too, now that you mention it."

Getting to his feet, he flashes me another grin before making his way to the bars. He's pulled on his jumpsuit halfway, over the top of his jeans and graphic tee. It hangs limp around his waist. Somehow he makes it work.

"Sy?" My cellmate taps the bars, jerking his head at someone I can't see. I don't know how they got real life cells assembled in the local community center, but they'll need a truck or something to pull them down again.

The real cop who fake-arrested me comes into view.

"Pass my backpack?"

The straight-faced officer quirks a brow. "Do I look like your fucking servant?"

"Please?" Even with his back to me, I can tell he's smiling.

With a grunt, Officer Sy turns away and after a beat or two comes back with an army green canvas bag. He opens the cell door, hands over the bag, and closes it again, smug satisfaction settling on his face as he secures the lock in place.

"Thanks, Sy. 'Preciate it. Tate been picked up yet?" The broad-shouldered hottie with his back to me jerks open the bag and sticks his arm inside.

Stifling a giggle at how much he looks like Mary Poppins right now, his arm disappearing almost all the way inside the canvas bag, I avert my gaze.

"Not yet. I get to pick him up later."

I sneak another glance in their direction at the tone of the officer's voice. Something almost menacing crosses his face as my cellmate chuckles, his shoulders bobbing. I'm missing an inside joke, but whoever Tate is, he seems to have pissed off this cop. He's going to take great pleasure in locking him up, even if it's fake jail.

When my cellmate turns back to me, he's holding something in my direction. "Here."

I'm almost sure there are sandwiches in the brown paper bag within arm's reach. And it's tempting. But just because he has a beautiful face, a strong jaw, and blindingly blue eyes doesn't mean I'm going to eat any old thing he hands me.

As though reading my mind, he sinks back onto the bench next to me, drops the pack at his feet, and opens the paper bag in his hand. Pulling out two halves of a sandwich, he makes yummy noises. Loudly.

After taking a huge bite out of one half, he beams at me. How does he even make eating a brown bag lunch look sexy?

Is he having an orgasmic experience right now? The bliss on his face would lead me to believe he is.

He slides closer, until his thigh touches mine, then offers the other half to me. With a growl of encouragement from my digestive system, I relent despite realizing that it's peanut butter and jelly. Having it damn near every day as a kid has made me generally not a fan.

Mom worked three jobs just to make ends meet, and when those ends met, PB&J was the flavor of the month. Every month. But something's different about this one. Something extra. An x factor I can't place.

"It's honey." His thumb sweeps across my bottom lip, then he sucks it into his mouth with a low moan. It's an incredibly intimate touch from a stranger without any buildup of mutual attraction or flirting beforehand.

He didn't even hesitate before doing it, and I'm too perplexed to jerk away.

Am I horrified? Turned on? I'm not sure. His close proximity is stifling even as the scent of cinnamon and peanut butter overpowers my senses.

"What is?" The words catch in the back of my throat. I'd love to say it's the thick peanut butter coating the inside of my mouth, but something's bewitching about this guy that suggests I need to put as much distance between us as I can.

"My secret ingredient." His gaze flickers to my lips for a beat longer than is probably acceptable before resting on my eyes again. "I drizzle honey on it. Sometimes I sprinkle sea salt, but this one," He waves his half-eaten sandwich at me. "This one has honey."

"Oh." My body sags as he sits back to finish his sandwich. I'm not sure what the fuck is happening right now. I'm not this doe-eyed, breathless fool when it comes to guys.

Sure, I dropped my life and moved to a school I had no interest in to support my hockey-playing boyfriend, but that's beside the point. In this moment, I'm not letting my vagina get the better of me. I'm in control. Me. Not my hormones. Not this grinning man-child with sandwiches in his backpack. *Me.*

He clears his throat, drawing my attention to another sandwich outstretched in his hand. He's already plowing through his half.

"You just carry sandwiches around, waiting for the perfect picnic opportunity?"

He shakes his head. "Did I expect to be incarcerated with a beautiful woman today? Absolutely not. Am I mad about it?" He shrugs. "Also no." He polishes off his sandwich with another bite. "But I'm always prepared." He pauses before hurling an exaggerated wink my direction. "For snack time."

Pretty sure tiny pieces of bread spray from my mouth as I snort out a laugh. "Does that line ever work?" He's hitting on me, right? While I'm not in the market for another relationship quite so soon after breaking up with Mark, I'm not averse to having a hot, one-night stand with my fellow prisoner.

Another head shake precedes him pulling two bottles of water from his bag and pointing one at me with a lazy grin. "Never tried it before today." This guy is so laid back he should be horizontal. I've never met someone who smiles as much either.

I suppose if my face looked like that when I smiled, I would smile as often as he does too.

He gestures at the phone in my lap. "Not making any more calls to escape lock up?"

"I'm stuck here for the duration, I'm afraid. Forty-nine minutes and counting." I wave my screen at him.

He chuckles. "I think you'll find that's one hundred and nine minutes and counting."

My stomach drops. Two whole hours? Motherfucker. I thought it was an hour.

His chuckle deepens into a laugh, shaking the bench under our butts. "Don't look so happy about it."

Ugh. I don't even have my books to do some studying. "You think your buddy Officer Sy would go grab my books from school?"

The open water bottle destined for his mouth pauses in mid-air as he gasps. "You mean you don't want to spend the rest of the next two hours in my wonderful company?" He lowers the bottle with a sad shake of his head and clutches his chest with his free hand. "I'd be offended, but you don't know how awesome I am yet."

The way he says "yet" makes something tingle in my stomach.

"And he's my buddy Tate's brother. Sawyer. Actually hates being called Sy."

"So naturally that's what you call him." I nod as though it makes perfect sense.

"Naturally." He twists the cap on his bottle. "It's a sign of affection. He's probably too busy doing important cop things to run and get your books."

At my sigh, he nudges my knee with his. "Don't sweat it. I'm not so bad once you get to know me."

"What about you?" I return his nudge. "Aren't you calling your boy squad to be rescued? Surely a guy like you can raise a hundred bucks in no time." I imagine he has droves of friends. Even if ten of them give ten bucks a piece into the pot, he could be out in fifteen minutes, twenty tops.

He watches me patiently until I turn so I'm staring straight into his captivating eyes. "I'm right where I'm supposed to be, Firecracker."

CHAPTER 2

Raffi

Cheese is my favorite food.

But even I cringe at just how tacky the words are that come falling out of my mouth. I usually have more game than this. Better game. Jeez. I'd take any fucking game at all right now.

Dunno what it is about the enchanting, fiery-haired goddess next to me in this pseudo prison, but she's got me tangled up in knots.

Her eye roll confirms two things. One, I'm most definitely lacking in game. And two, she has the most beautiful jade eyes I have ever had the pleasure of staring into.

A rap on the bars makes me jump.

"Bail's paid." Sawyer smirks at me.

Bolting across the cell, I shake my head before dropping my voice. "Got the wrong man, officer. I'm staying put."

"You'll have to match the bail to stay put for the duration. Them's the rules of the fundraiser." He shrugs like there's nothing he can do about it despite the fact we both know there's something he could do about it. That's what I get for pissing him off with the Sy thing, I guess.

A quick glance over my shoulder at the redhead who's pretending to assess her nails confirms it. The money I've been saving up to buy new Airpods is going to be spent on time with this woman. If I can't woo her in the next ninety minutes, then I deserve to lose the hundred bucks anyway. And the girl.

Even if the American Society for Deaf Children wasn't so near and dear to my heart, it's a damn good cause. "Give me an hour."

He shakes his head before holding out his hand. With a dejected sigh, I drop my wallet into it. I'm now officially on the hook for a hundred bucks. I can't say I've ever paid to have the pleasure of the company of a beautiful woman, but something about this one tells me she's worth it.

Unsure of how much my cellmate has heard, I pause to evaluate my next steps. How can I make her adore me in the next ninety minutes?

Mom tells me almost every day I have a winning personality. But she's my mother, and she's supposed to say that. Not only that, but the firecracker pretending not to stare at my ass has declared she hates hockey players. I'm already starting at a deficit.

Definitely don't lead with the fact I play hockey.

Considering this woman has—as recently as five minutes ago—sworn off men forever, most notably hockey-playing men, giving her a fake name feels safer than not.

"Loki." My outstretched hand hovers in the space between us.

She cants her head, not taking her gaze off my fingers for a long moment. "Really?" Her single, perfectly manicured brow arches high.

With a shrug, I try smiling again. Don't think she fell for it the first ten times, but if it makes her smile back at me, even once, even just a half smile, I bet it'll be worth it.

Another eye roll, a sigh, and her pale hand slides into mine. "Sigyn."

It's my turn to tilt my head. "Huh?"

"You went the Marvel route, didn't you?"

Heat fills my cheeks. "God of Mischief." Brushing the back of my neck does little to cool my face.

"Loki's wife is Sigyn in Norse mythology." She says it so nonchalantly, just tossing it out like it isn't the coolest thing someone's said to me today.

"I guess if he had a wife in the movies it would piss a hell of a lot of women off."

That makes her...not quite smile but there's a flicker of amusement that's hard to miss and I want to try harder. Damn, this woman is a tough nut to crack.

Her expression is locked up tight and surrounded by barbed wire. Her impassive face rivals Mom's, and that's saying something. It's a truth universally acknowledged that mothers have the best poker faces.

This firecracker hugs her stomach like she's protecting herself. The slight slump of her shoulders and how she holds herself, is she self-conscious? My mom used to contort herself to hide her body.

It's a guess based on nothing at all other than having lived with Mom my whole damn life and having seen her act the exact same way. Why the hell do beautiful women think they need to be skinny to be beautiful? I dunno. But lots of them certainly seem to.

"I mean, I'd do him." Her shoulder hitches and that flicker of amusement is back as the corners of her lips curve just a bit.

Him who? I got pulled out of the moment by the counterpoint of her vocal confidence with how she's defensively curling her arms around her stomach.

I doubt she's talking about doing me. Though it would kinda be nice.

Sy? Oh, Loki. Right. I mean, who wouldn't do him? "I'm straight, but even I'd consider doing Tom Hiddleston."

She nods. "Makes sense. I'm straight, but I'd totally consider doing Scarlett Johansson."

My heart skips faster. "You like Marvel?"

That impassive look tells me I asked a stupid question. Does she look at herself in the mirror and spend time practicing casual poker face?

"I might," she allows.

"What else do you like?" I'm leaning toward her now, like I'm being pulled into her orbit, as though one morsel of information about who she is, what she likes, might be the key to unlocking why I'm so drawn to her.

I can't say it's love at first sight, but I'm definitely smitten, and her cool, don't-give-a-fuck vibes only serve to lure me in even more.

"I didn't say I liked Marvel." She has me there.

"Didn't say you didn't either. Well, I know you like PB&J."

"I liked *your* PB&J." That tiny crumb of praise makes my soul leave my body. But I'm determined to play it cool. Or at least pretend to. Externally. If only my brain could communicate the message to the dumbass smile spreading across my face.

"And you don't like hockey? Or just hockey players?"

She levels me with a flat stare that shrivels my balls.

"Okay. Noted. What about other sports? Do we hate all sportsballs and sportspeople? Or just the frozen ones?"

Her eye rolls are so impressive I might make it my mission to outdo myself with every single one. She may even have strained her eyeballs with that last one.

"I like football."

"Go Hawks. Am I right?" Hope has my heart on a fraying

string. If she's an Iowa State fan, I'm going to cry right here in fake prison.

We have our own football team here at the University of Cedar Rapids, but it's fairly new. And we suck so damn bad that most of us wish we didn't have a team at all. Even though we outwardly cheer for our own school, everyone has an inside voice cheering even louder for the Hawkeyes.

Most of us cheer out loud for them too.

"I dunno." Her tongue trails along her full bottom lip as she flicks her auburn curls over the shoulder of her orange jumpsuit. "Cy is kinda cute."

Cy is the Cardinal bird mascot thing for Iowa State. I can't quite tell if she's fucking with me until she bursts into laughter so melodic I don't care that it's at me.

"I can't even say Herky is cute. Dude's kinda scary," I say.

She laughs again. "I wouldn't fuck with him."

"Please tell me you're not a State fan, Firecracker."

"Why's that?"

"I'm not sure I can date someone who cheers for the wrong team."

She laughs again. "I'd fuck you. But I won't date you."

I shake my already spinning head. So she'd fuck me, huh? Good. Glad to know whatever spark of attraction I felt goes both ways. Though trying to send the message to my dick that this woman is a lady, and we're in a public space is taking longer than I'd like. "Oh, yes. I forgot. No more men. Ever. Except..." I gesture to my crotch. "When you need to scratch an itch."

Her nose wrinkles and a stray curl falls forward into her face. "If it's itchy, it's not coming near my vagina."

Her frankness is refreshing. I take it back. It might be a love at first sight story after all.

I want to listen to her read random words from the dictionary, rub her feet, and eat her pussy until death threatens to take me from this mortal plane.

I've played guitar since I was five years old. I wrote my first song when I was eleven and Brianna Price broke my heart by dating my best friend instead of me. I lost both my crush and my best friend, and the only outlet I had was soothing my beat-up heart through my beat-up guitar.

Never once has the urge to write music about the stranger I'm staring at crashed into me like this before.

Have I just met my muse?

I haven't picked up my guitar since the summer. Hockey has taken up all of my time. Hockey and making sure my grade point average doesn't drop.

If I fail, I get kicked out. It's that simple.

When I first earned my hockey scholarship, I foolishly thought I was home free. But if I don't maintain my grades, I lose my scholarship, and if I lose my scholarship, I'm out on my ass. My family can't afford to pay for college tuition. It's become a whole thing.

I thought I'd be fine with the pressure, but the exhaustion weighing down my muscles and the bags underlining my eyes tell a different tale.

I didn't think college would be so fucking hard. Do they want to break us before we become real adults?

What happened to all the keg parties and coasting your way through class?

I guess whoever made all those stereotypical college movies weren't athletes. If they had to factor in practice, and gym time, and game time, as well as keeping the hockey house clean, as well as, as well as, well, everything on my plate makes my head spin.

"Oh my god, is it actually itchy?" My fellow inmate leans back, face contorted in disgust as she eyes my crotch.

"Huh?"

"You went all quiet and got this weird look on your face. If your dick has issues, I'm out." She shakes her head.

A chuckle rumbles through me. "It's not itchy. I was just thinking I want to write a song about you."

Her brows furrow. "Excuse me?"

My cheeks heat again as my brain-to-mouth filter seems to be all-the-way broken. "I'm a musician." That much is true. I'm a songwriter and guitar player. That's not a lie.

The lie of omission that I play hockey digs into my skin as she takes me in.

"And I want to write a song about you."

She snorts, derision as clear as the smattering of freckles across her nose. "How many songs have you written about women?"

I pop my hip with a dramatic flourish of my hand. "A bunch actually, but generally only after they've broken my heart into tiny pieces. Never when I've just met them."

Again, her eyes widen. I don't know if she's not used to people being as frank and honest with her as I am, or if she's surprised I've had my heart broken, or surprised I have the higher brain function to write songs. Either way, I wouldn't blame her. I haven't exactly put my most competent foot forward with this woman. She has me flummoxed.

I kinda like it.

"Anyway. My point is, nothing's itchy. And since we're on the subject, everything works the way it's supposed to. Y'know. In case that piece of information matters to you."

She smirks. "I'll be the judge of whether it works the way it's supposed to or not."

Her brashness is alluring. We're bantering back and forth, sure, but something about her tone tells me I'm going to be buried balls deep in this woman by the end of the day.

And my dick, along with the rest of me, is very enthused at the idea. "One date."

"I'm sorry?"

"I want one date. Let me take you out when we get out of here."

She does a slow shake. Head, shoulders, torso, they all move from side to side with a resounding *no*. "No dating."

"No date, no dick." I'm showing all my cards, stepping through brave and going right to stupid. It could very easily push this woman the wrong way, but something deep in the center of my chest tells me I need more from her than just a good romp between the sheets.

From the way her brow and nose wrinkles, she doesn't seem as convinced as I am. Not by a long shot.

She hisses air through her teeth, her assessing gaze weighing heavily on my face. "Twenty questions. Then I'll decide about the date...and the dick."

I do a gleeful dance that ends in a mid-air heel click. The resulting eye roll is a thing of beauty. She looks around, presumably to see if anyone's watching my dorky, semi-public outburst.

"Person, place, or thing?"

She rolls her pouty pink lips before tapping a finger on her chin. "Thing."

I have about sixty minutes, and nineteen questions to make this woman agree to come on a date with me. Convincing her she loves me and we're destined to be together is going to take a little longer.

That's okay.

I'll believe in it enough until she's ready to accept that love at first sight is a thing and can happen in real life. In the meantime, I'll write songs about her auburn curls and jade eyes and hope she doesn't shank me with a filed-down toothbrush she has hidden under her bright orange jumpsuit.

CHAPTER 3

Victoria

I've never seen someone so skilled at playing Pac-Man.

Like, ever.

Wonder if he's this good at Ms. Pac-Man. Guess we'll see, she's here too.

I can't say I have much experience with video games at all to be honest, but this guy— this "Loki"—he's kickin' ass and taking names.

He's also happy as hell about it. I can't recall being around someone who radiates joy from every pore like this dude does.

He's just so fucking happy, about everything. About food, about video games, about being temporarily incarcerated in a fake prison for charity, but most of all about me saying yes to one date with him.

Golden retriever energy. That's him to a T.

It's like I've just offered to throw a tennis ball for him for a whole hour.

If he started doing zoomies or chasing his tail in circles around the room I wouldn't be surprised. His energy is boundless, his joy is contagious, and if someone's smile could channel sunshine, I'd say that's what happens when Loki smiles. Warmth prickles over my skin like I've stepped outside on a summer's day.

We've been here at the Quarter Barrel Arcade for over an hour. It's still early, but the more time I spend with Loki, the more his glow thaws the icicle dangling in my chest.

Ugh. I need to walk away.

I don't want another relationship. I don't want to like anyone else, let alone date. Or god forbid, anything more. I don't have time for another broken heart.

So I just shut it the fuck down instead.

Can't hurt if you don't feel.

But every time I'm determined to step toward the exit, Loki says or does something to draw me in even more. He's adorably endearing. And the urge to scratch behind his ear makes my fingers tingle.

He's beaten me at Karate Champ and Pole Position. Repeatedly. I thought for sure I had him on that last lap of our last race, or he'd take pity on my loser ass and let me win, just one time, but he only pushed harder and topped my score even worse.

The fact that he doesn't back down, that he's so competitive, so driven, so intent on coming first that he won't relent even for a woman he's trying to get into bed, appeals to me for some reason.

There's nothing fake with him. There's also no malice either. When it looked like I might win, he didn't sabotage me. In fact, he even cheered like I was in the finals of the Olympics while he pushed himself harder.

I regret agreeing to this date already.

If I'm not careful, I could end up catching feels. And if I let myself listen to the constant drip of the defrosting heart in my chest, it might even be too late. Does this place have a freezer? I need to re-freeze.

Out of our prison gear, he's in sneakers, sweats, and a shirt that fills out across the shoulders and biceps but hangs a little around the waist. This guy's in shape.

A shape I like a lot.

A smack on the machine and a declaration of glee draws my attention from his cute bubble butt.

"I did it, Firecracker!" He charges at me. His warm arms curl around my middle for a split second before he lifts me off the floor and spins me around and around until my breath leaves my lungs and I'm dizzy.

Can't quite tell if it's the spinning, or the fact I'm in his lickable arms—huh, who knew arms could even be lickable?—but either way, I'm breathless and my brain is whirring.

"Did what?" At least that's what I was trying to say, but he's hugging me so hard it sounds like a half-squeak, like one of those noisy dog toys is on its deathbed.

"New high score, baby!" The words are barely out of his mouth before he comes to an abrupt stop. He slides me down the front of his very hard body, and before I can ask him what the fuck he thinks he's doing touching my curls, his fingers are tangled in my hair and his lips are closing in on me.

As his mouth presses against mine, his hands cup my face. My lips part on a sigh, my body sagging against his. My ex hated public displays of affection. Well, I guess he just hated them with me, but this...this is public, consuming. It's so intense that my body vibrates as his tongue pushes into my mouth and finds mine.

He swallows the sigh that falls from my lips as he backs me against the side of the nearest video game console. His kiss is fire, his tongue possessing every part of my mouth like he has kissed me a million times before.

Sparks of something I try—and fail—to ignore tickle across my skin as he nips and tugs on my bottom lip. His kiss is every bit as playful as his personality. Fun, sweet, tender, while also being scorching hot.

A group of guys erupt into cheers behind Loki—I assume because one of them got a high score on a machine—pulling me out of whatever fever dream I was in with this guy whose real name I don't know and dropping me back to reality. A reality where I'm dry humping a stranger's rock-hard cock against the side of the Ms. Pac-Man machine in broad daylight.

Mischief sparkles back at me when I finally rescue my lips from his. They're swollen, pulsing and tingling, but he's so close, so in my space that I can't reach up to touch them. He pinches my chin between his thumb and forefinger and kisses me again, hard, claiming, no tongue, keeping his eyes open and locked with mine.

It's a kiss filled with possibilities.

A kiss I'm not ready to have right now, maybe never, but also a kiss I can't walk away from. From the minute he walked into my jail cell, I've been cuffed to this man.

Experience has taught me it's going to end in tears. But years of Disney movies keep tiny embers of hope alive somewhere deep inside me.

His lopsided grin does me in. I can't even lie to myself that I don't have a crush on this guy. I do. A stomach-fluttering crush I want to explore after only a few hours of being in his company.

My stomach growls, but all the ambient noise makes it too loud for him to hear—thank fuck.

He leans forward, his mouth brushing against the shell of my ear.

"I could eat." His voice is laced with a double meaning that makes me clench my thighs together to fight the inferno he's already sparked between my legs.

"Do you like Brussels sprouts?"

I jerk my head back in surprise and slam into something hard. "Ouch."

Before I can answer his vegetable question, he's checking my head. "You okay? How many fingers?"

A laugh bubbles out of me. "I'm fine, you weirdo, it was just a bump. And I can't say they're my first choice of vegetable, but I don't hate them."

He taps me on the nose. "Prepare to be wowed. The Quarter Barrel does maple bacon Brussels sprouts that are blow-your-mind incredible. Fuel then fuck?"

It's more of a statement than a question.

I shrug, sliding my hands up the front of his shirt and linking them behind his neck. "I think you mean fuel then fart."

A blurt of laughter explodes from him, surprising me. He's smiled and chuckled, but this is a full-on laugh that has him stepping back and doubling over in a matter of seconds.

"This is true. But don't worry—if you fart while we're having sex, I'll just pretend I didn't hear it." He winks at me.

"You're a fucking liar." I wag my finger at him. "I've known you for a half a damn minute. If I decide I want to go anywhere near your bed, and happen to fart, you'll never let me live it down."

"I'll replay it in my mind every day for the rest of my life." He's still laughing. "Come on, let me buy you sprouts."

When I don't move to follow him, he stops in his tracks and turns back to me. Planting both hands on his hips, he purses his lips. "I can see you're not convinced by my offer of fart-inducing veggies." He folds his arms and taps his bottom lip with one finger. "Pretzel bites with beer cheese dipping sauce? Parmesan truffle fries? Frickle spears?"

Pointing at him again, I shake my head. "You made that one up."

He shrugs and backs a couple feet away from me. "Guess you'll have to come find out."

As we walk to grab a table, his words echo around my

mind. *Every day for the rest of my life.* He can't really mean forever. Can he?

Was my ex the exception to the rule? It never felt like this with him, not even when we started dating. Carefree, easy, fun. Those things should all feel like good things, but instead, they just feel like red flags, and I don't know why.

Loki stops at our table and pulls out a chair. "What's it gonna be, Firecracker? Are we eating or not?"

CHAPTER 4
Raffi

Is there anything worse than a girl who's afraid to eat in front of a guy?

Considering how reluctant Sigyn was to take my sandwich, and how she sat all bunched up on the bench in jail, I was scared she'd eat like a bird. Or worse, not eat at all. Especially when I led with fucking vegetables. Could I have been any more insensitive to her weight?

Hi, you're clearly self-conscious about your size, but let me offer you some green vegetables like I'm not thinking about your appearance.

Fucking idiot.

We've polished off a selection of appetizers so she could try a few different things. And to my absolute delight, she matched me damn near bite for bite.

I love a woman with an appetite.

For food and fucking.

It took her a while to come around on the poutine—I think it was the squeaky cheese that put her off at first. But once she got used to the strangeness that is the Canadian delicacy of fries topped with cheese curds and brown gravy, she couldn't get enough.

We ended up fighting over the last few spoonfuls of sprouts, used the mozzarella sticks as pretend swords to battle over the last one, and when I reached to pick up the bill she tried to stab my hand with a fork.

She's savage, and I fucking love it.

"What's that look for? Never seen a girl pay for dinner before?"

"Actually, you're the first. But the look was more satisfaction that you ate in front of me."

She sucks her cheek into her mouth and blows it back out with a pop, tilting her head. "Why wouldn't I eat in front of you? I ate your witchcrafty sandwich earlier, remember?"

"You did, but you felt a little reluctant, and you kept hugging your stomach. I got the impression you were...I dunno. Self-conscious? Then I fucked up with the sprouts thing. I wasn't being offensive—I just really like the sprouts here and think everyone should try them." I'm in full word-vomit mode but can't seem to stop myself. "You're absolutely fucking beautiful. You're sarcastic, funny, and smart as hell, and I don't care if you never eat vegetables for the rest of your life."

Her face softens as she flashes a rare and blinding smile. "I was reluctant because a strange man offered me something from a brown paper bag in a fake prison cell. Not because I was self-conscious about eating in front of you." She chortles. "I'm definitely self-conscious about my size. Sometimes. Feels like no matter what, I try to lose weight but it doesn't go anywhere, so I'm working on liking myself just as I am. Thanks for being considerate about it, though. My ex..." Her eyes fall to something invisible on the table in front of her.

Knuckle under her chin, I tip her head back. I'm not letting her shy away from this conversation or letting her think it's a conversation she *needs* to shy away from. "What about your ex?"

She shrugs, her shoulders slumping. "Hockey player. All protein, all the time."

I wince. While a healthy, relatively balanced diet is part of my life, I also work out so much I can afford to be more lax with what I eat. But some of the guys on my team, well, they sound a lot like Sigyn's ex.

"You're absolutely fucking beautiful." I repeat my words in the hope she'll believe them.

Her cheeks turn a dark shade of red, making her freckles stand out even more. "You're just saying that because you want in my pants."

"You're right. I do want in your pants. But you're also breathtakingly stunning. And I don't care what you eat, or what you wear, or whether you work out or not. Life's too short to be miserable about how we look just because society makes us feel like shit if we don't fit into a certain box. Remember that when you're deciding whether to come out with me for a second date."

"We aren't dating."

"We'll see."

The corners of her lips twitch as she gestures at my body, then at her own. "I have rolls."

My turn to shrug. "I'll bring the butter."

She cracks up into hysterical laughter, knocking her fork off the table.

"Are we fucking? Or am I taking you home?"

Her face grows even darker at my crassness. But there's no point in beating about the bush, I desperately want to take this girl to bed, and I need her to know it.

"I could definitely be down for some fucking." She's barely finished her sentence when I bound out of my seat, offering her my hand and grabbing the pizza I insisted we get to go with the other.

"No time like the present, Firecracker. Let's blow this popsicle stand."

She ignores every one of my directions to where I live and drives us back to the dorms on campus instead. I guess she wants to pass out in her own bed when I'm done making her scream Loki's name all night.

Just as well, because if she hates her hockey playing ex, as soon as she finds out I'm on the team, this whirlwind romance and my dreams of making it something more will come crashing around my head.

I need her to be in deeper with me so the fact that I happen to play hockey won't make any difference. And I'll just keep kissing her and saying sorry until she forgives me for neglecting to disclose that fact.

It's shitty and underhanded. I'd prefer to be upfront. But she won't give me the time of day if I don't keep the truth from her. She's said as much herself. And I need her to give me a chance.

So, we're at her dorm. Truth is, I don't mind being kidnapped by this woman.

In fact, if she wanted to chain me to her bed and make me her plaything, I'd be down for that too. As long as she let me out to play hockey, anyway. Shit. She'd never let me out to play hockey, would she?

Might need to rethink the whole sex slave thing.

As soon as I step into her room, her hand brushes my arm as she reaches to close the door behind me. She leans close enough for me to sniff her, but other than the lightest brush of her lips against mine, she doesn't come close enough for me to really kiss her. And I want to *really* kiss her.

The grin she flashes me before dropping to her knees is wicked. Stuttering protests clog the back of my throat as she makes short work of freeing my cock from its cotton prison. I want to worship her. I want to tongue her clit like she's a Double Stuf Oreo, and I can't pry the sides apart to get to the cream. But my dick most definitely wants me to kick back and let her have her way with me.

The door's cold and hard against my ass as I lean back, planting my feet as wide as I can with my pants and boxers trapping my ankles. She wants full access and I'm not about to interfere.

She licks her fucking lips, giving me a split second before she sucks my already leaking dick deep into her mouth and goes to fucking town. Her mouth is soft, hot, and accommodates my rock hard cock so well.

One of her hands is gripped firmly around the base of my cock, pumping up and down toward her mouth. The other cups my balls, gently squeezing, twisting, and tugging them. My breath hitches as she sucks.

"Fuck." My heart's racing so fast I'm out of breath. My balls are already tight, my muscles coiled and ready for release. Her tongue caresses the shaft of my dick like it's her favorite thing to do.

Some girls hate giving head, but Sigyn isn't one of them. She's in it for the long haul, seemingly with no idea I'm about thirty seconds from blowing my goddamn load in the back of her throat.

My fingers curl around her hair as I start to lose my grip on self-control. My head tips back with a thud against the door. Knees start to shake. Hips jerk in an awkward rhythm trying to chase the orgasm this woman fully commands.

I should just stand here, be the passenger, but the tingling all over my fucking body makes me needy, desperate, aching to come, to reward this beautiful woman for getting on her knees and treating me like a king.

"Gonna...come." Words gritted out through clenched

teeth don't sound much like the English language, but it's the best I can do to fend off the brewing orgasm making my balls heavy.

Instead of slowing down or pulling my dick from her mouth so I don't shoot my load right at her gag reflex, she flashes that wicked smile again around my length and pumps her hand harder, sucking me deeper. Her eagerness is so fucking hot.

Jesus Christ on toast, she's sucking my soul out of my cock. Short, panting breaths splutter out as my whole body explodes at once. A roar comes from my chest, so loud the only way I know it's mine is because the back of my throat burns with effort.

My hands hold her hair so tight I'm surprised she isn't breaking my fingers to release my grip. My knees flex, buckling, threatening to fail to hold me upright while my cock shoots jet after jet of my release into her mouth.

She hums as she swallows most of my cum before pulling back just as the last squirt hits her pouty lips. Our chests heave, breaths weighty in the silence. Her tongue snakes out to collect the remnants of my release from her mouth and her finger collects the trickle making its way to her chin.

No woman has ever enjoyed cum as much as Sigyn seems to love mine in this moment. Her eyes only leave my face when they roll back with a guttural moan as she sucks the last droplets from the tip of her index finger.

Fuck. I'm already back at half-mast. I've never been so turned on in my life. And I've seen more than my fair share of porn.

Glad to be leaning against the door, I let my body sag, sliding as I splay my hands at both sides to keep from descending all the way to the floor.

If I thought my heart was racing before, it didn't have anything on how fast it's galloping right now. Is this what heaven feels like? A funny, snarky woman with a killer smile, introspective eyes, tits I can't wait to suck and bite for hours on end, and an ass I want to come all over?

"Feel better?"

I don't answer.

Fingers back in her hair, I grip her unruly auburn mane and pull her to her feet without a sound. Whatever caveman lives inside my body has entered the chat. Kicking off my sneakers and socks and stepping out of my clothes, I smash my lips against hers, kissing her till her knees soften.

She braces herself against me, but I'm moving her across the small dorm room to the bed. I'd love to say I'm careful as I dump her ass on the bed, but I'm not. A fire's raging through my veins, and the only thing I need right now is to have my hands on her skin.

I strip most of her clothes off in record time, but she's hit by a fit of giggles when I can't get her damn shoe off and her pants get caught up in the damn thing.

"Need a hand?" She's propped up on her elbows, her pale skin calling for me to trace my fingertips over every goddamn inch. Her dusty rose nipples are almost symmetrical, and her creamy tits are everything I imagined them to be. I can't wait to bury my cock between them while she jerks me off.

My dick twitches. It's almost ready to go again, but this isn't about me or my dick. This is about the woman who just gave me the best blowjob of my fucking life. And my desire to blow her ever loving mind with my tongue, my fingers, or whatever toy she has lying around.

It's my turn.

And I'm not going to stop until her soul leaves her fucking body and finds mine floating somewhere above both of us.

I don't know if it's a growl or a grunt, but it's all the answer she's getting.

Hulking out over her stupid shoe, I finally free her leg and settle between her thighs, jerking her down the bed so she's right where I need her to be.

She spreads her legs wide for me, such a beautiful, small accommodation that makes me want to have her begging for mercy from my tongue even more.

I lock my arms under her thighs and stare up at her. The expectant look in her eyes is framed with challenge, like she's not sure what I'm going to do or if I'll get her where she needs to be.

I don't know what damage she has from her ex, but I *do* know I'm not stopping until she comes for me. Don't fucking care how long it takes.

Tipping my head in a silent question, I wordlessly ask for her consent to continue.

With a growl of her own, she drops her head back onto the soft bedding with a quiet puff of air. "Just fucking lick me already."

Don't mind if I do.

I plant my tongue just above her taint—what the fuck is a chick's taint called? Sticking my tongue flat against her entrance, press hard and drag it right up the center of her pussy.

She rocks her hips as my tongue makes its way to her clit. Pausing for a beat, I swallow, taking a moment to savor her salty flavor. She groans again, thumping both sides of the bed with a whimper. A fucking whimper. I want to hear that again, and again, and once more for good measure.

It's my turn to cast a wicked grin before I slide my fingers inside her and wiggle them around a bit. Her hips twist in response.

When I remove my hand and suck my fingers into my mouth, her protests die on her lips with a gasp.

"You taste so fucking good, Firecracker." I lick my lips. "So. Fucking. Good. I'm going to enjoy every fucking drop."

Dropping back onto the bed between her plush thighs, I don't waste another second before my tongue is spearing inside her, making her moan. By the time the tip of my tongue flicks against her clit, she's soaked and writhing.

"Yes. Yes. Don't stop. Don't fucking stop."

There's no "please," no begging, no biting down on her bottom lip. This woman races toward her orgasm the way she's been all afternoon, with a confident stride. She knows what she wants, and she's not accepting anything less.

She's not quiet. Any time she stops making noise, I change what I do. Move my tongue, slide my fingers inside so I can press against her G-spot, or tweak her nipples with my thumbs and fingertips.

Committing every single response and noise to memory, I eat her pussy like she's the most decadent meal I've ever consumed. Because she fucking is.

"Stop edging me and just make me fucking come."

Her demand almost makes me blow my load all over again. The friction of her sheets alone while I dry hump the bed with my tongue nestled between her folds is enough to push me over. But I want my next O to be inside her.

"I swear to fuck, Loki. Stop fucking around and make me—"

The primal scream that echoes around the room as her release crashes into her is the best sound I've ever heard. It's better than the goal horn in the arena, better than the swoosh of a puck through the air toward the goal, better than the smack of wood against rubber when you hit a slapshot. There is literally no better sound in the world than the orgasm of the redhead splayed out on the bed underneath me.

"Fuck me. Please. Please just fuck me." Her chest heaves with each breath, and a bead of sweat trickles down her temple, disappearing into her hair.

Looping my arms behind her knees, I grip both legs, lining

myself up against her pussy. "Protection?"

She arches her back, a whine falling from her on a long breath. "The pill. Just fuck me."

I'm balls deep before the notion of STIs and STDs hits my addled brain.

"I'm clear of all of those things rolling through your head. Just fucking fuck me already. Jesus Christ."

This woman.

Rutting into her like a pneumatic drill, I drive her up the bed until her head smacks against the headboard. She's tight, hot, and so damn soft I never want to stop.

"Don't stop."

Except that's exactly what I fucking do.

"What…? What are you doing?" Her shriek combined with her hips bouncing up and down off the bed in a clear bid to make me re-start has me rolling my lips between my teeth. At least I'm doing something right.

"What's your favorite position?" It takes every single ounce of self-control I have right now not to bang this woman senseless. But as tight as she's gripping my cock, as wet as she is, as needy and desperate as she seems to be for me, I want to destroy her for anyone who even looks at her after me.

I want to brand her, imprint myself inside her so the only dick she's ever going to need or want for the rest of her life is mine.

"Are you fucking kidding me?" She claws at my chest, her nails searing a path down my pecs, across my nipples, and down my obliques. Firecracker's got claws. And the burn sinks deep into my skin.

The temptation to make her wait even longer, to tease her, push her right to the brink of her patience is overwhelming. But I'm scared she'll go from clawing my chest, to my fucking eyeballs. Or worse, ripping my cock right off my body.

"I'm trying to fuck you. What. Is. Your. Favorite. Position.

Firecracker?"

"Doggy."

Without another word I pull out, flip her over, and grab her hips. I don't let her catch her breath before I slam back inside her. She's hot and wet and so fucking tight. When she flickers her muscles around my dick, stars prick at the edges of my vision.

"Hold on tight, Firecracker."

When she doesn't grip the headboard, I throw a warning shot across the bow, ramming my dick hard inside her, making her yelp as she headbutts the wooden panel.

With a growl she curls her fingers around the top of the headboard, and by the time I plunge deep inside her again, her head's thrown back, her hair's tickling me, and she's moaning.

One hand drops from the board, and soon she's eagerly bouncing on my cock, meeting me thrust for thrust. She tightens around me, moaning, demanding more, harder, faster, deeper. Sweat trickles into my eyes, stinging, but no amount of blinking helps. I'm not letting go of this woman's hips—if I go blind from fucking her, so be it.

Her velvet pussy has my cock in such an iron grip that I'm not sure I'm getting it back. With the fissures of pleasure skating across my skin and up my spine, I'm also not sure I ever want to.

Not sure if it's her screams, or oxygen deprivation to my brain from how tightly her pussy is clenching around me. But I'm pretty sure the blurring light fixture swings back and forth in time with my thrusts as I tip my head back to come on a heavy grunt.

As I rut into her, my jerky hips smacking against her ass, she splits the air with a roar that almost equals mine, then collapses face down onto the bed with a moan.

"I hope you're not done, Firecracker. We're just getting started."

CHAPTER 5

Raffi

My arm burns as I step out onto the street.

Brash? Absolutely. Impulsive is my middle name. It's not really but it kind of sounds cool to just go do something because it feels right. But this... Shit. Mom's gonna kick my ass over this one. I've always wanted ink, but never been brave enough to take the plunge. This... Fuck. This was kinda stupid, right? Definitely stupid.

The brightly colored firecracker emblazoned on my inner forearm with yesterday's date underneath it pulses. It's not huge, a couple inches at most, but Sigyn is the woman I'm going to marry.

The woman has been consuming my every damn thought. I should message her.

No. I should wait. I should definitely wait.

After significant deliberation on her part, I left with her number this morning. I don't want to seem too needy and clingy. She strikes me as the kind of woman who enjoys a bit of space. How long constitutes an acceptable amount of time passing before I can reach out?

I already miss her acerbic wit. And those captivating eyes.

Jesus. I got a tattoo of a fucking firecracker on my arm for her, and she'll probably slice my arm off when she sees it. But the heart wants what it wants.

My gut has never led me wrong. Never. I mean, occasionally it gets confused between decision and indigestion. But it hasn't let me make a bad call yet.

When I was applying for college, I was offered a hockey scholarship to a few different places. My gut told me to stay local, to stay home, to stay close to Mom. Two weeks after the term started, my grandpa suffered a major stroke and died.

Like I said, my gut is never wrong.

And my gut tells me this woman is important.

As I make my way to the ice rink for our game, I can't get her out of my head. The smoothness of her skin, how ticklish she is, twitching and jerking under my featherlight touch, and how she responded to my tongue.

If I had the choice, I'd still be in bed with her. Swallowing down a yawn, I loosen my shoulders. My muscles are heavy with exhaustion from a long and active night. Making Sigyn come is almost as good as playing hockey. Maybe even better. But if my teammates ever heard me say that they'd never let me live it down.

Rein it in, rookie.

So I'll tuck it inside my chest, and message the new woman in my life as soon as I get off the ice. Another few hours won't kill me.

With a groan, I grip the back of my neck.

It might actually kill me.

I want to know everything about her. From the moment she was born. Who is she? What does she like and dislike? Who are her friends? Her family? What does she want to do with her life? Who's the asshole that hurt her?

I want to thank him for being such a stupid fuck and letting her go.

Warm up is a blur. For the first time in a long time I'm distracted from the game that lives inside my veins.

"The fuck was that?"

"Leave him alone, Coop." Our captain, August Cade, smacks Cooper Duke on the ass with his twig.

"We're all thinking it." Coop points at me as he retorts. "Get your head in the game or their defense will destroy you."

They're the last words he says to me before he disappears into the locker room. No one else says anything, but I do get a couple concerned glances. Didn't think I was quite that bad in warm up, but I guess I was more distracted than I thought.

Fuck.

August takes me aside before we walk into the locker room. "You need to talk about anything?"

Definitely not. "I'm good."

"You missed morning skate." He pats my shoulder. "And you barely managed to stay upright for warm up. You gonna make it through the game?"

We're playing the Flint Flames. And AJ Williams is the toughest defenseman in the league. I've heard that if he checks you, you see literal stars. So far, he hasn't managed to land one on me.

And he's not starting today.

"I'm fine, Cap. Had the shits this morning. But I'm good now. Promise." I tap my gloves to my temple. "Scouts honor."

I need to be fine. My whole future is tethered to this scholarship. If I get benched, I'm fucked. I have to play my best, every single fucking game. No matter whose bed I'd rather be in. If things progress with Sigyn, I'm going to need to channel better self-restraint.

Starting to sound like Mom. Homework first. Hockey first. Then hobbies and fun time.

Ugh. So boring.

But she's not wrong.

The game starts with a buzzing energy in my stomach I can't tamp down. I don't want to. And before I know it, we've played almost three full periods of hockey.

We're up 3-2 in the final minutes of regulation time. Despite having scored one of our three goals, the coach skips over my line when calling for changes. I hover on the bench, poised and ready. He's got to call my line, he just has to.

I'm ready. Eager. Hungry. And I'm freakin' capable too.

When he finally calls our line, I explode over the boards like the bench is on fire.

Legs heavy, sweat streaming down the back of my neck, I refuse to give less than one hundred percent even just for one shift. Until that final horn blows, I'm going to give it my all.

When fellow rookie Justin Ashe sends the puck to the blade of my stick, I grin. I don't tend to use the long curl-and-drag shooting motion that a lot of forwards use. Instead, my motion is extremely compact, sacrificing some of the power for disguise and the ability to release it quickly in a restricted area. Just like one of the top twenty-five players in Nashville Predators history, Filip Forsberg.

The shot goes wide, and I chase the puck into the corner. Someone's breathing down my neck from the other team, but fuck if I know who. Don't care, either. Right now, I only need to regain possession of the puck and do whatever I can to get it back into the net.

I'm a heat-seeking missile, the goal is my destination, and my target has been acquired.

Puck gets stuck at the edge of the rink, so I chip it with the toe of my skate. Frustration bubbles inside me. No time for stupid-ass delays when we have a game to win.

Let's go, little puck.

Sometimes inanimate objects respond to being talked to, especially if you talk sweetly to them.

Someone shunts me from behind.

I slam into the plexi.

My legs go out from under me.

And everything goes black.

CHAPTER 6

Raffi

"Isn't this his third concussion?"

"Second since school started."

"I think he said he also had a couple in his last season in high school."

"What if he doesn't wake up?"

"Oof. What the fuck did you do that for?" Fabric rustles like someone is running their hand back and forth over something.

"Shhhhhhhhh. Keep it the fuck down."

If everything didn't hurt, this would be funny. But all I want to do is sleep. There's a drilling behind my eyes I wish I wasn't familiar with, and a deep ache through all my muscles.

"Common symptoms of recurrent concussions in hockey players include headache, dizziness, difficulty concentrating, memory problems, and sensitivity to light or noise."

Ugh. Someone's reading icehockeycentral.com. I can quote their page on concussion in my sleep.

"Memory problems? What if he forgets who we are?"

No such luck.

Another sharp exhale of air, likely due to an elbow to the stomach. "Stop fucking doing that."

The voices are all mixing together in my brain, but Cooper, August, and Justin are in the room with me. It's hard to follow who's saying what and to whom, and I'm still not brave enough to open my eyes.

"Players who have had multiple concussions may also experience symptoms such as depression, anxiety, and mood swings. It is important for players to report any symptoms to their coach or medical staff. Fuck, this doesn't sound good. Cap, this doesn't sound good."

That's definitely Justin's hushed whisper. Despite being a rookie, he's the worrier of the team, the mother hen. I'd smile if my face didn't hurt. I don't remember what happened, but from the throbbing in my nose and eye socket, I'd guess I hit the plexi at speed. It's not my first rodeo.

"Medical professionals may recommend players who have had recurrent concussions sit out for a longer period of time or even retire from playing altogether to prevent further damage to their brain." There's a whistle of air. "Cap, he's on the bench for a while."

No. Panic clutches my whole body, making me groan. The extra movement seizes the drill behind my eyes and shifts it up a notch. Fuck. I'm gonna hurl.

"Everyone out." The next time August speaks, it's so low I barely hear it. "Go get some food. Raffi needs rest. I'll sit with him while y'all eat."

"Want something brought back?" Justin again.

"Nah, I'm good. I'll tag out with someone when you're done. But no overwhelming him. And keep the fucking noise down, okay?"

Footsteps thump and squeak away. There's a swish of the door closing. If only their exit had also taken away the dread curling around my body.

If I can't play, I lose my scholarship. I swallow down the bitter panic lodged at the back of my throat with a groan.

"Easy, Raf. It's okay. Just rest." August pats my leg.

It's fine for him—he's not the one in this bed.

"Research has shown repeated head trauma can lead to chronic traumatic encephalopathy C.T.E, a degenerative brain disease which can cause symptoms such as memory loss, mood swings, and dementia."

Great. He's clearly reading the same fucking website Justin was before he left. August's words are spoken quietly, and they'd almost be soothing if they weren't so terror inducing. I know the risks. I *know* what I could end up like. But hockey is life.

"Hockey players who have suffered concussions may also experience post-concussion syndrome, which can cause headaches, dizziness, and difficulty concentrating, among other symptoms.

"These long-term effects can have a significant impact on hockey players' lives, leading to difficulties in their personal and professional lives. Some players may have to retire early due to the effects of their concussions, while others may struggle with mental health issues and financial challenges. Fuck. Raffi, we're going to have to keep an eye on you, kid. This brain shit isn't something to fuck around with."

While I appreciate his concern about my well-being, I'm also freaking out on an epic scale. I need to heal quickly so I can get back on the team. Without my scholarship, I can't afford college, and I'm far less likely to be discovered by the NHL so I can play professionally.

It's always been my dream to play big.

Wincing, I swallow down the half-truth. I'd love to play in the National Hockey League, I would, but I know deep in my bones I'm not cut out for it. My parents though, once they learned my childhood dream was to become a hockey star, they took it with both hands and ran with it. I can't let them down.

"I can hear your fucking brain working from here, Raf. Settle down and go back to fucking sleep."

But I can't settle or get comfortable. The pain in my head, my ears, encompassing my entire body, makes it impossible for me to "settle down."

"Okay, okay. Don't freak out. Let me help."

I don't know what he's doing because I can't bring myself to open my eyes, but there's a lot of shuffling around. The brightness of the room shifts, getting darker. I don't know what he's done, but my chest swells that he's trying to help.

"What happened?" My voice is croaky. I should probably drink some water.

As though he read my mind, a straw pokes at my lips, and I take a long, slow drink of the cool liquid. Fuck. That feels so damn good.

"What's the last thing you remember?"

Trying to recall memories hurts. It's like the piece of my brain that knows what happened earlier is on fire. Shrugging, I dare to crack an eye open, just a bit. My stomach tightens. I'm definitely not in the hockey house. And August has somehow jerry-rigged a blanket over the window to block out some of the extra light. He's nothing if not resourceful.

"I can't, I don't." Ugh. I start to shake my head but nope, that hurts. "I...did we do the jail-and-bail?"

August nods. "Raised a shit-ton for the ASL charity you picked too."

My sister in law's going to be so happy. My niece was born deaf, and the whole family has learned American Sign Language. It was a slow process, especially for Dad—old dog, new tricks and all that jazz—but we pulled together as a family to learn how to communicate to our littlest member.

We do a fundraiser for a different ASL charity each year,

and I roped my fellow teammates and friends at school into joining the cause this time. I'm glad we raised money, even if I can't remember it.

There's a prickle in my arm, an itch I want to sink my nails into and scratch like crazy. It's right under where the IV is administering fluids. There's a bright red firecracker tattooed on my inner arm, with a date—today, yesterday, last week?— inked underneath it.

"What's this?" My speech is slow, heavy like my tongue's too big for the inside of my mouth.

August shrugs. "No clue. You showed up to practice with it, smiling like a fucking idiot. No idea what it means. You don't remember?"

Even a slow shake of my head makes it throb harder.

"I'm sure it'll come back to you. Doc came in while you were sleeping. He couldn't tell us much 'cause we aren't fam-bam, but a quick Google told us all we need to know. We're experts now." He winks at me, and I try to laugh, but my body just says no.

"Memory loss could be permanent," he continues, "but it also may just be temporary. It's a waiting game."

"So the game was yesterday?"

His turn to nod. "You don't remember anything?"

"I don't even remember my pregame bowl of cheese." Closing my eyes, I rake through the spaghetti strings in my brain and come up empty. There's nothing in there. The last thing I remember was dinner at the hockey house. "Cooper made lasagna?"

"Couple nights ago," August confirms. "Probably best you don't remember the hit. It wasn't pretty."

As I try to pull myself up to a sitting position, sharp pain radiates throughout my whole being. Listen to your body, they say. But I feel like I've just started my car and all the needles in the dials are going haywire and every light on the dash is on.

"Easy." August pats my chest before helping shift me in bed to a more comfortable position. "You're going back to sleep in a sec, okay? You really do need to rest. This concussion shit is nothing to brush off. It's your fucking brain."

There's a joke about being a dumbass there, but it's just slightly out of reach. "Who hit me?"

He winces. "Williams."

Fuck. They weren't lying when they said he hits like a bus. I could probably lie in an ice bath for a month and still have bruises from the tank that crashed into me.

"Clean hit?"

He nods. "I've watched the repeats a million times from every angle, I can't see anything other than a clean hit. And believe me, I'd love nothing more than to go after him. But no one's taking this worse than he is."

He scratches his chin. "Dude's fucked up. He stopped in this morning but you were out cold. Wasn't sure how it was going to go—the guys were prickly. But AJ was on the verge of tears and so messed up everyone just gave him a wide berth."

"He came alone? What if they mauled him?"

"Pretty sure Jeremy Lewis was waiting outside for him. They're joined together at the hip. But he came in alone. Guess he figured if we kicked his ass he deserved it."

Knives are stabbing into my temples, and there's a constant blur on the edges of my vision. It's probably temporary, but it's scary as fuck.

"Close your eyes, rest. You did good."

"Did we win?" A yawn starts as my eyes flicker closed.

"We won."

"When can I play again, Cap?" Sleep's already pulling me under.

"I dunno, rookie. I really don't know."

CHAPTER 7

Victoria

(TEN WEEKS LATER)

"You're still staring at that fucking phone."

Jazz points at the device that's been all but surgically attached to my hand since the day I met the elusive Loki. She's not wrong. Part of me still hopes he's going to reach out. As much as I didn't want to get attached to the stranger at the fundraiser, I thought we connected.

Can't say I thought he was going to be *the* one, but I figured he'd be a good booty call. Dude was talented with his light saber.

With a groan, I push my lunch away and drop my forehead to the table.

"Still nauseous?"

My forehead makes a squeak on the table as I try to nod. "That's what I get for eating cold leftovers three days in a row for breakfast."

Jazz's eyes narrow. If her head tips slightly to the right, I'm in trouble. She's got this shrewd awareness that I envy. The stink-eye, head-tilt combo means something's brewing in her brain. I'm not normally on the receiving end of her deep thoughts.

Her head tilts.

Oh no.

"What?"

"Gimme ten. Don't move." With that, she disappears out the door of the cafe.

I must fall asleep, because when someone's hand touches my shoulder, I bolt upright in my seat. "Ugh."

Moving too fast brings a new wave of nausea. The half-bagel I managed to force down threatens to make a reappearance.

"Come with me." Jazz holds her hand out, and I stare at it for what feels like an entire minute before I meet her eyes.

"Are you kidnapping me?"

"You wish. I left my duct tape in my other backpack." She shimmies her shoulders at me. "Plus, we both know I don't need to kidnap you. Come on, princess. On your feet."

The very fact that she's helping me stand up has alarm bells ringing in the back of my mind. She's never this maternal. Do I look that bad?

I must if she's so determined to be nice to me. Maybe she needs something. Maybe she wants my notes from class this morning. She was distracted by the guy two seats in front of her.

She doesn't stop until we get back to my dorm room. It takes three tries to get the key in the lock, and as soon as the door opens, I drop my bag and make a beeline for the bed.

"Ah, ah, ah." Jazz intercepts me, redirecting my trajectory to the bathroom. She turns me to face her, cups my cheeks in both her palms and her face softens.

Am I dying? I've never seen her be so concerned. She's all party all the time. What the fuck is going on?

"When was your last period?"

"I had one last month. It's been about four weeks."

Her head's already shaking before my sentence ends.

"I haven't missed one." I finally catch on to where she's going with this, and my stomach drops. "No." The word falls from my mouth on a heavy sigh. "I can't be. It was one time. Just one. And we were protected." And I really did have a period last month. Sure, it was on the light side, but it was a period. There's just no way.

Ice fills my veins. Not wanting to confirm her suspicions, still firmly planted in denial, I take in what she's holding in her hand. It's a bag from the local pharmacy.

Oh no. No, no, no, no, no.

"Yep. We're doing this right now. I'm not letting you avoid this. Pee on the stick, and we'll know one way or the other. One of us is right. Let's see which it is." She unboxes the pregnancy test and points the stick at me.

"Do you know how unlikely it is to conceive from a one-night stand? Especially considering I was on protection?" I try to stand up straight, to seem dismissive, indignant, confident. But my insides churn so hard that I'm not any of those things.

"Actually." Her face darkens as she wiggles the stick. "I know exactly how unlikely it is." There's something in the tone of her voice that makes me think she's speaking from experience. But Jazz doesn't have any kids.

"Even if you have wholly unprotected sex on the right day of the month, there's only a twenty-ish percent chance of conceiving from that session." She arches her brow. "Ask me how I know."

No. Fucking. Way.

She's unrelenting with the pregnancy test, so I just whip down my undies and plant myself on the fucking toilet. If she's going to make me do it, she can tag along for the whole ride.

"Sixteen-year-old Jazz. My boyfriend at the time swore it'd

be fine that we ran out of condoms. Turns out, it wasn't fine. Not by any stretch of the imagination."

That makes my jaw drop open.

When I'm done taking a sample and dipping the stick, I set it on the counter and tell my phone to set a timer.

"What happened?" I ask and turn to the sink.

In the mirror, she shrugs, but her face turns red. "I got an abortion."

The admission hangs heavily between us for a long moment.

"It was the right decision at the time." Her voice is thick with an emotion I can't place. "My parents didn't force me into it, they told me it was my life, my body, and I could make the choice."

She takes my hand once I'm done drying. "I have been where I suspect you're about to be. You're going to need to make a decision, Vic. And it's not one anyone else can make for you."

Shaking my head, I wring my hands in front of my stomach. There's no way. All this panic and anxiety is for nothing. It's going to be the stomach flu or a virus—there's no way the stick will say I'm pregnant. None.

It's bad enough I didn't get Loki's number, but the fact that he hasn't reached out seeps a little deeper under my skin. If I *am* pregnant, how can I tell him? How can I give him the option to be a part of his child's life when I don't even know his real name?

The timer goes off, and Jazz and I lock gazes for what feels like an eternity.

"You've got this."

I most definitely don't got this.

With a shaky hand, I pick up the stick from the counter. "See? I told you." I smile, relief sinking in. "There's no way I'm—fuck."

The test clatters into the sink, my numb fingers unable to hold it.

The sympathetic stare from my best friend is nearly unbearable.

"Jazz." My voice cracks as my jaw trembles. "I'm pregnant."

CHAPTER 8
Victoria
(THREE YEARS LATER/PRESENT DAY)

The worst thing about getting pregnant in my freshman year wasn't the leg cramps, or the nausea, it wasn't the night feeds on top of assignment deadlines. It wasn't the permanent bird's nest of matted curls on top of my head, the constant lukewarm meals, or even the lingering smell of baby puke that followed me around everywhere I went.

The worst thing about getting pregnant in my freshman year was the unspoken judgment, the shame, the overwhelming loneliness.

Jazz and I drifted apart as soon as I decided to keep the baby. I guess it was too hard for her to be a character in an alternative life to the one she chose. It was never anything direct, no outward confrontation, but "all party, all the time" didn't quite vibe with boob feeding a teething tiny parasite going through a growth spurt.

It got worse when I dropped out of the business program. I had to pivot from studying to be a paralegal into photography. Jazz and I drifted even further. As much as I wanted to go into a legal career, I just couldn't keep my head in the game enough to make it happen.

Not to mention the fact that I needed to study something that would earn money faster. Becoming a photographer wasn't my dream, but I'm good at it. I have a good eye, and can capture the mood of a session as easily as breathing.

And when my adviser "kindly" suggested I had missed too much of school to catch up in my original classes, it was both a relief and a gut punch.

Over three years later, I'm freelancing on the side of finishing up my photography course, while raising a tiny human to not be a dick.

It's harder than you'd think, raising kids to not be dickish. It's like they're born with all your worst traits, and you've gotta spend your life deprogramming them so they don't end up in prison.

The real kind.

Ugh. I need a friend. Mom's great, and we're close, but sometimes I just want some girl time with someone my own age, y'know?

I'd kill for an hour with a similarly-minded human being. Throw in a Hawaiian pizza, peanut M&Ms, and a nice bottle of Pouilly Fumé, and I'd be in heaven.

I'm not a complicated creature, but I am an exhausted one. A bored one. A lonely one.

There's a tiny pink-haired fairy sitting about ten feet from me. She's been coming to Bitches Brew to study for a while now, and I've never seen her come in with anyone else. She's always alone when she arrives, always alone when she leaves.

Is she a loner, or just lonely?

I'm contemplating buying her one of those fancy hot cocoas she seems to be somewhat addicted to when it occurs to me that I'm being a creeper right now. Watching another human being from a distance, getting to know their processes, their preferences, their habits.

Creeper. With a capital C.

I need to channel Wyatt, my inner toddler, who walks up to damn near anyone—and everyone—and requests, nope, demands they be his friend. I'd say he has a ninety-two percent success rate. But he's also far cuter than I am.

If he was here, pink-haired fairy girl would absolutely want to hang with us.

Or maybe the fact that I'm a single mom might send her running for the hills.

It's safer to stay in my lane. To leave her and her hot chocolate the hell alone. You can't be rejected if you never introduce yourself and put yourself out there. But she seems as sweet as pie.

And I need to get back on the friendship horse. I'm a social being, and while I have friends, I don't have any *friends*, y'know?

She's muttering something while chewing on the end of her orange highlighter. Orange highlighters are my favorite too, so that seals our fate. I'm making this woman my bestie. Even if it means gaining thirty-five pounds from drinking hot chocolate just to get to know her.

Challenge accepted.

I dunno why my palms are sweaty and my mouth is dry as I cross the few feet to her table. When the squeak of the chair I pull toward me outs my presence to her, wide, confused eyes meet mine.

Please don't turn me away. Please?

I'm not a psycho killer. My worst crimes are that I let my toddler have too much screen time, and I love pineapple on pizza.

When she doesn't speak, I drop onto the chair, offering

what I hope is a warm, friendly smile that doesn't come across as "I ate a burrito for dinner last night and have gas today."

Her hand twitches as her eyes follow my auburn waves down my shoulders. Not sure if she's going to touch my hair, or her own short hair, so I keep smiling. Now that I'm up close, I get a better look at her. She has a jagged scar down one side of her face.

It's pretty badass. And instead of blending into the background, she's dyed her hair a vibrant pink. If I had that scar, I'd shrink into obscurity.

I barely resist the urge to reach across the table and tuck her hair behind her ear. She's fucking stunning. Hiding behind hair on her face... I dunno, I get that she's probably self-conscious, but she has no cause to be.

My new best friend's eyes are wide, like she's trying to silently communicate to me that I'm sitting at the wrong table. If I sit here for much longer without saying a word, she might lose her mind or break out into actual sweats.

"Hi, I'm Victoria." I stick my hand out, hovering over the pile of books and notes she has littered across the table. "Or Tori. I've seen you come in here almost every day I do, and I figure since we're both here a lot, and we're both studying alone, we may as well study alone together, right?"

There's no way she can say no. I'm an absolute fucking delight. I'm a hard worker, I can sit quietly, and even if she thinks she never has to talk to me, I'll win her over one day at a time. The tension holding my neck muscles hostage dissipates as her face relaxes.

But she doesn't speak or move. Not dropping my smile, or my hand, I tilt my head just a smidge. "If you'd rather I take myself back to a table by myself, I can do that too." Pretty sure no one's walked to my old table behind me, but I glance back just to be sure.

Still like a deer in headlights, she cautiously accepts my hand and shakes. Her hand is so bony compared to mine, and she's cold.

"I'm Eloise."

She speaks! And she has such a pretty name, to match her edgy, striking vibe.

"Let me guess—introvert, right?"

She gives me a slow nod. "How'd you guess?"

I can't help but laugh at the terror etched across her delicate, doll-like features. "I thought so. Don't worry, I'm not some weird energy vampire or anything, and I'm not going to talk and talk and talk at you when you're trying to study—ugh, isn't that so annoying? But I wanted to say hi and get the ball rolling by telling you I'm your new best friend."

Not waiting for an invitation, or giving her a chance to change her mind about letting me be in her space, I pick up my backpack and yank out some books. She hasn't left me much space to work with on the table, but I'll make do. I mean, of course she hasn't, because she didn't invite me to the table in the first place, but that's neither here nor there.

Making do has been my MO since two lines popped up on the fourth pregnancy test, cementing the fact that the "pregnant," the smiley faces, and the extra lines were all accurate, and I was, in fact, pregnant.

Her stare is heavy on me when I jam a pen between my teeth as I flick through my notebook. I want to launch into conversation. Ask her about her hair color, why she chose pink over every other color out there. I want to be incredibly rude and ask about her scar, what degree she's working on, if she has any secret children lying around that could be besties with my Wyatt. But I chew on the fucking pen so I don't scare my new best friend away.

It doesn't last long. A need to break the silence crawls over me. I want to get to know this chick, and to do that, I've got to lure her in with the hot chocolate. "You're empty. You want a drink or something?" I hook my thumb over my shoulder toward Jake the barista.

Yes. I know them all by name. A lot of my time is spent here in Bitches Brew. "I'm going to get something. Full disclosure: possibly more than one something. Spoiler alert: *definitely* more than one something. Have you tried their hot chocolate? It's orgasmic."

It's part sarcasm, part hiding the fact I've been watching her for days. She's not going to turn down her favorite drink.

"I love their hot chocolate. I've already had one though. I should switch to tea."

"You only live once. Have the second hot chocolate if you want it." I pat my tummy. "This chunky girl doesn't judge."

After a long pause, like she's evaluating her decision, she nods. "Okay. I'll take another."

"Something you're going to learn pretty quickly about me, Eloise, is that I'm an enabler." Dropping my voice to a whisper, I give her an exaggerated wink. "So, if you ever need to be talked into something, I'm your gal."

When I'm halfway to the counter with my wallet, I stop in my tracks and turn back to her. "No allergies, right? If I get something with nuts in it, I won't find myself having to dig through your bag for an Epipen or anything?"

"No allergies."

Allergies are no fucking joke. Wyatt's daycare has a boy named Arthur who's allergic to both eggs and nuts. I don't know how his parents do it. I'd stick him in a plastic bubble and never let him outside the house.

I'm enough of a helicopter with Wyatt as it is without having to read every single food label for the rest of his life. Eating out must be a nightmare too. Those parents are the real heroes.

Just as well Wyatt has no allergies as his favorite foods are dirt, months-old McDonalds fries from the depths of his car seat, and Mom's cat food.

A couple minutes later, I turn back to the table with overflowing mugs of buttery hot chocolate, and my stomach falls through the floor. My new best friend is making eyes at the hockey god goaltender.

The de la Peñas are famous in our school. The hockey playing twins, the prodigy younger brother goaltender, the boss bitch older sister, rich parents... It's like something out of a movie. Please don't let my new bestie be a hockey fan. Please.

I send up a quick prayer. You can never be too cautious when it comes to the influence of the big man upstairs.

I've very carefully avoided all things hockey, including players, since my ex. And I've very carefully avoided all potential, dateable, real-life-penises since the night I conceived Wyatt. Fine, not all, just most.

I fuck around sometimes. Not often, but every now and then I hook up with someone from a dating app for a quickie. A girl's got needs. Needs a battery operated boyfriend can't meet. They just can't successfully recreate a human tongue in toy form.

But I never date the same guy more than once, and I never give out my real name. Even though I have PCOS, I'm on the pill, and insist he wears protection. His toy soldier can't come anywhere near my vagina if it ain't gloved.

Lightning won't strike twice in this one night stand space. It's highly unlikely to conceive while having PCOS and on the pill, but it's not impossible. It's a freak occurrence that's already shifted the trajectory of my life once before.

I also don't have time to devote to a man-child, or an asshole, or worse, a man I might fall in love with.

I have a man in my life. He's a two-and-a-half year old tornado who loves cars, trucks, and *Paw Patrol*. That little fucker Ryder gets on my nerves every damn day of the week. But Wyatt adores him and his pack of dogs.

"Why are we staring at Ares de la Peña like he hung the moon?" I manage not to spill hot cocoa over the sides of the ginormous mugs as I place them on the table.

Eloise doesn't answer.

"I can see you behind that shield of pink hair. I know exactly who you're staring at." I'm trying not to judge. Just because I had a shitty experience with my hockey-playing, asshole ex doesn't mean everyone else in the world will too.

I'm sure there are some half-decent hockey players out there. Heck, maybe even mostly decent. Loki wasn't a hockey player, and he still turned out to be a ghosting prick.

Flicking a glance toward Ares—who's leaning so far back on his chair I hope gravity comes for him so I can get a good laugh at him falling on his ass—I question whether he's an asshole or not.

I've heard stories. And if he fell on his butt I wouldn't be mad. Not like, hurt himself fall. But just a small fall, like, enough to take some of the ego out of his sails.

I'm sure he's a great athlete, worthy of all the accolades and countless articles and brouhaha. But he's just so...ugh. Arrogant. It makes me want to twist his ear and kick his feet off the fucking table.

"I can see it. You'd be cute together." They'd make the most beautiful babies the world has ever seen.

She visibly flinches. "I couldn't ever be with him."

There's tea there. And while I don't like hockey players, I love how this woman's face has turned as pink as her hair. I poke just a bit harder. I want her to spill the tea.

"But you want to be."

No matter what she says, she definitely wants to be with him. She's practically salivating as she watches him lob his dumbassness around the coffee shop with his frat boy friends.

"He's the youngest. The bad boy." When the only response I get is a frown, I know my new bestie's in trouble.

Oooooh boy. She has no idea who she's dealing with. Her eyes flicker with something that could be judgment or caution as she pulls out her phone. Probably to google him. How she has a crush on him when she doesn't know his name would be curious to me if I didn't have a similar history. I still remember the taste of Loki's kisses, three years later. And it all started with a stupid fucking crush in a fake prison cell.

"I can see your screen."

Her face is on fire as she slaps her phone against her body.

"You should totally shoot your shot with him."

She's probably going to pitch the damn phone at my face. "But he's gay."

"I can see why you'd think that, but click the photos tab. You'll see him with both men and women. He's bi." Hot chocolate tastes even better when it's drunk over girl talk.

Would I rather she had a crush on someone who *isn't* a hockey player? Absolutely. But I've missed this. And I like this chick. So I'll pretend Ares de la Peña is some rockstar or a famous chess player instead of a hockey player.

Something shifts on Eloise's face. Suspicion replaces the concern sitting heavily on her brow. Her eyes narrow, crinkling her face.

Ah. She thinks I fucked him. Ha. Hell no. "Don't look at me like that. I have a kid at home. I don't want any part of your nasty boy. I mean, he's a fantasy come to life. Athlete who moonlights as a stripper. Bad boy who takes gender studies. He's a walking contradiction."

After a few more clicks on her phone, she puts it face down on the table while we finish our drinks in silence. Have I steamrolled this new friendship before it's even gotten off the ground?

Huh. It's not me, it's him. Her furtive glances across the

coffee shop aren't fooling anyone, Ares included. He clocks her watching him. For sure. I can't help the smirk that spreads across my face. She's got it bad.

"No." She folds her arms.

Rolling my lips barely stops the brewing laugh from escaping. "If you say so."

We work in silence for a while, each sipping our drink, and Eloise casting sneaky looks over at Ares until he and his posse depart the building, and a calm returns to our space.

After about an hour, I glance up to find her staring at me.

"Can I ask a question?" Her face is pale, and she looks like she might puke just from asking that, never mind whatever she really wants to ask.

"Sure." I drop my pen onto my notebook. I'm so over the history of photography anyway.

"You said you had a child. What's their name?"

This poor woman has no idea what she's getting herself into. Asking me about my son is like asking Hermione to tell you all about her favorite spells.

"His name is Wyatt."

She smiles. "Cute. And...uh..." She wrings her hands on the table. I know what's coming, it's the question that always follows my disclosure that I'm a mom. "What about his dad?"

The urge to snap brews deep inside me. It's not her fault. Even after three years I can't temper the urge to break shit when he comes up in conversation.

"We don't talk about him."

"Never?"

"Ever."

She nods. "Okay."

"Just like that? Okay?" It's my turn to narrow my eyes.

She shrugs. "We all have things we aren't comfortable talking about. Why would I force you to talk about something that hurts you? You say no, it's no."

I knew I chose a good one. Leaning forward, I plant both fists under my chin. "Tell me this. How do you feel about pineapple on pizza?"

CHAPTER 9

Raffi

(PRESENT DAY)

The Rockford Rockets are in the house. They're not my favorite team to play against, but they're also not my least favorite. They fall somewhere in the middle, just like using regular peanut butter in a PB&J versus using crunchy.

What's the point if there's no crunch?

Just like a mediocre sandwich, the Rockets have no crunch. But we're on high alert because Coach has been trippin' lately and seems to be roasting our asses for no goddamn good reason.

No one has said anything directly, but I feel like things have slipped. I feel slower. I feel like I'm spending more time warming the bench than on the ice.

It's probably my mind playing tricks on me, but I need to up my game. I need to make it impossible for Coach to bench me. I need to make it so my team doesn't have to compensate for a slip in my performance. I need to make it so I don't let anyone down.

The speed of the Rockets gives them a chance inside the first twenty-five seconds as one of their top scorers gets in behind our defense. He flips a backhand effort on the net that's casually saved by de la Peña.

Somehow two of our guys get called for coinciding penalties. It happens in the corner and no amount of craning my neck at the melee or the replay helps me figure out how Tate gets called for interference while Scott sits for two for holding.

It's a tied game, goose eggs all around by the time we get to the final few minutes of the first period. Two of the Rockets get sent to the box for interference and a third for holding, while Apollo heads to the box for roughing.

We head to the intermission scoreless, and I've barely broken a sweat. Am I being benched?

No one looks at me differently as we head down the tunnel, there's no judgment or accusation in my teammates eyes as we hit the locker room. But I'm not getting the same ice time I used to. Why?

It's probably paranoia. Nothing has changed except the frequency of my headaches. And the only person who knows that, or is going to know that, is me.

My leg bounces when I'm nervous. Not both of them, just the left one. And no matter how much I glare at it, it doesn't let up.

Tate plops on the bench next to me, tipping the blade of his stick at my knee. "What's that about?"

Shrugging, I focus on the tape at the end of my blade. It's suddenly the most important thing in the world to me. "Who's your personal trainer again, Phil someone?"

Nodding, he bumps me with his elbow. "Stop changing the subject. What's going on?"

Lowering my voice, I lean closer to my friend. "I didn't get as much ice time as I usually do. Am I...? Is there something...?"

Tate's been pretty good at pretending he isn't observing my behavior for signs of concussion syndrome, or whatever the fuck it's called when you hit your head a few too many times on the ice. He's a great friend, but every now and then, he'll pay closer than usual attention to me like he's making sure I'm not losing my shit.

How he can tell the difference between my regular terrible memory and concussion memory loss is anyone's guess, but he makes for a great work wife, and I know without question, he's got my back.

"You're in your head about it." He pats my shoulder. "I haven't seen any sign you're slipping. And we both know I've been watching you." He gives me a grossly exaggerated wink like he's hitting on me.

"Not my type, Tate." The mood has lightened, but inside I'm heavy, mulling over every shift I skated in the first. "Tell me about your trainer."

"After the game. But there are only so many hours in the day, man. You can't spend all of them at the gym."

But I can try. If I'm stronger and faster than everyone else on the ice, there's no way I'll get benched. It's dumbass logic, even I know that, but it's the only thread I can cling to that won't shunt me off the cliff into depression. That murky fucker stays at bay most of the time, but every now and then it sinks its tendrils into my skin and tries to fuck with my mind.

Not today, Satan.

We start the middle period on a 5-on-3 powerplay, but our best chance falls right after the Rockets return to their full complement. Apollo de la Peña puts the puck right in front of me, but the best I can pull off is a midriff shot at their goaltender.

Goddamn motherfucking shit.

Chances keep falling our way, but we can't capitalize on any of them. Tate on the left wing is only able to put his back-handed effort into the chest of their Hulk-sized netminder before we're stuck on another penalty kill. Artemis goes to the box for delay of game by flicking the puck over the glass.

From the surly glower on his face I'd say he's as thrilled about how this game is going as the rest of us. It's like the puck is coated with butter, or oil, or... I can't really say something slippery considering we play on a giant-ass sheet of ice, but none of us are doing well with the puck handling today.

The skills coaches are going to be thrilled.

The end of the period becomes the Ares Show as he makes a set of back-to-back stops to deny the Rockets, followed by an incredible save to stop their top scorer as he's fed what looks to be a back door tap-in on the breakaway.

The whole bench is on the edge of their seat—for both teams—my blood pressure is through the roof as Ares barely has time to recover before another wave of shots comes at him.

Guy might have an ego, but he's got the fucking skills to back it up. Kid's talented as hell, and I'm glad he's on our side.

A late "too many men" call at the end of the second, followed by a high sticking penalty puts the Raccoons on another 5-on-3 powerplay we still can't convert, although it needed a big stop from their netminder to deny Tate's powerful right circle one-timer.

It's not until we're back to full strength on both sides that we finally make a change to the zero-zero score taunting us from the board with back to back goals from Apollo and Tate to put us up by two.

At last. I got assists on both goals which should make me feel better about life, but it doesn't.

"Watch your six."

I'm not sure who Artemis is warning until I'm crunched against the boards by some big ape of a motherfucker who takes a two minute penalty for boarding.

Realistically, my teammates know as well as I do that any big hits can be dangerous. But I've kept the extent of my...

condition to myself. Fucking hate being treated like I'm broken or weak. Or worse, being benched and not allowed to play. It hasn't been much of an issue the past couple years. I've earned my place on the team. My stats have spoken for themselves. I settled into a routine that kept my headaches at bay, and for a while there I even thought making the big time was possible.

But lately something's shifted. Everything feels harder. Training feels tougher, games take more out of me, and my headaches are becoming more frequent. My stats no longer speak for themselves, every game is a fight to protect my space on the team. Nothing feels comfortable, or safe.

As I skate back to the bench, a headache brews in my temples. What else can I do to make sure I don't end up permanently benched?

Coach gives me questioning eyes as I take my seat on the bench. I nod at him. I'm fine. But the pain already prickling in my head tells me otherwise.

I can't outrun this.

But if I'm fitter and stronger, perhaps I can better outrun the defense of the other teams so I don't end up out on my ass. While I'm pretty proficient at American Sign Language, I really want the degree behind me. I want the protection of having a college degree no one can take away from me. And to do that, I need to maintain my scholarship. And to do *that*, I need to keep my pretty head out of the boards, and in the game.

I just need to figure out how to do it.

CHAPTER 10

Victoria

(PRESENT DAY)

"We're going to do a quick internal ultrasound, okay? From the list of symptoms it sounds like your PCOS is off the rails a bit, and we need to figure out what's going on."

For such a commonly diagnosed and suffered condition, it feels like it's so stupidly misunderstood by so many. It's taken three different OBGYNs but I finally found one who speaks polycystic ovary syndrome. Once my ultrasound is complete, and she's shown me the pretty pictures of my "very beautiful" uterus, as well as the cysts all over my ovaries, I'm in the stirrups all over again for my pap smear.

Shortly after Wyatt was born, Mom had cervical cancer. Since she was adopted and we don't know her family medical history, and since I have my own up close and personal relationship with cysts on my ovaries, it all makes me high risk. So I like to keep on top of my annual well-woman exam.

I want to live a long and healthy life, not just for my baby boy, but for myself as well.

"We've talked about your diet, Victoria. But we haven't really mentioned exercise."

Tension sinks its claws into my muscles as I go stiff. The assumption by most doctors, hell, most people, is that because I'm fat, I eat like shit and don't move at all. But it's actually not the case. I'm hoping because my new OBGYN, Dr. O'Flaherty understands the condition, she'll actually listen to me when I tell her I'm not a lazy shit who sits in the drive thru of McDonalds all day every day eating Big Macs and drinking milkshakes.

Ugh. Fuck. I could definitely go for a strawberry shake right now. With super salty fries. And a Big Mac.

Okay, fine. Fat girls like shitty food too. But it's not *all* we eat. Or at least it's not all *I* eat.

"I swear I've tried everything." My palms are slick as I wipe them on the thighs of my jeans. I'm so tired of being fat shamed and judged. I really just want to find someone who's going to help me. "I've done Couch to Five K twice. I've done cardio classes."

She sits back in her chair, nodding, no sign of judgment or disbelief on her face. "Have you ever lifted weights?"

"No." I fucking hate exercise. As soon as I realized Couch to Five K wasn't working for me, I wanted to quit. Walking is a pointless waste of time. And I don't have the patience or self-confidence to learn how each of the torture devices in the gym work.

"I have PCOS too." The admission takes me aback, but it makes sense now why she's more sympathetic to my story, since she's lived the same issues I've lived through. "And I can out-lift my husband in the gym."

She goes on to tell me that with PCOS there's a surplus of estrogen in my body, and—long story short—if I lift heavy shit in the gym, my muscles will absorb the excess hormones and "crap" in my body to repair the micro-tears you get from weight lifting.

"I recommend you try thirty minute sessions, three times a

week. That should be enough to start. And I'm going to put you on Metformin for insulin resistance. We'll start at 500mg for two weeks and then step up to 1000mg, okay?"

Tucking the piece of paper with my notes about Metformin into my purse, I nod, tears welling in my eyes. It's so nice to finally be listened to by someone who knows what the fuck they're doing. She's answered every question I had on that piece of paper, before I even got to ask them.

"I'd suggest you get a personal trainer for the first while, too. So you can learn how to do things the right way."

That's never going to happen. I'm so tired of buff gym people with their judgy judgment, and their side-eye shade. Okay, fine. That might not be completely accurate, but that's how it feels. Anytime I go to a gym, I feel judgment.

I wouldn't know where the hell to start to find a personal trainer in my area. There are flyers on bulletin boards all over campus, but I'd never train where people from my classes might see me. Cringe. Can you imagine? There could be someone near Mom's, but how much will that cost? I don't have that kind of money or time.

I thank Dr. O'Flaherty, pick up my prescription, and read about the delightful side effects of Metformin when I get back to Mom's.

"Mama!" Wyatt has no chill. He runs at a solid eighty every day. When he's really feeling it, he dials it up to a hundred and three.

The kid is a bundle of joy and sunshine. Sometimes it's a hard pill to swallow, as it reminds me of his father. Loki's big vibes are hard to forget—his lopsided smile, his zest for, well, everything, every single thing made that boy freakin' happy.

Except, as it turns out, me.

What feels like shards of emotional glass slide under my nails and deep into my skin. Reliving the memories about my one-night stand with Wyatt's father never ends in a good place.

It's always a back and forth battle in my chest. I wouldn't trade Wyatt for the world, but I just thought—

"Mamaaaaaaaaaaaaaaaaaaaaaa!"

I guess not answering him the first time made him go bigger for round two. If I keep ignoring him, he'll just get louder and louder.

He launches himself at me, giggling uncontrollably when I blow raspberries against his neck. "Hey, buddy! Did you have a good day at school today?"

He's only two and a half, but with me in college and Mom working, he started daycare pretty early. Another mom-fail. I wish I could raise him by myself, but in today's world, it's just not possible.

I'm grateful for the social interaction and learning he gets at daycare, but I'd give anything to spend all day with my son. He's my favorite person in the whole world, but I need to earn money. And that means he's gotta go hang with other kids throughout the day.

He's every bit as social as his dad seemed to be, so as hard as it is for me to let him go every morning at drop off, he takes it in stride and doesn't look back. He loves his teachers, he loves his friends—except that one kid who threw a duck at his head on day one, and Wyatt has never forgiven her for it.

Don't blame him. I wouldn't forgive someone for splitting my head open with a toy duck either.

"Hey, sweetie."

"Hey, Mom." Squishing Wyatt against my chest, I smile at Mom.

She looks tired. She always looks tired. Working multiple jobs always seemed so cool when I was a kid, but as an adult, it just makes me want to do more, be more, earn more, so I can give back to her. I'd love to earn enough so she could quit one of her jobs and spend more time with Wyatt. But she gets good health insurance, and she's stubborn as hell.

Thankfully, kids are covered under her medical plan until they're twenty six. That gives me five more years to set myself up for success. She's shouldered so much of the weight for years on end—I want to give back. And I want to be everything to Wyatt that Mom was to me, even with all her jobs and spinning plates.

"Eloise called over on her way to visit her dad. Said she has tickets for the game tonight and was wondering if you'd like to go."

Oh no.

"Which game?"

Mom angles herself so her back is to me. "I think she said it was hockey," she says with false levity. She knows how much I loathe the game.

That's not true. I loathe the players, not the game. As a sport, hockey is my favorite. But I'll never admit it out loud. I miss the smell of the ice and the sound of bones crunching against the boards. But I can't risk running into my ex.

"It's a Minnesota game. So she said."

That's code for "I Googled to make sure your ex-boyfriend wouldn't be playing so you can go but I'm saying your friend said it so you don't get upset at me for looking up your ex-boyfriend's team."

Mom-child-code is a hugely complex language.

"That so?"

She doesn't turn toward me. I'm not sure what she's doing in the kitchen, but it apparently needs her whole attention. "Mmhm. You should think about it."

The forced upbeat tone in her voice starts to waver. "You need to go out and do something...uh..."

"Normal?" I supply. We have this discussion every now and then. She thinks my childhood was cut short and that I've missed out on the typical college experience because I got pregnant.

And while both of these things are true, she also seems to not believe me when I tell her I'm fine. My kid is my whole universe.

For some reason, I think that's what she's afraid of. Not sure why. Isn't that the whole point of parents? To adore their children?

"Please, Victoria? For me?" Something falls into the sink with a clatter. "I'd love to see you go out with Eloise more. Let me spend time with my grandbaby while you go and do regular college kid stuff. She seems like such a sweet girl. Did you know her mom died?"

She turns to me, eyes red-rimmed and welling. "Such a tragedy. I stupidly asked about her parents." She sniffs. "Didn't mean to step on an emotional landmine, but she handled it with such grace."

"You chatted with her?"

Mom nods. "Made her tea and fed her snacks. Thought you might come back early. Such a sweet girl. And beautiful too. When she's not hiding behind that curtain of hair to cover her scar."

Eloise's mom died in the car crash that gave Eloise the scar down her face. I'm determined to convince her to tie her hair up at some point. She has the best cheekbones. People spend hours with a million makeup products to get that look. And she's hiding it behind her bright pink hair.

"So...is that a yes?"

She's not going to give up. My phone vibrates on my lap.

> Eloise: Have you talked to your mom yet?
> Please come to the game tonight? Please?
> I'm nervous and really don't want to go
> alone.

I'm kind of out of excuses not to go. I like the sport, I have childcare for Wyatt, and I'd walk through fire for my bestie.

Ha. I'd walk through ice for her, too. I can't let her face the big, bad hockey players all by herself. If someone hurts her, she'll need help hiding the body.

The sigh that comes out of me is so heavy it's exhausting.

"Excellent. I think I have your uncle's old Raccoons jersey in the closet."

My sigh turns into a groan. "I didn't say yes."

"Your sigh of resignation says otherwise."

"Fine. But no shirt. I need to make sure I like them and want to cheer for them before I drape my precious body in their colors. They gotta earn my support."

Mom knows not to push. She holds her hands up.

While dinner cooks, I reach out to the moms group for Wyatt's daycare and ask if anyone has recommendations for a good personal trainer. One who isn't some bodybuilding lunatic who's going to yell at me or shame me into working out. I need someone supportive. Someone who listens. Someone who works with super hormone-charged bodies.

A couple hours later, I shuffle through the row of seats and plop down next to Eloise. Despite subtle differences, every rink is kind of the same, right down to the faint smell of popcorn, hotdogs, and beer lingering on the chilled air.

Eloise is so nervous her whole body shakes with excited energy. Or fear. I can't quite tell. Whatever she's got going on with the goalie is adorable. And as long as he treats her right, I won't need to snap his neck like a pretzel stick.

I brought my camera. It's an older SLR model, but it takes pictures just fine. I want to work on capturing some at-speed shots during the game. Taking a good photograph is hard enough, but while someone's in motion, that requires a different level of skill.

Out of all the sports out there, I'm pretty sure hockey ranks as one of the fastest. Formula One is probably top of the pyramid, but if I can nail taking good shots of giants with knives on their shoes, I could start selling pictures to media outlets.

The first period passes with minimal fighting. I remember it being more aggressive when I was in high school. Did they change the rules? Not that I mind the lack of blood sport on the ice. It's interesting how the game has evolved in the few years I've been away.

To my left there's a guy mansplaining the game to a girl who seems to be his date. She's wearing a hockey jersey, but it's a Snow Pirates shirt, not a Raccoons one. Can't hold it against her when I haven't decided who I'm cheering for either.

About forty five percent of everything he says to the girl is utter bullshit. And for the most part, I ignore it. Not my circus, not my monkeys. I'm just here with my bestie so she can ogle her boy. I'm a snack-consuming spectator.

But when he gets a basic icing call wrong in the second, I can't bite my tongue any longer. The truth is important to me, and this douche is talking out his ass. He has his chest puffed out while he points at the ice and commentates at the top of his lungs for everyone to hear.

And he's fucking wrong.

About damn near everything.

Jesus fucking Christ.

I want to shove my pretzel in his mouth. And that's not even a euphemism. When I'm not absolutely certain on something, I keep my goddamn mouth closed. I'm way too afraid of being wrong. I'm mouthy and confident, sure, but I'm generally not wrong, and if I am, I can be humble. Unfortunately, this guy doesn't seem to suffer from the same affliction.

Leaning into his space, I speak quietly, slowly, using small words he should understand—assuming he shuts the hell up enough to hear me. "You're wrong."

A derisive snort is all I get in response.

When the play resumes, so does his running commentary.

Would anyone notice if my elbow accidentally slipped and broke his nose? He's such an arrogant prick. UGH.

A penalty is called, and this idiot makes up his own penalty explanation for his date. Since he's not open to listening to the truth, I reach over to his date. "That's not what it was. If you want, I can explain the game to you. He's only right about half the time."

She giggles, pulling a headphone out of the ear farthest away from me. "I know. That's why I'm listening to the commentary." She points up to the media box. "They're not always right, but close enough."

The guy between us goes bright red, stands up, and storms off, pausing for a beat to return and pick up his beer from the floor between our feet.

When he leaves, the girl moves into his empty seat. "Thanks for the rescue. Penelope."

"Tori."

She smiles, and I've made a new friend.

It's almost the end of the period, which means I don't have long to grab a few more shots. I'm not having much luck getting in-motion snaps. Gonna have to work harder on that, maybe spend a day in Wyatt's daycare following toddlers around. Nothing moves faster than a toddler with something they shouldn't have clutched in their tiny little hands.

I turn my attention to the bench to work on some more candid shots of the players. Focusing on the first guy, one of the de la Peña twins, I get a great shot of beads of sweat trickling off the tip of his nose. Don't know them well enough to know who's who, but one thing is for sure—they have beautiful genes.

I snap a picture of the line change, catching Twin One and Twin Two glove-bumping as they switch places. When Twin Two sits on the bench, someone leans across into the shot.

My stomach free falls with a jolt.

Those twinkling blue eyes, that firm jawline, the "everyone's friend" casual smile that lights up the whole world.

Fuck.

It's Wyatt's father.

The lying fucker is a hockey player.

And he's been here this whole time.

CHAPTER 11

Raffi

The win doesn't matter.

Okay, that's a lie. It does matter. It actually *really* matters. I've been falling behind on the ice. My legs have been heavier, my headaches more frequent, and the puck hasn't been going where it's supposed to as often as it should.

No one's said anything, but I feel it. I *feel* it. Everywhere.

In every missed pass, in every clink against the crossbar, in every training session where I slip behind by another fraction of a second.

I feel it.

But right now, it doesn't matter. The W doesn't matter. The goal and two assists I got don't matter. The bubbling headache behind my eyes doesn't matter.

What matters is the stunning woman sitting at the edge of the bench in the bar. She's got thick, curly auburn waves rolling over her shoulders. I can't see what color her eyes are from here, but they sure as hell are expressive.

When I scooch down the bench to sit next to her, her expression darkens. There's definitely murder in those eyes.

I can't for the life of me figure out who it is she wants to murder.

There's a distinct lack of hockey colors on her person, but I'm pretty sure I can convince her to cheer for our team. I'm kind of charming.

Or so I'm told at least.

Perhaps if I'm really nice, I can convince her to let me buy her a drink.

Before I can make my move, a flicker of red in my periphery catches my eye, drawing my attention from the beautiful woman I want to kiss.

The tattoo. I grab the stranger's forearm. He has a similar firecracker tattoo to me—there's no date underneath it, but his ink is close enough to my own that he might know why I got it.

"Dude." The guy moves to lift his fist until he clocks who I am. "Raffi Shaw. Great game."

"Thanks." My cheeks warm. I'm no more used to people knowing who I am in the bar now than I was in my freshman year. But I might be closer to knowing what the fuck this tattoo on my arm means.

"Your ink." I jerk my chin at his forearm.

"Yeah? Cool, right?"

Nodding, I drag my hand over my face. "It's great. Hey, did you get it for any reason?"

His brows bounce then crash into a frown. "Uh. No. Did you?" He points at mine.

With a shake of my head, my face gets hotter. "Nah, I just liked it the day I was in the tattoo parlor. I thought we might have gotten it together or something. You know, tattoo twinsies?"

"I wish." He pats my chest. "Hit me up if you ever want to get some new ink though, yeah? I have a list of tattoos I want to get."

It's never going to happen. Having art on my body and no fucking clue as to why it's there or what it means was enough to turn me off getting ink ever again. Much to Mom's delight.

I thought about getting it removed, but if I did, and it means something really fucking important, and I don't find out until later, I'll be pissed.

So I live with the firecracker ink on my skin. A constant reminder that I have a very delicate relationship with my own brain. Forced retirement is only a concussion or two away.

The doctors have suggested it over the years, but it's not going to happen. I'm not giving up the sport I love, that I need to play, just because I *might* get hurt again at some point. I can't spend my life living in fear of the outcome of something.

Mom's already saving for tickets to the NHL. For real, she's already started a savings account. NHL tickets aren't cheap, and she's so determined to watch me play she seems to forget that when I play for the National Hockey League, I'll be able to give her complimentary tickets.

But that's not the point for her. She wants to be able to hand over money to watch her son play on the ice for whatever team I manage to get signed to.

The idea of skating on NHL ice is fucking terrifying, but there's always a glimmer of hopeful excitement in my chest when I think about it.

It's similar to the glimmer of hope that ignites every time I look over at the gorgeous redhead sitting side-on to me.

I'm going to make my move. I am. As soon as I find my balls. She's just sitting, not talking to anyone, except occasionally the pink-haired woman chatting with Ares. She seems very...wholesome for his tastes. Could the hotshot goaltender be ready to settle down?

Almost laughable, but anything is possible.

Red is sitting next to Athena, Ares's sister. They aren't

really engaging in conversation as much as they're staring at Ares and the pink-haired woman.

Okay. I'm going to do it. I take the final slug of my beer and set my bottle on the table before rubbing my cold, damp palm on the side of my dress pants.

Something compels me to talk to this woman, and sooner's better than later.

I gently touch her elbow to pry her attention away from Ares. Hopefully she doesn't have a crush on him or isn't in some love triangle with the pixie and the goalie. Wouldn't that be a cool book to read at Get Lit?

Speaking of, I need to catch up on this month's read. Dammit.

Cold, hard jade eyes meet mine, as a single eyebrow arches.

I'm about to die.

"Hi." My tongue is coated in peanut butter, and my brain no longer remembers basic communication. Which would be funny if it wasn't a potential outcome from taking too many hits to the skull.

She tilts her head to the side, remaining quiet.

This chick is about to rip my head off and feed it to a pack of wild dogs. "I'm Raffi."

More silence.

"Can I buy you a drink?"

She purses her already flat lips, flaring her nostrils. I wouldn't be surprised if flames burst from her mouth when she opens it. There's a rage brewing between us that is going to explode any second, and I fear I might be on the receiving end of it if I don't haul ass out of her space.

Resting bitch face is one thing, but this...this is just next level loathing. She could simply be in a bad mood in general, but it feels more like she hates men. And right now all her rage is focused right on me.

She picks up a full glass of dark liquid, maybe Coke? And moves it over my head.

There's no way.

Except when the first drop of liquid hits my head she proves me wrong. There's absolutely a way.

She dumps the whole glass of liquid on my head, drops the glass—which I'm not fast enough to catch before it hits the ground at my feet and splinters into a million pieces—and grabs her shit and starts to leave.

When I make a move to rise, to follow her, to ask her if she has the right person, she holds her hand up like a stop sign. "If you follow me, I'll call the cops." She spins on her heel in a blur of curves and fury. The urge to go after her is strong, but last thing I need is to be arrested for harassment.

A hand appears in front of me with a stack of napkins. "What the fuck did you say?" Tate asks with a wide smirk.

The sticky liquid trickles down the back of my neck, all over my face, and onto my lap from my nose and chin. "I asked if I could buy her a drink."

"Guess she had one of her own."

"Guess so."

Who is that woman, and what the fuck just happened?

CHAPTER 12

Victoria

If I stand here for just a couple minutes longer, I'm going to be late for my appointment with Phil. That's the name of the owner guy the moms from Wyatt's daycare recommended I go to for personal training sessions.

Phil.

He doesn't sound like an asshole drill sergeant who's going to make me cry, or puke, or dislike myself more than I already do. And yet I can't convince my legs to carry me through the front doors of The Fit Factory.

Two different moms recommended I come talk to him. But when you're a big girl stepping into a new fitness place, and when you've been made to feel like shit about your size so many times over the years... It's hard walking through the doors of a new gym to meet a new, fit person you secretly hope will somehow change your life without being a judgy prick.

Stepping into the building, I suck in a steadying breath. My hands shake, my stomach hurts, and I might puke—before I've even met the guy.

There's a huge chalkboard facing the main entrance to the gym with brightly colored messages of gratitude and encouragement in numerous handwriting styles. Clearly the people who come to the gym are happy here, or at least they're not miserable enough to write horrible messages on the chalkboard like "save me" and "Phil sucks." Hopefully that means he doesn't actually suck.

The walls are covered in photographs, smiling faces both inside and out of the gym. It sets a welcoming tone, and the terror clutched in a heavy knot in my stomach relaxes just a tad.

A sign over a doorframe says, *"You don't have to see the whole staircase to take the first step."* It's a Martin Luther King, Jr. quote that makes me roll my eyes. Phil's a funny fucker. I know this already because there's a staircase through the doorway, and you can't see all of it, just the first few steps.

It leads to his torture chamber. I'm going to be out of breath by the time I get to the top.

Ugh. What am I doing here?

Stepping through the doorway I'm met with a bright light in a small alcove. Giant yellow letters on the wall tell me this is the selfie spot, and I can see why.

If I were big into social media, this would be the perfect setting for a selfie. Maybe in the future.

A winding staircase lined with yet more smiling photos of people in various stages of fitness leads me up to a black door.

Once I open it, there's no real turning back. If I try to flee, I'll likely fall down the stairs and won't ever be able to show my face again due to overwhelming embarrassment.

Hey, wait a sec, there might be something to that.

Every now and then, Wyatt needs a pep talk. When he's trying new food, or going somewhere for the first time, using the potty, or even going back to daycare for the first time after a break.

Today, I need the pep talk, and my little cheerleader is at school.

It's just me, pep talking me.

Not sure how this is going to go to be honest. I'm not good at pep talking myself at all. But at the end of the day Phil's just a human being like I am. Sure, he might have perfectly chiseled abs, and can probably lift a fucking car off the ground—I honestly have no clue since I've never seen the man before—but he had to start somewhere, right? Doesn't everyone?

He can't have been born able to lift cars, fully equipped with bulging biceps. And surely the moms from school aren't pranking me. He's got to be decent enough for a couple of them to recommend him as being down to earth and not a dick.

Not a dick, that's where the bar is. That's what we're aiming for, and poor buff-as-fuck Phil on the other side of this door has no idea.

Pulling open the door, I swallow down the fear tickling the back of my throat. I hate this. It feels like I'm walking into a new doctor's office and having to start from the beginning, all over again.

Turns out, Phil's not buff-as-fuck after all. He's just a regular human being who is also muscular. He's not like, the Hulk, or anything. He's just a guy. A nice guy from how our introductory conversation goes. I told him my history with PCOS and that my OBGYN recommended I start lifting weights to help insulin resistance, and that building muscle will help with the balance of estrogen in my body.

Fuck knows if he believed a single word that came out of my mouth about why I'm a fat girl, but he nodded and listened, and most of the time that's more than half the battle.

I might like him.

It's too soon to tell, but we'll see how things go.

For the last part of our thirty minute session, Phil makes me actually do things. I mean, I came dressed and ready to work out. Okay, I might be over stating the "ready" part, but I'm dressed for exercise at least.

We do squats and push-ups and planks and squats and kettle bell single arm rows and squats, and did I mention the squats? I've worked out a bit before, but it never took. Mostly because of the second and third day agony from waking up dormant muscles. I'm for sure not going to be able to sit on the toilet tomorrow. I'll have to work on perfecting hovering above the toilet and then dropping onto place movement.

Sweat is pouring off me by the time the fifteen minutes of devil-squats are up. Not sure what Phil was looking for from that quick run through of a number of exercises, but the temptation to lie on the gym floor and tap out was strong.

Didn't cry, didn't puke. Those are both wins.

My muscles are already screaming, asking what the fuck I was thinking just using them after all this time being inactive. This body was not designed for fitness. Fit-this-whole-cookie-in-my-mouth more like.

Gonna hurt like hell tomorrow.

"I'm dying." I want to starfish on the floor, but at this point I'm not sure I could get back up.

"You're not dying, you just can't think of anything good to do."

"Uh...?" I can think of at least thirteen thousand better things to do than be right here at the gym with sweat trickling down my sternum and into my sports bra.

Phil raises an eyebrow at the confusion on my face. He's got a look on his face that says, "Why did I take this woman on as a client?" I have no idea why.

"Ferris Bueller?" Phil's eyes rise up his forehead, but I don't know why.

Still nothing. I mean, I know of the movie. Pretty sure I watched it once, but from the way his eyes go wide it's like I just kicked his puppy, or his favorite pair of Asics.

Shaking his head, he sighs with a laugh. "You're not dying, you just can't think of anything good to do is a quote from Ferris Bueller."

He shakes his head again, clearly despairing at my lack of Ferris Bueller knowledge. I mean, I enjoy movies as much as the next person, but I'm not a diehard movie lover. Perhaps Phil will give me a couple of good recommendations to watch with Mom.

Could talking about his love of movies save me from this torture chamber?

By the time I leave, my limbs are shaking. I've finished two bottles of water, need to pee, and my shirt is sticking to my back.

It's my first session, and while the OBGYN said to trust her, right now, I'm not sure I'm cut out to be a gym rat. The idea of doing that all over again, even just one more time, never mind for months on end... Ugh.

Can't pizza just make me skinny?

No. This time's different.

This time isn't about being skinnier or prettier. It's not about fitting into pre-pregnancy clothes I've held onto for years in the hopes I'll finally get back into them. It's not about what I'm *supposed* to look like by the unrealistic standards of social media influencers.

It's about getting my PCOS under control, not bleeding through my fucking clothes and sheets every month when I get my period, living a longer and healthier life for both my son and myself.

This time is different. It has to be.

And if doing all the right things means I end up losing weight, and fitting into old clothes, those are bonuses I'll happily take, but it's not the goal. And I need to keep reminding myself of that.

Dragging myself through the front door of the house is

hard. My legs feel like I crammed my feet into the holes of those stupid kettlebells, and they're weighing me down as I move.

Why the fuck do people do this to themselves?

That's when it hits me. During my time at the gym, I never once thought about Raffi fucking Shaw or the fact that he's a lying, ghosting, scumbag hockey player who tried to hit on me in the bar like he's never had his dick inside me.

Bringing my thoughts back to the lopsided smile and twinkling eyes makes my blood go from gym-hot to ready-to-boil-over.

I already agreed to go to another game with Eloise, and she suspected something was very wrong from how I stormed out of the bar the other night. To her credit, she hasn't pressed me for information, but that's not going to last forever, especially if I flake on her this weekend.

I'm definitely not ready to see Raffi again. I might slice his throat with the heel of my shoe if I do. Or, I dunno, something more effective at the murder thing.

It's hard enough to look into Wyatt's eyes every day without looking into the eyes that started it all. I'll have to pretend I'm sick. Mom won't cover for me if I don't tell her why, and I'm not ready to talk about him yet either.

Ugh.

Why does he have to randomly appear back in my life again and fuck things up?

CHAPTER 13

Raffi

Being from the Midwest there are some culinary delights we take for granted that other states don't have the pleasure of experiencing. I know this because guys I've played with over the years have made some weird faces at our Midwestern delicacies.

Midwesterners can turn just about anything into a salad—I don't know how cottage cheese, Jell-O, and a can of fruit constitutes a salad, but the Midwest says it is. Salads, tenderloin, and Maid-Rite, those are my top three.

Still remember the first time I took the de la Peñas to Maid-Rite, a Midwestern institution. They're from the Dominican Republic, and while they loathed Taco Bell—probably because their family owns an *actual* Mexican restaurant—they *loved* Maid-Rite.

We come here at least once a week as a team. Or as many of us who can make it. It gets rowdy, and most of us order the same thing to the point the nice folks at the counter know what we're having before we do.

It's part of the routine. Same day, same place, same food,

same seats. No one says it out loud, but it definitely feels like a superstition.

The only reason people miss Maid-Rite Mondays (MRM) is if they're sick, or if they have something better to do than ensuring the Raccoons win their next game.

If someone misses MRM and we lose a game, the loss is firmly on their shoulders, and they're shamed for all eternity.

It's a heavy burden to carry. But it is what it is if you fuck with MRM.

The Cheese-Rite is the only way to go. *"A perfectly seasoned ground beef loose meat sandwich served on a warm bun, then choose your cheese."*

Depending on who's working behind the counter, the amount of cheese on my sandwich varies. If Jaden's working, it's almost equal parts meat and cheese—he's my favorite. Most of the time I get a basket with cheese curds, or rings, or sweet potato fries. Okay, the sides are the hardest part to figure out because they're just so damn good, and I generally want them all.

So when I walk past a table, clutching my precious MRM meal on a tray on my way to the hockey table, and spy someone eating a chicken salad and drinking a water—in Maid-Rite—I almost grind to a halt.

Someone behind me grunts as their tray jabs them in the stomach, so I keep moving. Can't risk my root beer float hitting the deck. But as soon as I sit down, I examine the poor soul who doesn't know how to Maid-Rite right.

Holy shit, it's her. The girl who dumped a drink on my head at the bar.

My eyes don't linger on her chicken salad for much longer. Her hair's pulled onto her head in a messy top-knot thing, it looks on-purpose messy, not straggly. I learned the hard way that the distinction is an important one for some women.

She doesn't have a trace of makeup on her face, and she's smiling down at...

Jesus fucking Christ, it's me.

I mean, it's not me, because, well, I'm me, but it's a tiny version of me. He has the same button nose, his hair slicks up in the front like in the millions of photos Mom has of me as a kid.

His hair is red like his mom's, but everything else about the kid is me. The shape of his face, the slope of his nose, the cheeky grin with adorable dimples. He's like a mini me. I must be hallucinating. It's not one of the symptoms of concussion, but maybe something's playing with my brain right now.

I need air. Pushing to my feet, I mutter that I'm going to take a leak and beeline for the bathroom. Leaning over the sinks, I stare at myself in the mirror. I can't have seen what I thought I saw, right?

I'd know if I had a child. Especially one that's walking, talking, and eating a Kids-Rite like a badass.

I splash water on my face, as cold as I can get it, dry off, and do it again. There's no way I have a kid, pretty sure I'd remember if I conceived a fucking child. For a long moment I stare at the ink on my arm, tracing over the numbers etched into my skin under the firecracker tattoo. Is that his birthday?

Math could fit, but how can I not remember my own child?

They're gone by the time I get back to the table, and my food's gone too. That's what I get for leaving it unattended around these assholes.

My stomach's queasy though, and I don't even want my half-empty float. The background noise of the restaurant is suddenly deafening. Every fork clinking against a plate, every glass being placed on the table, every time the front door opens—it's all magnified. My head throbs.

There's a nagging at the back of my brain that what I saw

is what I fucking saw. But I don't know the first thing about reaching out and contacting her. If I did, what would I say? Oh, hey, is that my kid? She'd probably dump another glass of something on my head.

I have no idea what the hell to do. If he's my kid, I want to step up, be his dad, but taking on a kid while I'm in college trying to get a break and get into the NHL... Fuck. That's a lot.

It's more than a lot.

There's a chance I'm overreacting, seeing things I want to see. Maybe there's some day-dreaming analyst who can tell me what it means to see yourself in the face of another woman's kid.

On the other hand, there's a chance he's really mine, in which case, I at least need to have a conversation with his mom. And while I have no clue where I could find her, there's at least one person on the team who could help me.

"Hey, Ares?"

Our goaltender slurps the last of his milkshake before meeting my stare.

"I need your help."

CHAPTER 14

Raffi

She's not at the game. Ares's girl is in the stands, but there's no sign of the redhead whose name I have come to learn is Tori.

Not sure if it's short for anything, but it's one of the questions I've added to the list of things I'd like to talk to her about. Didn't Eloise give her my number?

Eloise shrugs when she catches me staring. She mouths something, but I can't make it out. I wave it off. No biggie, right?

My gut stirs. It has been unsettled since I saw the child I'm almost entirely sure is mine. Fuck. I don't know whether to be angry or sad. Did she try to find me? Did she just let me live my life this whole time and not bother telling me? Did she have a hard time during her pregnancy? Was his birth okay? Has she spent this whole time alone and raising our kid?

I need answers. Questions swirl in my brain, not letting up.

Jackson Gilbert comes up behind me. "You okay? You look a bit green."

"I'm good. Too much cheese."

His face contorts. "You're gonna stink all fucking night."

Probably accurate.

I'd love to say that was my best game ever, but it wasn't. There's a heaviness in my bones I can't shake. Pretty sure I zoned out for chunks of the game, staring into space. Not really great when you're trying to make an impression on the coaching staff. At least not if you want to make a positive impression.

Tonight, I'm heading to Mom's after the game. I need to talk to her about things with Tori, how to proceed, what to say, what to do. I don't really know if she's going to be ecstatic or lose her shit. Might not even mention it to her at all. Depends how I feel when I get there.

Before I get in the car, I head to the hockey house to dump my gear and grab my overnight bag. The guys are all at the bar post-game, so it's just me and the low-key odor no one can figure out that lingers in the hockey house.

My bag's all ready to go, but I feel like a sandwich so while I'm eating slices of turkey straight out of the packet, I pull up tonight's match report, which is already written and online by the one and only Tabitha.

I don't always agree with what she says in these things, but it'd at least be nice to fill in some of the blanks from the night.

Tonight, the UCR Raccoons return to home ice at The Trash Can and welcome the Minnesota Snow Pirates.

Resident hot-shot goaltender Ares de la Peña made 41 saves and the Cedar Rapids Raccoons bagged another 'W' with a 2-0 win. This reporter had to ask how it felt to have another win under his belt. "You make your own luck," said de la Peña. "You could have the exact same set of circumstances every night, same team, same players, same everything, but there's an element of luck in every game. That keeps me humble."

A snort bursts out of me. "Humble" isn't exactly a word I

would use to describe Ares de la Peña. In the silence, I'm convinced someone sniffs. It's probably Bacon, our team's pot-belly pig mascot. Usually he stays in Ares's fancy-ass apartment across town, but every now and then he'll bring him to a game, and drop him here before heading out.

Raffi Shaw had an assist and Brady Faber scored his first goal in his third game for the Raccoons as a recent transfer to the team from Michigan.

Faber, 18, made it 1-0 with a snap shot from just inside the blue line at 7:54 of the second period.

"The Snow Pirates are such an aggressive team as far as how much pressure they put on you," Coach Bales said. "We didn't get out of our zone as quickly as we'd have liked in the first period. But we started to get forward and into their zone a bit more."

Raccoons Captain, Apollo de la Peña, had nothing but praise for the visiting team. "They're a solid team, hard to play against. They play fast and tough. They've got really good sticks. Unfortunately for Séb, he took shots from some of the best. And there is no goaltender better than Ares."

Part of me wants to roll my eyes. Sure the guy's going to say that about his brother. He's also not wrong. We're championship-heat hot right now, without a shadow of a doubt, and it's in large part to Ares between the pipes.

Someone blows their nose, and I know for damn sure pigs can't do that. Bacon's smart as hell, and if we teach him to do something, he's pretty quick on the uptake, however, to my knowledge, no one's ever taught him to blow his nose.

Plus, pigs don't have thumbs.

"Hello?" Dropping the slice of turkey on the counter, I lick my fingers. Probably rude to punch someone in the face with turkey-juice fingers, but it's equally rude to break into someone's house to blow your nose, so I guess we're even.

We have a couple baseball bats lying around the house.

Not necessarily for protection, some of the guys play in their spare time. But right now, it's the closest thing on hand to confront The Sniffer. I probably don't need it, but it's coming with me, just in case—I'm definitely not our team's muscle. If there's trouble, I'll need a weapon for sure.

The first three bedrooms I check are empty. The light's on in the main bathroom, shining through the door that's barely cracked open. Movement, sound, light—safe bet whoever's home is in there. Just call me Detective.

If they are a robber, that's not where we keep the meds, so they're shit out of luck if they're looking for a quick high.

"Hello?"

"Shit." It's a female voice, but I'm on alert so I don't lower my bat. There's a scramble in the bathroom, Bacon screeches —whoever's in there probably stepped on his tail. He hates when people do that. "Be out in a minute."

The door snaps shut, the faucet turns on, there's a couple splashes of water, and it's not long before the door opens again.

Athena de la Peña—whose brothers and closest friends call Hen—steps out in sweats and an oversized hoodie that falls all the way to her knees. I've never seen her so casual before.

Her hair hangs limply around her face. There are dark circles under her eyes, and if I'm not mistaken, a bruise blooming on her cheek. But I'm not close enough to look, and she's staring at me like if I don't stop looking at her she's going to stab me.

"Could you put the bat down, Raffi?" She puts her hands up. "I'm unarmed." She jerks her head at the potbellied pig at her feet. "Bacon might disagree. There was an incident with the tail."

Wincing, I nod, lowering the bat. "Are you—?"

"I'm waiting for Scott."

We speak at the same time, our words colliding in the thick

air between us. She's very clearly not okay, and I don't know her well enough to get in her space. All I want to do is hug her. She looks like she needs a hug. But Athena doesn't do hugs.

"Scott," I repeat his name slowly in case I misheard. Scott isn't one of her three brothers, and while he's a close family friend, I wouldn't guess he'd be her first call when she needed something.

The de la Peñas close ranks hard and fast when something goes wrong.

"I can call one of your brothers if you want?"

She shakes her head for a long moment before she speaks. "I need you to pretend you didn't see me, Raffi."

I'm not hugely comfortable with the suggestion that I lie to my brothers, the guys who have my back on the ice. But when her voice cracks on the word "please," the decision is made. I've never heard her say please to anyone, ever.

"Sure. No sweat. I won't say anything. You want some Gatorade? I was just making a sandwich." As I point behind me to the staircase, I shake my head. "That's a lie, I was planning to make a sandwich but I got sidetracked eating lunch meat straight from the packet."

That gets the smallest smile from her. I suck at making tea, but I'll make her ten cups right now if it makes her feel better. She looks like shit.

She walks down the stairs in front of me in silence. In the kitchen, she leans against the counter, folds her arms, and stares blankly at a spot on the wall in front of her. If she doesn't want to talk, I won't force her. I'm not going to make her make small talk if she just doesn't have the energy. Scott can't be too far away, and when he gets here I'll haul ass and give them their space. But first, I'll feed her. Everyone loves sandwiches.

It's very clearly not a sordid, secret, sexy rendezvous between them. If anything I'd say she needs a friend, and that friend currently isn't me. I'd almost prefer it was a sordid affair to keep secret from her brothers. Her energy is all off, and she's sad. It's disconcerting.

Snagging my slice of meat off the counter, I wiggle it at her. "I left this here when I thought we were being robbed."

She stares at the piece of meat dangling from my fingers before I cram it into my mouth. Definitely doesn't want to chit chat. I make the sandwiches in silence, making enough for Scott when he gets back. Nothing worse than getting home and finding other people eating something you really want to chow down on.

"Bright eyes?" Scott's panicked voice echoes through the otherwise empty house. Bacon makes a shuffling dash toward the newcomer and crashes into something with a thud, probably Scott. Bacon's always ready for scratches. Because of course Scott is only there to deliver attention to the piggy. "Athena?" A pause. "Hen?"

"She's in here."

Her head snaps up like she realized he's really here and sad, red-rimmed eyes meet mine.

"Doubt he's calling me bright eyes." My attempt at lightening the mood falls flat.

Her face pales.

"Don't worry. He's not my type." Humor's all I've got in this situation. I grab my sandwich, my go bag, and offer what I hope is a reassuring smile before I walk past Scott. "Sandwiches are on the counter."

He doesn't take his eyes off Athena. "Thanks, man. And I hope it goes without saying..."

I shake my head. "Never saw a thing."

"Thanks." Athena's voice is small as I leave the room.

The last thing I hear before the door to the house slams shut behind me is a fresh wave of tears hitting the most badassest of bitches any of us have ever met.

Twenty minutes later, my mood hasn't improved. I'm distracted by whatever the hell has Athena crying to Scott, and the possibility of having my own kid, but I'm standing outside my parent's house. Mom's spied me through the window, so I'm on the hook for a visit.

"Hey, sweetheart." She rushes out in her robe and slippers. "How's my favorite superstar hockey player?"

My chest caves a little.

Can't I just be her son? It's like a constant reminder of the weight of their expectations holding down my shoulders. What would happen if I didn't become a superstar hockey player? What would I be to her then?

She'd still love me, right?

Would they complain about all the money they invested in me, in the game, their time, all the driving to and from practices and games? It's been quite an investment all around.

Fuck. That's unfair. My mood is sour, my mind so distracted with everything going on.

Mom releases me from her bear hug. "What's wrong? Moms always know, sweetheart. What is it?"

With a shake of my head, I follow her inside. My ass is barely on a stool at the breakfast bar before she's in a blur of motion, pulling stuff out of the fridge. "Are we talking cheese and crackers level, or...?"

I can't lie to her. Apparently I can't school my face either.

"Alrighty then, time for the big guns." She bends over into the freezer, digging in the shelves for something. "Travis. Travis! Get in here, Raffi's back. Traviiiiis." She won't stop yelling until he answers or appears.

"Ani, I'm right here. There's no need to yell."

Mom's Armenian—her name means "very beautiful," and her mom, my *tatik,* is named Heghine, which means "luminant and radiant." I've never really seen people as their names, but *mayrik* and *tatik* are the two most beautiful women I've ever seen.

The contrast of Mom's dark hair, dark eyes and pale skin is striking when she stands up from the freezer next to Dad. He has red hair, bright blue eyes, and skin so white it's almost transparent. Not to mention that Travis is the most un-Irish name for a man with Irish heritage, but I guess his mom really liked the name when she moved to the US.

My brother Razmik, Raz for short, is an ice road trucker who lives in Canada. We see him once a year when he and his family come south for some sunshine. He got red hair and brown eyes, and I got brown hair and blue eyes. Some days I wonder if we both came from the same parents, but then I see pictures of our grandparents and there's no doubt we're all from the same family line.

"What's wrong?" Dad's forehead wrinkles as he takes me in. "You take another hit?" He rounds the breakfast bar and grabs my face. He's not a doctor, but you bet your ass he knows what the symptoms of concussion are, and he quizzes me regularly to make sure I'm not losing my memory.

"Dad." I flap at his arms but he doesn't let go.

"Are you getting enough sleep? You look tired."

Jesus, here we go.

Mom drops whatever she's pulled from the freezer onto the counter and shoves Dad out of the way. "You're not sleeping? Raphael this isn't like you. Next you'll be telling me you aren't eating."

Dad laughs. "Then we know the world is ending."

They back up. Dad pulls a couple beers from the fridge, Mom goes about defrosting whatever deliciousness she's cooking up and they both just kinda wait, staring. The pressure of their silent gaze makes me crack.

Taking a long slow gulp of my beer, I damn near choke

when it goes down the wrong pipe. I thump at my chest for a couple seconds while swallowing a few times.

"I think I have a kid."

Mom gasps, her brows shooting up and grabs Dad's arm. Dad's face doesn't change. I hate that he has this unnerving ability to shield what he's thinking and feeling. I can't do that, and I never know if I'm in trouble with him or not.

"You didn't glove up?" He shakes his head. "Raffi, we've always preached safe sex in this house."

Mom rubs her cheek with her palm. "Well, we have a few months to get ready, right? They don't just come out full sized. They've gotta cook in the oven for a while."

Holding up a hand, I shake my head. "I didn't get someone pregnant. Well, I may have, but not recently. The kid's a toddler. And I'm like, almost sure he's mine."

Dad pulls out a stool and Mom sits on it. She's clutching her chest now, her face contorted, nose scrunched, lips pursed. "Raffi, I don't understand. How can you have a child?"

Shrugging, I shake my head. "I don't know. But I think it's something to do with this." Pulling up my sleeve, I brandish my ink at them. "The date. I think this tattoo may have something to do with it." Rubbing at my face with both hands, I grunt. "I don't remember." My whisper is quiet, but since it's the only sound in the kitchen, they hear me.

A squeak of a chair against the tiles suggests either Dad sat down or Mom got up. When a warm hand meets my spine and rubs soothing circles, I know it's probably the latter.

"We've got you, Raphael. It's all going to be okay. Whatever happened, or happens, you have our full support." She leans close. "I have another grandbaby?"

I nod. "He looks just like me, *mayrik,* I can't see how he's not mine. And his mom," I heave out a sigh. "She hates me. She's so angry at me like...like I got her pregnant and left her to fend for herself." I know it's probably a stretch. There's probably no way he's mine, but something about the moment I saw that child and his mom that tickled something in the depths of my chest. It hasn't left me alone since.

Dad hands me a tissue for the tears I didn't realize were coursing down my face.

"What do I say to her? Hi, I think that might be my kid. Know I haven't been around for a while but can I take him to a hockey game?" My shoulders shake.

"No, Raf." Dad reaches out and takes my hand. "You tell her you suffered memory loss from an incident on the ice. There are news articles, pictures of you in hospital, hell, there are medical records, witnesses. She'll know you're not making it up."

"What's more." Mom puts the container of food into the microwave and pushes buttons. "You know this. What's this really about? You're fearless." She wipes her hands on her apron before coming over to me again, gripping my shoulders. "Ah." She stops. "You're afraid of this. A tiny child."

"They are fearsome little creatures to be fair." Dad tips his beer to mine before tossing back a drink. "But you've got this, Raffi."

"And whatever you don't have, we've got you."

There are too many words building at the back of my throat but none come out, only tears. Mom pulls me against her, letting me cry on her shoulder. I can't remember the last time I broke down to my parents, or needed The Mom Hug deployed, but right now, in this moment, she's all that's holding me together.

"I don't have time to have a child." The words come out jerky, fragmented between sniffling sobs.

Dad chuckles. "No one does, Raf. You *make* the time. They're eating, crying, shitting machines that cost a fucking fortune. But they're also the very best parts of you and are worth every second, every penny, every sleepless night." He cuffs my arm. "And if we've done our job right, you've got nothing to worry about. Is it hard? Yes, absolutely. But it's also the most rewarding and educational thing you'll ever do in your life."

Mom's dabbing at her eyes with her apron. "He's not wrong, sweetheart. You and your brother were the best gift God could have ever given both of us. Do you want us to come with you?"

Hard pass. I don't want to blindside the poor girl with a ready-made family of in-laws.

With a shake of my head, I offer a small smile. "No thanks. I've got to approach her myself. We'll see where it goes though." I pat her arm. "One step at a time."

Her eyes sparkle with excitement. I know what she's thinking. Seeing her grandkids only a couple of times a year drives her up the wall. Raz only brings them down once, but she and Dad make the trek into the Canadian tundra a couple times annually to see everyone.

Having a grandkid on her doorstep would bring her so much joy. But I can't fuck this up again. I need to figure out what to say, how to say it, and where to approach Tori. I need to find a way to get her to let me meet my son.

My son.

The more I think about it, the more I know he's mine. It settles into my chest with an ease, a warmth. There's something about this woman. And I'm determined to find out what it is.

CHAPTER 15

Victoria

"I can't."

"Yes, you can."

"What the fuck do you know?" I've only been to see Phil for a couple sessions, and already we've exited the honeymoon phase. Truthfully, I'm not sure we had a honeymoon phase.

This man is Satan and makes every part of my body hurt, every time I climb the stupid stairs.

"If you'd've stopped running your mouth for thirty seconds you could have been done by now. Instead, you're telling me you can't, when we both know you can. So woman up, channel the womb fury, and lift the damn kettlebells." Satan gives back as good as he gets. It's one of the things I like about him.

He's fluent in sarcasm and banter and all out of fucks. Plus, when he says things like "womb fury," my pelvic floor muscles threaten to up and quit on me. He doesn't like Abba or Megan Trainor though, so I'm not sure I can ever fully trust him, but he's funny as fuck, and from what I can tell, he knows his shit about this gym thing.

"If I lift it, can I swing it at your head?"

He grins at me, but takes a step back. "If you can catch me."

We both know that's never going to happen.

"I watched that movie you mentioned." Sweat's already trickling down my forehead. Why am I at the gym again? Whose bright idea was this?

I've only had a few sessions with Phil, but each time, movies come up. He's a big movie buff. He told me his girlfriend found this one on a streaming site and suggested I watch it.

"Which one?"

"*Love at First Sight.*"

"You like it?"

"Made me cry." If my arms worked right now I'd smack him, but considering I've just done a bazillion step-ups onto a bench with three million pound kettlebells in my hands, I'm not sure I even have arms.

Also, that may be a slight exaggeration. They were twenty pounds each, but they most definitely felt like three million. My burning shoulders and forearms can attest to the fact.

"I haven't seen it." He's already lost count of how many step-ups I've done. I might not know him well yet, but I know he can't fucking count, and I need to pay particular attention to my number of reps.

"You should watch it, grab the tissues though."

Phil strikes me as a sensitive soul. I tend not to cry at much of anything, so I'm a terrible judge of whether something's emotional or not.

"Watched *No Hard Feelings,* too. Love Jennifer Lawrence so much."

"Wasn't it great?" Phil's clearly lost count of the reps. Not that I blame him, the movie in question has a full frontal nudity scene when Jennifer Lawrence runs out of the ocean onto the beach to chase some kids who stole her clothes.

Damnit, now I've lost count, too.

When I finally finish my last set of step ups, I've gone over my time by a few minutes. There's something about this gym that doesn't feel like a gym. It's a wide open loft, there is equipment lining the perimeter and a wide open space in the middle the instructors use for spin classes, circuits, and various other activities.

Loud music and bright purple and blue lights make it feel less like a clinical, same-old gym, and more like somewhere fun. My muscles don't currently agree, but I always leave in a better mood than when I arrive.

"You have someone else coming in?"

Phil slaps his palms together and rubs them. "Conveyor belt of pain." The glee in his eyes cracks me up. The guy's a sadist. For sure.

When I turn to cross the space to get my jacket and bag from the front desk area, my eyes land on familiar bright blue eyes and my stomach plummets. Raffi Shaw stands staring back at me.

Can't even pretend I didn't see him, he's looking *right* at me. He's standing next to someone who could also be a hockey player, but without his name emblazoned across his shoulders, I don't know who he is.

"Raffi." Phil waves across the room to the man who sucked every bit of oxygen out of it. "You're up. See you Wednesday, Tori."

Raffi nods, but holds up two fingers at our personal trainer. "Can we talk?"

If my stomach wasn't through the floor already, it would be twisting up in knots.

He waits for me to grab my stuff and follows me out onto the landing outside the door.

"You workout here?"

His brows flinch. "What? No. Why would you say that?"

"This gym isn't near campus. You have no reason to be here."

"Neither do you." He points at me, the corners of his lips threatening to turn up into a smile.

I'm not telling him I live near here. He doesn't need to know that. "I heard Phil was a great trainer." And I got an intro package for classes at an absolute steal so there were no more excuses not to get my ass to the gym.

"Me too." He scrubs the back of his neck, eyes cast to the floor between our feet. "I gave Eloise my number. We should talk." His eyes are swimming with emotions I can't read and imploring me not to lose my shit at him.

It takes all my fucking strength not to shove his ass down the stairs. "About what?"

He casts a tentative glance over his shoulder. "Please? Can I just have your number? We can talk."

Is this fucker for real? Flexing my hands by my sides, I need to finger the edges of my clothing so I don't deck this asshole. "Where's your phone?"

He whips it out of the pocket of his sweats and holds it out to me.

With a shake of my head, I point at the damn thing. "Unlock it, and go to your contacts."

His head starts moving slowly from side to side as all color drains from his face. "No." It's barely a whisper. He turns the phone to me, he's at 'T' in his contacts, and my name's not there. "Short for Victoria, right?" He scrolls further into the alphabet and there's no sign of my name there either.

I can't even with this dumbass. "You're kidding me, right?"

His eyes are pleading with me. "I—uh."

"Go to 'F'"

Confusion pinches his brow as his thumb works the screen. It takes a long minute of scrolling the names on the list. Scroll up, head tip, scroll back. His eyes are working up and down while he nibbles on his bottom lip.

I see the exact moment when he realizes he's had my number this whole time. How did he not know that? It's literally *right* there. Regardless, it's the final nail in the coffin for this ghosting prick. I'm already turned on my heel and halfway down the stairs when a single word falls from his lips that brings tears to my eyes.

"Firecracker."

CHAPTER 16

"Thanks for agreeing to meet with me." Dunno why the words coming out of my mouth are so measured, clipped, and formal when my insides are like they've been pushed through a shredder.

I swallow.

She doesn't move, doesn't say a thing.

We're the only people in Get the Fork Out—the local, secret, tiny pie cafe inside a dry cleaners—and we've both ordered a slice of savory pie. It's the first time I've been here since ownership changed. Apparently the old owner wanted to move home to Ireland to be closer to his family, so he sold the business and left.

The new owner, Megan, is a bubbly young woman who seems to know her pie stuff. Apparently she was Brian's sous chef, and the key to all the amazing pie secrets. But the proof is in the eating.

Victoria just stares at me, silent loathing seeping out of her body as she mentally plans various ways to kill me. At least that's how it feels, like she's plotting my murder. Repeatedly.

I guess it's time to come clean. "I don't remember you."

She recoils like I smacked her.

"I have a history of taking bad hits during games and getting concussions. From what I can piece together, I met you, then I got concussion and lost a few days of my memory."

Her face is twisted by emotions. Anger, suspicion and heartbreak all flicker across her beautiful features.

She leans toward me. "You don't remember me?"

A shake of my head is all I can manage in response.

"At all?" Her voice is loaded with grief, like I reached into her chest and gripped her heart with scissors.

Another shake.

She opens her purse and pulls out her phone. While she searches for something—probably a news article about my face colliding with the plexi glass—Megan brings our pies, but I can't stomach a single bite until we figure this out.

"Th-that's the day after..." Her voice is quiet. Her face falls as she reads. Her chin trembles, and before I can blink, tears stream down her face. She pushes back from the table, grabbing her purse as she does. She's going to bolt.

Not gonna happen. If I have a chance of connecting with this woman it needs to be now, while she's emotional, showing something other than repugnance toward me.

I bounce out of my chair and onto my feet. "Please don't run, Victoria."

Her eyes flex wide as I open my arms. I'm not letting her run. She's a stranger, but we have history. There's a pull in my chest when I'm near her that tells me I can't just let her leave.

She presses against my chest with both palms flat, but I don't relent. I curl her against my chest and just hold her.

She falls apart. Heaving sobs wrack her entire body, so I hold her tighter. Her bag drops to the floor with a thud and Megan steps out from behind the counter to see if she needs to help somehow.

Or at least that's what I think she's mouthing over Victoria's head. I mouth back that it's okay, but from the down-turned lips and the frown she's sporting, I'm not sure whether she believes me or not.

"Easy, hey, come on, you're going to pass out if you keep this up. Can you take a slow breath for me, please?"

Victoria shakes her head against my body, so I squeeze even tighter. After a few long moments, her shaking shoulders slow to a stop, and when she eventually lifts her head and meets my eyes, hers are watery and red-rimmed.

"Don't leave."

She nods, but it's shaky, and her focus is on the door behind me.

"I mean it. We'll figure this out."

"You forgot me. You didn't ghost me."

Her words drive ice picks through my chest. "Victoria." My thumbs brush tears from her red, blotchy cheeks. "I would never, in a million years, ghost anyone. Let alone someone as beautiful as you."

She casts her eyes at the floor, and my heart splinters. What's going through her head? What misbeliefs about herself has she held onto for the past couple years that are untrue all because I hit my head and forgot who she is?

"He's mine, isn't he?"

Wide eyes flicker back to my face. "H-how?"

"Saw you with a kid that looks very much like me at Maid-Rite. He's mine?"

She sniffs, reaching around me to a napkin on the table to blow her nose. "Wyatt. But I didn't know who you were." She shrugs. "To be honest even if I did I thought you ghosted me, so I probably would have kept your name off the paperwork."

I have a son named Wyatt.

"I'm not ready for you to meet him." She shakes her head. "This is a lot. Too much. I-I need to process."

Nodding, I can't help but agree. It's a lot for both of us.

"Are you okay enough to fill in some of the blanks for me? Or do you need some space and time to clear your head first?"

Her gaze flits to the table. "I really want pie."

A girl after my own heart. My stomach rumbles in response, and she laughs. The sound is glorious after the past few minutes of gut wrenching tears.

She sits, but I stay standing, half poised to tackle her if she makes a run for it.

"Sit down, Raffi. I'm not going to leave."

Slowly, I lower my ass onto the chair and relish the yummy sounds she makes after she takes a huge bite. Leaning towards me with a smile, she points her fork at me. "You know, Megan might make better pies than Brian did."

Wow. There's no higher accolade. Brian's pies are unrivaled.

She narrows her eyes at me. "You called me Victoria."

"I did." I carve a giant bite from my slice of pie. "Is that not okay? I feel like you're more Victoria than Tori, but if you hate Victoria..."

"What?" She tilts her head to the side.

"I don't want to give you any more reason to plot my death."

"That obvious?"

Chuckling, I pause the fork on its way to my mouth. "You don't have a resting bitch face, you have a resting murder Raffi face."

She laughs again, and it melts the icicles that speared my chest. "In my defense." She pauses to take another bite of pie and leaves a trail of crumbs along her bottom lip.

Reaching out, I capture the crumbs with my thumb before they fall to the table.

She gasps, her body popping back as she stares at my outstretched hand.

"What?" I lick the buttery pastry debris from my thumb.

Her jaw trembles again. Fuck. What did I do? Did she really want those crumbs? I mean, the pastry is delicious, but it wasn't that big a piece. She can have mine if it'll make her better.

There's a familiarity with her that makes me uneasy. I don't like how my body instinctively wants to protect this woman I can't remember, yet at the same time, I want to get to know her.

There's a reason she's the mother of my child, and I'm not superficial enough for it to simply be because she's a beautiful woman.

And she fucking well is.

She touches her fingers to her lip where I brushed off the crumbs. Have I done that before? Is that why she's so upset by the movement?

"Peanut butter and jelly sandwiches."

Good choice. One of my top five sandwich fillings.

"You really don't remember?"

Dredging the corners of my mind, I come up empty. Nothing. Nada. "I'm sorry." It's the only thing I can think of to say.

She takes another bite of her pie before she launches into our story. She tells me about the jail and bail, how I shared my sandwiches with her, and convinced her to let me take her on a date.

"Wait. Why didn't you want to date me? I'm a catch." Puffing out my chest makes her laugh again, but it's the eye roll that sets my soul alive. That eye roll was freakin' impressive.

"I *am* a catch. I mean, so my mom says."

She snorts. "My mom does not." She winces. "But she also doesn't know...everything." She shakes her head. "Are you okay now? The article I looked at said you got hit pretty badly."

"Hazard of the job." I point at her. "We're not skipping the point where you didn't want to date me. Don't you think I'm pretty?" I clutch my chest with a gasp.

She searches the table, probably for something to throw at my face. "I'd just broken up with an asshole ex who did a number on me. I didn't want to date anyone. Especially hockey playing someones who didn't tell me they play hockey."

My stomach falls. "Why wouldn't I have told you I play hockey?"

Her face turns red again. "I was pretty vocal about my loathing of hockey players."

"So you never knew I played hockey. But you knew my name was Raffi, and I went to school here?" I can't figure out how she couldn't have tracked me down. There can't be all that many Raffis here on campus.

She shakes her head, toying with a piece of pastry crust. "We gave each other fake names."

It's a fucking Greek tragedy. I'd say it's Shakespearean, but so far, no one's died.

Please God tell me no one dies.

"Because of course we did."

"You really didn't want me to know you played hockey."

Nodding, I give past Raffi both a high five and a head slap. "If I'd told you that, you most definitely wouldn't have dated me. Was it a good date?"

Her mouth snaps closed, fork poised in front of her face loaded with her last bite of pie. Her eyes brim with tears. "The best. I gave you my number. And despite myself, despite my cheating asshole ex leaving me damaged, I wanted to hear from you so badly."

There goes the chin again.

Nooooo. Can we go back to banter and eye rolls please? Please? Anything that isn't this stunning woman crying. It hurts on a level I'm not sure I'm ready to accept yet.

"So I ghosted you, and a few weeks later you find out you're pregnant, don't know who the father is, and have to make a decision about whether or not to be a single, teenage mom? Fuck." Anguish sears my skin as I scrape my hands over my face. This woman has a titanium spine. The past few years couldn't have been easy for her, and yet, she's in college, she has a gorgeous kid, and she hasn't stabbed me with a fork.

It's not my fault. Rationally, I know this. But at the same time, it is. If I hadn't lied to her off the bat, if I had just given her my fucking name, I could have helped her.

Did she get morning sickness or those stupidly painful leg cramps my cousin got when she had all three of her kids?

Who was with her in the hospital?

The pie in my stomach sits like a lead weight.

"What?" Her piercing jade eyes nail me with a hard look.

"I just... I don't know how you did it. You're a fucking badass." There's no other word for it, she truly is a gladiator. "Were you completely alone? Did your friends and family at least rally around you?"

It's my turn to fight tears. If she says no, if her family kicked her out for getting pregnant, or her friends abandoned her... My heart can't take it.

"Mom had my back the whole time." She gets a far off look in her eyes. "Friends drifted away. But I'm getting back out and making some new ones."

"Like Eloise."

She nods, smiling. "We're like oil and water in some ways, but we work well together."

An awkward silence hangs between us. I'm not sure where to go from here. "You want a dessert slice?" I'm half out of my chair, ready to snag us round two of pies, but she shakes her head.

"I should get back."

Of course. She has a little boy to look after. *Our* little boy. My stomach flutters. It's not the time to ask to meet him, not yet anyway. She's flighty, and emotional, and she's probably going to have to wade through a lot of trauma before she's ready to talk about me meeting him. But the thought of getting to hang out with a piece of me… It's almost too much to keep contained inside my body.

Should I ask to see a picture of him? Is that too far?

A photo might keep the rabid grandmother at bay for long enough for me to figure things out with Victoria—Tori, gah, dammit.

"Tori or Victoria?"

She stares at me for a long beat. "Either's fine. From you. I think. But I reserve the right to change my mind. Mom calls me Victoria when I'm in trouble." Her lips purse like she's fighting the urge to say more.

"What is it?"

A shake of her head dislodges a springy curl from her ponytail. "We'll work up to it."

I dunno what that means but it sounds like some time in the future which means she's not walking out of here with no plans to ever see me again. That statement unwinds tension in the crease of my neck. I hadn't realized how worked up I was over the outcome of this get together.

There's every reason for this woman not to believe me. The news articles all say I took a hit, but nowhere in them did we release the information that I lost my memory. She's just going on my word alone for that. And it's awfully convenient for me to hit my head, forget about a woman I knocked up, and never reach out to her again.

For all she knows, I saw her waddling around the store one day and actively decided not to be a participant in their lives.

She's taking a lot on faith right now, and I don't want to take that for granted. For all I know, I scared the fuck out of her by refusing to let her leave, and she's telling me whatever I need to hear until she gets outside and can run fast and far away.

"Do you think I could have a picture of Wyatt, please?"

When her head cants to the side, I can't help but feel like I'm about to lose a ball.

Maybe even both of them.

"For my parents." I shrug. "I know they'd love to see him. And I'd like to have a picture on my phone, for, you know, me."

She taps her screen a couple of times as I recite my number to her and about ten pictures appear in my inbox. A quick scroll of them has me smiling and a lump swelling at the back of my throat. "Thank you." Resisting the urge to pull my phone to my chest and give it a hug, I smile at her. "He's amazing."

She nods, and I can't tell whether she's choked up with emotion, or she's ready to stab me for overstepping.

Where exactly are the boundaries with a woman whose vagina you don't remember?

"Can I call you?" My face burns as I rub my damp palm along my pants. "I'd like to see you again."

I don't add "both" into the sentence, but the implication is heavy. At some point, I'm going to want to meet my son, *our* son, and get to know him, make up for lost time. But we need to take it slowly. We need to rebuild whatever trust she had in me before, and add to it.

If I had raised my kid by myself, I wouldn't just let any rando take him out for ice cream. Even if they shared the same DNA.

She stands, grabs her bag, and pushes the chair in against the table with a nod. "Yeah." She slides her purse onto her shoulder. "That might be okay. Text me. Because what kind of animal calls people these days?"

Facts. But considering how much I love the sound of her voice, calling her feels like something I want to do every fucking day. Reining in my enthusiasm, I contain my shit-eating-grin to a regular sized grin.

"Okay. I will."

CHAPTER 17

Victoria

Hazard of the job my fucking vagina.

Raffi downplayed his injury. When I got back from the pie place, I pulled open my laptop and did some digging.

He wasn't joking when he said he hits his head a lot. That much was true. There are a number of news articles spanning back to his high school hockey days where he'd taken heavy hits against the boards during games.

None of the articles mentioned memory loss, or any other symptoms of concussion. So I dug deeper, and that fucker seems to be the fucking King of Understatement.

Why the fuck is he still playing hockey?

I get enjoying a game. I get wanting to play professionally —which is what all his interviews online indicate he wants to do—but this... This is sheer lunacy.

Why aren't his parents stepping in to protect his fucking brain? Or his teammates?

Nothing defined as a "traumatic brain injury" is anything to mess around with.

According to the internet, physical signs and symptoms of a concussion may include:

Headache

Ringing in the ears

Nausea

Vomiting

Fatigue or drowsiness

Blurry vision

Other signs—because apparently the first list isn't enough—and symptoms of a concussion include:

Confusion or feeling as if in a fog

Amnesia surrounding the traumatic event—this adds heft to his story. Not that I didn't believe him, it's common sense. If you take too many hits to the head, you're probably going to damage your freakin' brain.

Dizziness or "seeing stars."

You may observe these signs and symptoms in the concussed person:

Temporary loss of consciousness (though this doesn't always occur)—according to the internet this has happened at least three times since Raffi's hockey career started getting documented online. Why does he keep doing something with such a high risk of getting knocked out? And the list isn't even over yet. It keeps going.

Slurred speech

Delayed response to questions

Dazed appearance

Forgetfulness, such as repeatedly asking the same question

Concentration and memory complaints

Irritability and other personality changes

Sensitivity to light and noise

Sleep disturbances

Psychological adjustment problems and depression

Disorders of taste and smell

None of this sounds fun. Not even a little bit. Most of the symptoms can last for days, but with post-concussion syndrome (PCS) it can be weeks, sometimes even months.

But the fact that there's a clear gap in his memory—I'm doing my best to believe he genuinely has no recollection of our night together, and he's not just pretending because he thinks I'm shit in bed—suggests it's doing more long term damage to his body.

No one knows the full extent of how the human brain works, or how injuries can impact the brain.

The exact reason why some people develop PCS after a blow to the head is not clear. One theory is that it is caused by tiny areas of bruising or other damage to the nerve cells in the brain, caused by the initial head injury. Another is that the head injury causes an imbalance of chemicals in the brain that leads to the symptoms.

I read on, my eyes lingering when I see a short list.

Having a history of mental health problems.

Being a sportsperson.

My dude hits at least two out of the five risk factors that may make a person more likely to have post-concussion syndrome.

Fuck.

About 1 in 10 people still have problems one year after the injury.

One in ten people. And he's that one.

Jesus fucking Christ. The more I read about PCS the more concerned I get. This guy, the father of my son, the man who seems intent to come back into not just my life, but our son's life, is playing Russian roulette with his fucking brain.

Every time he steps onto the ice he takes a huge risk.

Why would you not just do something else? Something safer. Something less likely to make you, oh, I dunno, die?

"I can hear your teeth grinding from here." Mom picks up

her coffee cup and sits across the table from me. "What's up, buttercup?"

Slamming the lid of my laptop closed, I try to force my jaws apart. All I can do is snarl.

"Victoria?" Concern laces her voice. "What is it?"

"He's a fucking idiot."

"Who?"

"The father of my child."

Her eyes flex wide. "You know who he is?"

Nodding, I open my mouth and everything falls out. When I'm done telling her, she dabs at her eyes with a tissue. "That's so tragic. You thought he disappeared on you, and he forgot who you were. That's...brutal."

She doesn't need to tell me that. It's all I've thought about since I learned the truth about what happened with Raffi.

Bad luck, that's all it was. It wasn't anything sinister or cruel, it was nothing personal. We slept together, he hit his head, and he forgot I ever existed.

What a kick in the crotch.

"Toooorrrriiiii." Her voice stretches my name out so it lasts for far longer than a two syllable word should last. "I've seen that look on your face before. That's your 'someone's going to die' look. You can't murder the father of your child."

"Why not? Saves him killing himself on the ice."

She holds up her hand, but all I see is red. "You don't know what his circumstances are. Playing hockey could be all he's ever dreamed about doing since he was a little boy."

"When your dreams come with the risk of death, it's too high a price to pay." My body shakes with inexplicable anger. I'm not sure whether I'm actually angry at Raffi, or myself, or the universe for being such a shithead and doing this to me, to him, to all of us. But most of all, to Wyatt.

Other than being a complete dumbass and putting his life on the line every time he plays on the ice, he seems to be every bit the nice guy I thought he was when we first met in fake-prison. But if he's going to be so careless with his own life, what would that mean for Wyatt? For me?

Should I let Raffi into Wyatt's life when there's every goddamn chance his dad will bump his head and forget he ever existed all over again?

That's something I'm going to have to think about. But right now, I need to release some aggression.

Standing up, I almost knock the chair over.

"Where are you going?" Mom's concern hasn't abated. Don't blame her, I'm spitting fire.

"Lauren, one of the Fit Factory trainers, is taking a pump class at the gym. Maybe I'll be less homicidal when I'm done lifting weights."

Wouldn't bet on it.

CHAPTER 18

Victoria

I might puke.

Don't know why I agreed to come here when I inherently disagree with his decision to step out on the ice at all.

I settle into my seat between Eloise and the girl who seems to be here by herself. Same girl we sat beside last time—minus the mansplainer. What was her name again? Something beginning with P...Penny?

Quite the impression to make on someone who looks to be around my age. Definitely a college student. Warm, friendly smile. I'd return it if I didn't think moving my mouth would enable the blowing of chunks.

Bet the one thing she didn't bank on by coming to the game tonight was a stranger puking all over her Chucks.

My stomach is tight, threatening to eject the hotdogs and mac and cheese Wyatt convinced me I needed to have before I left.

I had one day with this man. One fucking day. I didn't know his real name, didn't know he played hockey, never saw him again after he knocked me up, and yet I'm twisted up in knots at the fact he might splat all over the fucking plexi.

My kid doesn't know him, he doesn't know my kid. If he wants to throw himself around the ice and smush his face into inanimate objects at high speed, that's his business, right?

Right.

So why the fuck is raw rage consuming my entire being? Why do I want to shake him—albeit gently so I don't rattle his brain around in his skull—until he sees sense?

What business is it of mine whether he skates and puts himself in harm's way or not?

None of this is my circus, and Raffi Shaw is most certainly not my monkey.

A not-so-tiny voice at the back of my mind calls me a liar. He might not be my monkey, but he could be. I want him to be. But the nausea inducing fear engulfing my nervous system right now isn't worth it.

I might pass out.

Eloise silently slips her hand into mine. I guess I look as bad as I feel. My hand is clammy in hers, and there's a bead of sweat trickling down my temple.

Why is this so damn stressful?

She's such a good friend. She hasn't pressed me for information. She knows something's there between Raffi and me, but she hasn't prodded. It's one of the things I love about my bestie—her ability to sense when I need some space to handle my own shit. I'll tell her when I'm ready.

All these guys take this risk every time they step out onto the ice. It's part of the job, just like he said. No amount of telling myself I'm being unreasonable and need to calm down is helping. As far as I'm concerned, the father of my child—who I just got back—is going to come out onto the ice, get hit, and die right in front of me. Completing our tragedy.

Fuck.

This isn't worth it.

When I stand, everyone around me stands too. The team is skating out onto the ice for warm up, and as soon as his skate touches the ice, his eyes find mine like magnets drawn together.

There's a flurry in my chest as my breath catches. The pre-game intensity brewing in his gaze is hot. That's a lie—it's super-hot.

Mercifully, he doesn't skate over to me or make a scene. I don't care how delicate his brain is, but if he does something dumb, or calls attention to me in anyway, I'll ram his stick up his ass and turn him into a fucking flag.

It's too hot. Taking my eyes off the ice, I contemplate trying to pull this jersey off. Eloise borrowed it from someone for me at the last minute. As soon as I do, though, I'll start to shiver because I'm in a goddamn ice rink.

I'd love to say I pay attention to the warmups, but I don't. I focus on a space in the distance and work on getting my shit together. This might be my first panic attack. Which is so not cool considering I'm surrounded by thousands of people.

So not cool.

After warmups but before the game, Eloise heads to the bathroom. While she's gone, a hot guy in a suit comes scooching down the row toward me with a bag in his hand.

Nope.

My gut tells me he's coming right to me, and whatever the fuck is in that bag can fuck aaaaaaall the way off.

He kinda half-squats next to me, ignoring the ruckus a few kids are making behind us. Guess he's one of the players. "My buddy tells me you're wearing the wrong name on your shoulders."

Oh, does he indeed?

He snorts. "Told me you'd eye roll when I said it too."

Of course he did.

He places the bag on my lap. "How about you give the jersey with my name on it"—he jerks his chin at the shirt I'm wearing—"to your friend here." He winks at Penelope next to me, and she turns the color of the sun. "She needs to replace that dish rag she's wearing with a good team."

Once again, she is wearing the shirt of the opposing team. Last time I saw her she wore a Snow Pirates shirt, and this time she's got a Flint Flame's shirt draped on her. My dude here has a point—she sticks out like a sore thumb.

"Tate." He flashes a blinding grin at the girl to my left.

"Penelope." She takes his outstretched hand and shakes it.

Knew it began with a P.

"Not my shirt to hand over I'm afraid, lover boy."

He shrugs. "Did my part. Got the shirt to you. What you do with it is up to you."

It's my turn to grin. "Tell your *buddy* it'll make great kindling for the fire pit in my back yard after the game."

His face falls. "That's cold. Ice cold."

"I'm a complex woman."

"I'll say." He gets up and leaves, casting one last hesitant look back in my direction as Eloise returns to her seat. I cram the bag between my feet, willing her with the strength of my eyes not to ask.

I don't want to support the fact Raffi is playing hockey by wearing it. But I also kinda hope the shirt smells like him so when I get home I can roll around in it and pretend I'm snuggling him now that I don't have to hate him for leaving me a barefoot and pregnant freshman.

"We're going to have to talk about it all at some point, you know."

"Not yet."

CHAPTER 19

Raffi

It's nil-nil here in the second in Cedar Rapids. With Tate injured in the stands, there's a chance for one of our rookies, Angel Ferrara, to get a shot in but the Flame's goaltender is quick off his line and closes the door. Begrudgingly, I concede it's a nice save. Not only is it a great save, but he's able to hold onto the rebound despite both of us chipping at him to get it free.

After the line change, Apollo controls the puck, sending it back to the blue line for Jackson Gilbert, who skates it back down into the circle, tipping it over to Apollo who tries to create space in front of the crease.

The Flame's goaltender's back door is wide open, and none of the Raccoons can ram it home. Apollo picks it up and feeds it out to Scott Raine close to the blue line, but the netminder smacks it away into the corner.

Ferrara sends the puck down the wall to me. I have options. Quick assessment and I send it back to Angel. Apollo's on the far side, Ferrara heads down ice, gets it to Apollo, there's a tip in front, two tips, and gets it back to me. As I pass it back to Ferrara, my calf muscles burn under the weight of the second period. Ferrara looks for a backdoor play, takes the shot, and puts the biscuit in the basket.

The crowd goes wild. Well, almost all of them. There's one redhead who seems to be chewing on her thumbnail so much I'd be surprised if there's a thumb left by the end of the game.

Did something happen? Why is she so anxious? And why the hell is she wearing Tate's shirt? She might not be mine, but she sure as hell isn't his either. Not sure what it is, but seeing a girl you like wear another man's number does something to a guy.

Part of me wants to hop the goddamn plexiglass and make her change her shirt right here and now. It wouldn't end well for me, but fuck is it tempting as hell.

Two big saves from Ares has the crowd on their feet yet again, solid, high quality catches. The guy's a fucking wall. Morris from the Flames strolls almost nonchalantly into the zone but is robbed by the de la Peña between the pipes once again. Ares is bailing out our D across the board right now and they really need to work on tightening up our defense.

On our next shift, Ferrara falls on his ass, his legs going out from under him. He recovers quickly, but the Flames picked his pocket and snagged possession. One of the Flames gets a shot off, and there's a scramble in front of the net but it's cleared out by Raine.

The tide is turning against us. The Flames are picking up momentum and with each play we seem shakier. On our feet, on the blue line, the only thing holding us up right now is Ares between the pipes.

Scott's on his knees. That was a big block kneeling on the ice and from the wince on his face it hurt like hell. A turnover at center ice brings possession back to us, and we aren't fucking it up. Flanking Ferrara as he skates to the goal, I cover his wing. He passes it to me before getting in closer to the net to find a better position.

Back to Ferrara, Apollo now joins us in front of the crease. We're chipping at the puck, but it feels like it's not actually going anywhere. I try to toe-drag it around and break away but there's not enough gas in the tank to make it happen.

My limbs are like lead.

A stupid ricochet from the back wall misses the Flame's stick and meets mine. Stepping out in front of the net, I've got nothing but time. The goaltender's on his face, their defenders are marked and pushing my teammates, and if I miss this shot I'll be laughed off the ice.

The puck sails easily into the net. It's a goal anyone could have made, but the stars aligned to make it mine. I search the club for my redheaded firecracker, but her seat's empty.

She's gone.

The rest of the game happens to me, around me. I'm not an active part of it, despite not missing a shift and chalking up another assist, my mind is elsewhere.

Is Victoria okay? Did something happen to Wyatt that she had to leave? Is he okay? Should I call her? At least text, right? I mean, offer my help if something happened to him? It's the least I can do.

Stepping out onto the street after the game, I make a beeline for my car. My body feels heavy, there's a knot in my chest, and I don't know what the fuck to do. There are no messages on my screen, no missed calls, just silence, and it's deafening.

Familiar curves and loose red waves meet me at the side of my car. It takes all I have not to rush to her and check she's okay. She seems it, other than the scowl darkening her features.

"Are you okay?" I stop a few feet from her to give her space and drop my hockey bag to the ground.

She crosses her arms and somehow her frowny face gets frownier under the street lights. "Why are you still playing hockey?" She purses her lips, tension radiating from her person, but I have no idea why. She's picking a fight with me over hockey?

"I...uh... Better question." I hold up a finger. "Why wouldn't I play hockey?"

"Because you could get hurt."

A match flares to life in my chest, a flame flickering and warming my body. She cares. She's worried. And despite believing I abandoned her and our kid a few years ago, she doesn't want to run me over with a Zamboni. This is all fucking amazing news and makes me want to dance.

But her face tells me if I dance, I will die.

"Is that why you left? You were worried I'd get hurt?"

"This isn't about me." She waves a hand with a flick of her wrist. "This is about you. Why are you being an idiot? You shouldn't be on the ice. You could really hurt yourself. You *did* really hurt yourself. Your memories are gone, Raffi. Does your coach know that? Do your teammates? Do they know how dangerous it is to skate around like you do just waiting to get your face shoved into the glass?"

There's nothing I can say right now to calm her fears. I know this, because they're the same fears I push down deep in my chest every single time I step out onto the ice. It's easier to ignore them when it's just me. I can pretend I'm exaggerating or overreacting, convince myself it's no big deal. I'm doing what I love to do to secure a future for myself and a better future for my family than they've had.

"I'm scared, Raffi." She rubs her forearms with her palms. "I don't know you all that well, but it doesn't matter. We have a child together now, and if you want to be part of our lives, you've got to step up and show us you're not going to disappear again. Or forget about us." The way her voice breaks on her last sentence crushes my soul.

She turns to leave, and I pounce forward. "Wait, Victoria, please?"

Hesitation slows her feet, allowing me to grab her arm and turn her to face me. The temptation to kiss her senseless without asking permission is strong, because if she says no to me right now I might die. Actual, heart-stopping death.

But I wait, cupping her face in both my hands and staring at her lips like they hold the key to the universe. Please don't turn me away, Tori. Please. Silent pleading, heart in a vise, breath stopped right at the back of my throat.

Her breath is heavy in the silence, her eyes flickering between my lips and my eyes. She wants to kiss me, but until I have her explicit permission, I'm not making a move.

"Raffi." My name sounds painful as it falls from her quivering lips. Her hesitation is short lived. She grabs my shirt and pulls me toward her, our lips colliding in an explosion of strawberries and cinnamon.

Her kiss is cautious at first, timid. Maybe she's not sure I want to kiss her, or she's not sure she wants to kiss me, but her lips are pressed against mine and I'm not wasting it. Backing her up until she bumps into the side of my car, I pin her with my body.

"Raffi." This time my name sounds more like a plea than pain. Is she pleading for more or for me to stop? Her breathy voice speaks straight to my cock, and there's no controlling that thing as it pokes into her. There's also no hiding what she's doing to me.

She melts against me, quiet moans dropping from her mouth between hungry kisses. Her lips are velvet soft, her tongue firm and curious, and her fists grip my shirt in tight balls. She's not letting me go until she's done with me, and I'm absolutely okay with that. There's nowhere else I'd rather be.

She shivers when my hands skim her waist under her jersey. I'm not risking going another layer deeper, not yet. I need her to know I don't simply want her naked, but it's fucking hard. The urge to kiss every inch of her pale skin is as consuming as it is distracting.

When she moves my hand down between her legs and grinds on it, I almost make a mess in my dress pants. She's eager, hungry, and not afraid to put me exactly where she needs me to be.

My needy little firecracker. Victoria dry humping the heel of my hand is the hottest thing I've ever fucking seen.

She's chasing her orgasm, her breath coming in short bursts between our kisses. Heat from her core seeps through the fabric of her pants. She's wet under these clothes. I'd bet she's got a perfectly pink pussy dripping just for me. As though she's reading my mind, she tugs my hand and shoves it into her panties, spreading her feet for balance and access.

A beautiful woman riding my hand in the parking lot wasn't what I had on my bingo card for today, but I sure as hell am not complaining.

Her head tips back, and my lips trail sloppy kisses down the column of her neck as her phone rings. Without missing a beat, she pulls it from her pocket and answers it.

This fucking woman. She thinks she can get fingered by me and be lucid enough to talk on the phone?

Her pussy is soft, silky, and so fucking perfectly wet. As she's speaking, I pinch her clit, and a small yelp escapes before she coughs to hide it.

She mutes her side of the call. "I will murder you."

"Uh huh." I mumble against her throat as I make my way down to nibble at her collar bone, fingers working against her clit. Her body bucks, her spine bending, her hips rolling as she chases release against my fingers. "We don't take calls when we're fucking around, Firecracker."

The person on the other side of the line, who sounds like Eloise, is repeating Victoria's name over and over. "Answer your friend, Victoria. You thought you could take a phone call, so take the call."

Kissing Raffi in the parking lot after the game sounded like such a good idea at the time. Putting his hand in my pants and riding his very talented fingers—because I wanted to know if my memory had played tricks on me after all this time—felt like an even better idea.

At least until I started melting against him, trying to one-hand brace myself against his chest so I didn't collapse on the ground while trying not to drop my phone. I was so cocky thinking that I could talk to Eloise and let him get me off at the same time.

Fuck.

I was very, very wrong.

"Eloise, I'm fine."

"You don't sound fine. Where are you? I'll come and take you home, we can pick up your car tomorrow."

Raffi's teeth scrape down my clavicle, taking all the strength I have not to let out a feral moan. This man. One hand's in my pants, fingers circling my clit like he's right at home. The other's up my shirt, thumb flicking over my nipple through my bra, driving me more and more furiously frustrated with need.

My legs tremble, threatening to buckle. Sweat prickles across my forehead as he looks up at me with nothing but smugness in his beautiful eyes.

The chemistry's still here. And he's every bit as skilled with his digits as I recall him being from our one night stand.

A low rattle bubbles in my throat.

"Tori?" Eloise's concern would be touching, if I wasn't seconds from bursting apart on Raffi's fingers. Fuck.

"Eloise, I swear I'm okay. I'll call you later." I'm not proud of the fact I hang up on my friend, but if I didn't, she'd hear me come, and we aren't those kinds of friends.

"Much better," Raffi announces with another pinch of my clit. "Do I have your full attention now?"

I want to claw his eyes out, but I'm too busy gripping his biceps so I don't crumple onto the ground at his feet. People are leaving the rink, and I don't want to call attention to the fact I'm getting fingered in a public space.

Is it possible he's gotten better over the past three years? That's not a thought I want to dwell on. The idea that he's been with other women, improving his fingering game would make me white-hot with jealousy if I wasn't hanging over the edge of an orgasm cliff. He's controlling damn near every breath I take with just the movement in his fingers.

"Stop fighting me, Firecracker. Just come for me." His words tickle the skin of my throat as he kisses his way up to my earlobe and bites down. The nip of pain pushes me over.

My forehead drops onto his shoulder, mouth open in a silent scream in the dim light. My teeth clamp onto the sliver of bare skin peeking out from his shirt, biting through the undulating pleasure charging through every cell in my body.

I'm leaving a mark, but neither of us seem overly

concerned about it. In fact, from the way Raffi rolls his fingers around my clit faster, harder, I'd say he's hot for being bitten.

He's holding me up, taking all my weight as I'm just too fucking jelly-legged to stand up by myself right now. If the car wasn't behind me, I'd be in a puddle on the asphalt.

"I want to see where this goes, Victoria. You, me, our son. I want us to be a family. Together." He's saying the words I've been dreaming of hearing him say for three years. But I need to be clearheaded when I make a decision about what to do with the father of my child.

I can't make orgasm-haze decisions that will impact my kid's life too.

It's a bullshit line I'm feeding myself—my heart's already decided to give Raffi a shot, despite the fact he's a hockey player. But I need to stay grounded. Last time I let him under my skin, I was crushed and spent weeks staring at my phone for him to reach out.

This time we're taking it slowly.

No, really, we are.

If only someone could communicate that to the racing heart skipping along in my chest, that'd be peachy. The way he's looking at me, hope in his pretty eyes, that slanted goofy smile, it's too much. He has a bruise blooming on his cheekbone from what I can only imagine was a stick, or an elbow on the ice. All I want to do is get naked with this man and make another adorable baby for us to raise together.

It's ridiculous. This man strips me of every ounce of common sense.

I'm a smart woman, an independent woman, but when Raffi Shaw comes near me and my eager beaver, all I want is to abandon all logic and launch myself at him. Consequences be damned.

He still has his hand in my pants. As he slides free, I gasp, craving more, needing more, almost demanding it, but I need to get home. I need to reset.

When he sticks his middle finger in his mouth, it draws a low moan from both of us. There's nothing hotter than a man showing you just how much he appreciates the mess he caused you to make in your pants.

But when he curls his hand around my head and pulls me to suck his index finger while he's licking my cum off his middle finger, I damn near come again. "Taste yourself, Victoria. You're fucking delicious."

A pained noise escapes his mouth as he's licking his fingers clean. "How could I have forgotten how good you taste?"

He doesn't give me time to answer before he presses me back against the car, hard, and kisses me until I'm gasping for air. Our salty tongues collide in a give and take dance as our bodies rub against each other.

I definitely don't get this hot from a vibrator.

My phone's shrill ring in the night air pulls us apart. It's Mom. Disappointment, quickly followed by concern, flits across his face as he watches me answer.

"Mom? What's wrong?"

"Nothing's wrong, everything's fine. Wyatt's sleeping. I'm just checking to see if you're okay. I expected you back by now and thought something might be wrong."

My heart swells as Raffi's body relaxes. "I'm on my way. I got sidetracked talking to someone."

"No rush. Have fun. I was just making sure you didn't get a flat or something on your way back."

Raffi mouths "I love her" at me, making me eye roll.

"I'm good, Mom. But if you've jinxed me and I get a flat on my way home, I'll let Wyatt wake you at five am tomorrow on your day off."

Raffi laughs quietly as Mom gasps. "You wouldn't."

"Uh huh. See you soon."

"Love you, Tori."

"Love you too, Mom."

"She seems nice." Raffi's lips quirk into a smile.

"Single mom of a single mom. She's protective."

"I'd like the chance to change that." His face turns serious. "Think about it? Please?"

It's the only thing that's consumed my thoughts since I re-met him. But he doesn't need to know that. "I'll consider it."

CHAPTER 21

Victoria

Sweat streams down my ass crack, and all I want is a hot shower and a burger.

What is it about working out and feeling stronger that makes you want to eat all the shit in the whole world? On leg day, my appetite is unrelenting. I haven't turned into a calorie-counting, protein-obsessed gym bunny at least not yet—but I try to lean heavier into protein on leg days because otherwise, my muscles get jittery.

I was going to pick Wyatt up from daycare at the gym and eat on the way back to the house, but I stink—like, "What the fuck is that smell? Holy crap it's me!" kind of stink. And I need to rinse off.

Wyatt won't come near his mama if she's a stench-ball.

I can't help but walk past daycare and watch him through the window for just a minute. Some parents can't wait to have some time away from their kids, but if every moment of my time was spent with my son, I'd be a happy woman.

He's playing with a little girl that is leading him across the room by his wrist. It's adorable. He's such a sweet boy, so easy going and loves making new friends. Like his dad, I'd guess.

As I turn to leave, movement catches my eye, and I can't help but stare as Raffi stands in front of a woman with a kid wrapped around her leg. Raffi's arms are moving as he communicates to them in sign language. Digging deep in the corners of my memory, I vaguely recall him saying that the jail and bail where we met—which raised funds for an ASL charity—was important to him. But I can't remember why. Is someone in his family deaf?

The girl answers him, letting go of her mom's leg for long enough to answer whatever Raffi has said and duck back behind her. Raffi squats down in front of her and signs something else. The little girl's smile lights up her whole face as the mom bites the inside of her cheek like she might cry.

My ovaries might explode.

After Wyatt was born, I said I didn't want any more kids. Like, ever. He was my one-and-done. Raising a kid by yourself—even with the best mom in the world for support—isn't easy. But standing here watching the man who made Wyatt with me, I can imagine a whole future together. Green pastures, picnic blankets, kids using Raffi as a freakin' play horse. And all he's doing is being adorable and communicating to a shy kid at the gym.

What the fuck is this sorcery?

Grounding myself in late night feedings, exploding diapers, teething, fevers, trips to the pediatrician, and my heart stopping while I watched him sleep to make sure his chest was moving wasn't easy.

This man is so charismatic, people are instantly drawn to him.

Spoiler alert: It's me. I'm people.

I was drawn to him the minute he joined me in lock up, and I'm drawn to him now. The more I stare at him and the little girl, the more my heart yearns for that to be our boy. I want Wyatt to have a relationship with his father, I want them to be close, to play T-ball, and soccer, and make sandwiches together.

But one hard knock on the ice could ruin everything all over again.

As far as I know, Raffi doesn't see me as I make my way into the changing rooms to get ready for my shower. My tears blend with the hot water washing away my sweat.

Am I holding myself back from happiness for myself and my child over something that may never happen? Perhaps.

I'd never make him choose between me and his dreams. He can have a relationship with Wyatt, but I need to keep my heart locked up safe. I can't let him break me all over again. I can't go through that heartache. For as long as he plays hockey, Raffi and I can't be together. It's just that simple to me.

Once bitten, twice shy.

Once forgotten... I dunno how to finish that sentence, but I'm not sure I'm willing to take the risk.

Is it a deal breaker? It might be.

CHAPTER 22
Raffi

When I get to the gym, my Firecracker is bent over a bench doing single arm kettlebell rows. Her ass is pointed right at me. If I was a lesser man, I'd grip her hips and grind against her perfect butt until I covered her in my cum. But instead, I'm just going to think about it inside my brain and probably rub one out to the memory when I get home later.

"You made me cry again, you fucker," she's spitting at Phil, who is undoubtedly losing count of her reps as she talks to him. "That movie made me bawl."

He smiles despite her venom. "Which one?"

"*Coda*. It hit me right here." She kneels up and thumps her chest.

"Told you it was an emotional one. You should watch *Life as a House* next. It's one of my all-time favorite movies."

"Are you trying to break me?" Her wail draws a few looks from people who are working out around the gym.

"You'll love it."

Phil's pop-culture references are unrivaled. He's seen more 80s and 90s movies than anyone I know, and he can recite almost every word of Ferris Bueller off the top of his head. Guy's a legend.

I open my notes app and write down the two movies they're talking about so I can watch them later. It'll give me something else to talk to her about.

Impatience claws at my skin. I want to meet my kid, I want to get to know him, bring him home to meet Mom and Dad, have a relationship with him. But it's not my call, and if Victoria isn't ready for me to meet him, I've just gotta stay patient. Coming around to the idea that I didn't abandon them both must be a huge shift in thinking for her. And it's going to take even longer to convince her she doesn't need to do everything by herself anymore.

Working out at the gym, personal training, then doing practice or a game is killer, but it's necessary. I need to train harder, to play better. I'm paying attention to what I eat. Protein bars, protein pancakes—it all tastes like shit. Give me a PB&J any day. But I need to fuel my muscles so I don't get injured and lose my place on the team.

I'm so tired I fell asleep in the bathroom the other day. One of the guys found me on the shitter, pants around my ankles, and the imprint of the toilet paper holder on my face.

It's alright for most of them. A lot of them come from money, or have money. They don't have to worry about keeping their place in college even if they may have had concerns about keeping their place on the team. Some of them are like me, on a scholarship, hard at the grind, counting pennies, and falling asleep in the back of some of my classes.

I'm behind on two assignments, but my professors will give me extensions, I just need to find the time to ask. Everything's slipping through my fingers, like when you drop a roll of toilet paper and think it won't travel that far away, then it's across the room.

My life is currently like fucking toilet paper rolling across the room.

And yet, all I want to do is spend time with Victoria and convince her to give me another chance.

Fuck.

This isn't good.

I don't have time for a girlfriend, never mind a readymade family. Wyatt is a toddler, which is probably a lot of work, and yet, I want to teach him about sticks and pucks, about how to line up a shot and skate. Man, I want to teach my kid to skate so badly.

How do people find balance between the things they should do, need to do, and the things they love? Because I'm coming up short across the board, and I'm fucking tired.

"You okay?" Ares levels me with a look that says his question is more than just being polite.

"I'm good. Just tired."

He nods, but says nothing. We're gearing up for training on the ice, he's a weird one at the best of times—comes with the territory of being a goalie—but today he seems on edge for some reason.

Could be me. Maybe I'm projecting, maybe I'm the one who's on edge, and it just seems like he's off.

"You know you can talk to us if you need anything, right?" Ares is a playboy, a joker, a fun loving guy who rarely gets serious like this. Am I in the twilight zone?

"Sure. But I'm fine."

He grabs my arm. "I've seen you fine, man. I know you're not fine. It's cool if you don't want to talk to me. We aren't that close. I'm younger than you. Whatever. But something's going on, and you should talk to someone about it. I'm here if you need me."

Then he pushes away to bend himself into unreachable positions. My groin winces at some of the saves he pulls off. Like...just how?

Taking a huge bite out of my protein bar almost makes me cry. This shit is for the birds. I need real food. As soon as practice is over, I'm going for a fucking burger. Or nachos. Nachos sound good about now.

The first of today's drills makes me dizzy as fuck, and even watching my teammates do it makes me want to hurl that gross protein bar back into my helmet. We split into teams, and skate around the edge of the giant circle in the middle of the ice, passing the puck back and forth. It's a drill designed to work on speed, but so far all it's doing is making my stomach hurt and dots dance behind my eyes.

The second drill is a three person exercise, in a triangle formation. The person who starts with the puck skates between the other two people, passing the puck to the person at the top of the triangle, takes back possession, then passes it back to the person at the bottom of the triangle, regains possession, then shoots.

Usually, it's a great passing breakout drill for the whole team, to develop players' flow, quick one and two touch passes, communication, as well as one timers in the slot.

The skating player—the one who starts with the puck—should focus on keeping their legs moving throughout the entire drill without pausing their crossovers in the pivot. Speedy skating throughout.

We have four sets of players running the drill in each corner of the rink. Mercifully, there's no whistle piercing the air as it's a continuous drill, but it takes all I have not to blow chunks on the ice.

Fighting off a migraine is impossible, but somehow I make

it through practice without passing out, vomiting, or crying. Though at various points, I felt like doing all three.

I spend what should probably be considered a criminal length of time in the showers when we're done on the ice. Partly because my body is so heavy I'm not sure I have it in me to dry off and get changed right away.

Dunno how much later it is when I step out of the rink, but something makes my feet go into the store. I don't need anything new, but I find the hockey rink store to be like Target for Mom. I never *need* anything, but I always go in for a look and end up coming out three hundred bucks lighter.

Ha. I wish. I don't remember the last time I had three hundred bucks to blow on anything. But if I did have three hundred bucks, chances are I'd blow it in this tiny store right here.

The kid at the checkout jerks his chin at me in hello, but it's the red waves standing at one of the racks of shirts that draws my attention. Victoria's in the hockey shop. Curious.

She's also looking at shirts and if memory serves, I already gave her one with my name on it, so she has no reason to go shirt shopping.

Whoa, nelly. I don't own that woman, she can buy whatever the fuck she wants.

As long as it has my name on it.

Yup. Okay. Fine. There's no calming the possessive beast in my chest. That woman is mine, even if she doesn't accept it yet. There's no way she can wear anyone else's name on her shoulders. Not from my team, or anyone else's.

I'm about three seconds from beating my chest like a caveman. I doubt she'd respond well to being hit over the head by my stick, but it's worth a shot. Right?

Eloise holds up a shirt for Victoria, who wrinkles her nose. I'm moving in her direction, only a few feet away when a tiny voice demands more goldfish. My heart stops beating in my chest as I stutter to a stop.

The ba-dum of the brewing headache is drowned out by the tiny person's voice.

The squeak of my shoes on the linoleum draws Victoria's attention. Frozen in place I glance down at where the voice came from then back to his mom. She's far more relaxed than I am in this situation.

Do I run? Do I stay?

Eloise catches my eye, and her brows peak.

Instead of yelling or shooing me away, Victoria beckons me closer. Can't tell if it's to punch me in the face or to say hi, but she nods, and I take that as an invitation to step into their space.

"Hey." It's one word, and I'm already breathless.

"Hey, yourself." Her returning smile is almost shy, it's not like her. She's probably nervous about how this is going to go. She's not the only one.

Eloise's surprise has shifted to intrigue but she stays quiet, observing the scene unfolding.

"Hi." The miniature version of me steps out from behind Victoria's legs and beams up at me. Guess he's not in the least bit shy or scared of strangers. "I'm Wyatt."

Crouching down to his level, I offer a fist bump. "Hi, Wyatt. I'm Raffi. I'm a friend of your Mom's."

Returning my fist bump with his tiny clenched fist, he smiles. "You like fish?" He offers me one of those food catcher containers that are impossible to get your hand out of once you put your fingers in.

"I *love* fish. But I'm good, thanks."

My dude isn't taking no for an answer. He shoves the container at me, making his mom laugh. "He doesn't want a goldfish cracker right now, buddy. You have them. Great sharing, though."

Wyatt looks at me for a long moment, like this guy said he loves fish but he doesn't want fish. His little brain is trying to figure out how someone could *not* want fish.

He turns his attention back to cramming crackers in his mouth, and tears fill my eyes. This kid is part of me. He's a walking, talking, goldfish-cracker-eating miniature copy of his mom and me. What the fuck do I do with that?

Every bone in my body wants to swoop this little guy up and smush him until he punches me in the face to put him down. But that's not cool. Not yet. Maybe never. And I need to be okay with that. Even if my heart aches to just breathe him in.

Victoria's jade eyes are watering like mine when I stare up at her. Her face softens, and for a moment, there's only the three of us. My girl, my kid, and me, right here in the hockey store.

"You free tomorrow night?"

My headshake is so slow because I'm half tempted to blow off practice and the gym for whatever she might want me to do.

She scrunches up her face like she knows what I'm doing and isn't cool with it. Don't blame her— if all she's known of hockey is misery, there's probably no changing her mind.

Have I blown my chance? "Next night?"

She nods. "How do you feel about tenderloin?"

A woman after my own heart. "It's a date." The words are out of my mouth before I can stop them. It's a commonly used phrase, but here and now, in this context, it's more, and we both fucking know it. So does Eloise by the small gasp that escaped from behind her fingers as she tried to cram it back into her mouth.

Victoria's bright red face almost matches her hair, but she nods and my soul takes flight. "It's a date."

CHAPTER 23
Victoria

"So Raffi, Raffi Shaw, from the Raccoons hockey team, is Wyatt's—your son's—father?" Eloise points at me across the table in Bitches Brew, her words half whispered and half mouthed so the kid in question doesn't hear or repeat her words back to her. "Oh, wow. I mean, it makes sense. I can see it now you've pointed it out to me. But considering I still struggle to tell Ares's brothers apart that doesn't say a lot." She smiles, picks up her large hot chocolate and blows the cream on top before taking a sip and hissing. "That's...a lot, Tori."

She stays quiet for a long moment before she opens her mouth. Nothing comes out, and she snaps it shut again. Takes another sip, more carefully this time. "And you didn't know? Like...this whole time? That he was right here? Playing hockey?"

Biting my lips between my teeth to stop the threatening tears from falling, I shake my head.

"Wow."

Yeah. She's about where I've been since I found out who Raffi is.

"And he wants," She points at me, then at Wyatt, who's sucked into Blippi on his tablet. Yes, I'm that mom, so sue me. "To be a family."

Another nod.

"And you hate hockey, hockey players, and all things connected—loosely or otherwise—to the sport?"

I'm starting to feel like one of those nodding toys people put on the dashboard of their car.

"But there's obviously still chemistry between you." She holds up her palm to my face. "Don't even try to lie, Tori. The whole hockey store felt the sizzle. If you couldn't feel it you need to get your—" She looks around. "Girl parts checked out," she finishes in a whispered hush.

"Mama?"

"Yes, sweetie?"

"What are girl parts?"

Eloise turns a shade of red I'm not sure I've seen before and drops her head into her hands muttering "Sorry," over and over again.

"Nothing you need to worry about until you're older, kiddo." I ruffle his hair as he goes back to staring at his screen.

"Of all things he picked out to repeat, it had to be that one?" Eloise is beet red.

"Kids are dicks, man."

"I'm not a dick, mama!" My son swats indignantly at my hand caressing his hair.

For fuck's sake. He can multitask when it comes to parroting cuss words but not when I tell him to turn his screen off or come for dinner?

Kids really are dicks.

Eloise groans, her whole body now shaking with laughter.

This is first class parenting right here.

When Eloise finally stops laughing, her stare grows distant, and she's quiet for a while.

"What is it?"

She sips at her hot cocoa, shaking her head. "It's not my place."

"Eloise…?"

"Ares is worried about Raffi. He mentioned it." She flaps her hand like she's talking a while ago, in the past, not today or yesterday. "He says he's pushing himself too hard. Training all the time, either at the gym with the team, with a personal trainer, practice, games, eating stuff he doesn't normally eat."

"How the hell can he afford to pay for a personal trainer?" I only ask because I know he doesn't have a lot of disposable income, and if it wasn't for the killer sale I got for sessions with Phil, I couldn't afford to go.

Eloise doesn't miss a beat. "Ares and his brothers pay Phil for whoever on the team needs training. Kind of like a retainer I guess. If you want personal training, you go, and they foot the bill."

I don't know what to process first, the fact they have *that* much money, or the fact they're using their super powers for good. If they keep this shit up I'm going to have to fully rescind my 'hockey players suck' thing.

"Ares says he thinks Raffi is afraid of losing his place on the team and going too far to keep it."

Nodding along with everything she's saying, I sigh. "I think he's still having symptoms from his concussion."

She flinches.

"I'm sure the guys on the team are looking out for them, and I don't know him well enough yet to spot them. But he's going too hard for too long, and I'm afraid he's not going to be there for us long term." The weight on my shoulders lifts just a little at sharing the fears I've been keeping inside.

"Am I attracted to him? Absolutely. Do I want to be a family together? I dunno. Maybe. I don't know him well enough yet to see all of his annoying habits to know if I can survive with him and not k-i-l-l him in his sleep. Do I want to date him to see? Of course. And I want him to be an active part of his son's life, especially considering he's missed the first couple years. But I'm really scared, Eloise. What if he d-i-e-s because of these injuries?"

With a nod, she reaches her warm hand across the table to cup mine, giving me a firm squeeze. "Talk to him? Find out what's going on in his head? Perhaps he's chasing a dream so hard he's missing everything else around him. Ask him why? I dunno."

She shrugs. "I don't know him at all, and neither does Ares really. But he's worried. I'm not sure if he's talked to his brothers about it or not, but they're a tight knit family, so I wouldn't put it past them. You might be the one to get through to him. You never know."

I almost laugh out loud, but a snort comes out instead. "I don't know him either, Ellie."

"True, but things are different now." She gestures at Wyatt. "Sometimes things like that change a person's perspective on things. Your fears are rational. You need to hear that too. You've been through a lot—it's only natural to be afraid history will repeat itself. Especially when he hasn't changed the behavior that caused it in the first place."

Her words make sense, but she's placing a lot of importance on me and my kid with this guy I barely know.

My head says he's not my problem and to keep him at arm's length.

Except my heart wants him much closer.

"The Blind Pig or Joensy's? You got a tenderloin preference?" Raffi kisses me on the cheek. It's adorable, romantic, and makes his cheeks go pink.

This is most definitely not Raffi's car. I don't know who owns it, but it looks pretty new. Smells it too.

"Whatever you want is fine. I'm not picky."

"You should always be picky, Victoria." He sounds so stern when he's scolding me. "Especially about food. Life's too short to eat subpar tenderloin."

At this point, I just want to hang out with him. I don't care about the food, I don't care about the car, I just want to get to know him to see if we could work together as a couple. Or at least co-parent. That's non-negotiable.

"It's Apollo's car." He casts a glance across at me. "Apparently I wasn't allowed to take you out in something that was older than his grandma or likely to break down."

He told his friends we were going out? I'm not sure how I feel about that.

He pats my thigh. "They don't know who you are, just that I'm going out. I guess the fact that I didn't leave the house in gym gear was a giveaway. Apollo just tossed his keys at me and told me not to get cum on the seats." His eyes widen. "Fuck. Sorry. That's not... I didn't. Jesus. I'm nervous. I don't wanna fuck this up."

I'm laughing so hard I might pee my pants. Ever since having Wyatt those muscles haven't been as reliable as I'd like them to. They always tell you to work on your pelvic floor when you're pregnant, but they don't quite tell you why. And by the time you figure out the why, it's almost too late.

"It's fine. But now I'm tempted to leave a stain on the seat just to prank him."

He weaves his fingers into mine and holds my hand on my thigh. Bold move, but one I'm more than comfortable with. I want to be close to him. I've spent three years thinking he wanted nothing to do with me, so his overt affection warms me like stepping inside after being outside shoveling snow for a few hours.

My skin tingles. I opted for jeans, boots, and a shirt. Casual, but at least three steps up from my daily mom-wear. Raffi's wearing jeans and a button down. He looks handsome as hell, and there's a part of me that wants him to find a gravel road and make all kinds of mess in Apollo's back seat.

But we need to talk, reconnect.

As we wait at a red light, Luke Combs's "Hurricane" comes onto the radio. I haven't heard Raffi sing before, but the more he gets into the song, the more I realize he can really carry a tune.

"What?" That lopsided grin is going to be the death of me. It's the same one Wyatt gives me when he wants snacks or screen time. If the two of them ever pull it on me, I'll die right on the spot.

"You weren't bullshitting about songwriting, were you?"

He shakes his head. "Gotta get all my feelings out somehow." He tilts his head. "I'm better at the guitar than singing though. Some of the other guys are way better singers than I am."

"Don't downplay your achievements, Raffi. You have talents spanning beyond scoring goals on the ice." It's a shot across the bow, probably a tad unfair, but also true.

He falls silent as he pulls off I-380. "How's it going at the gym with Phil?"

I grunt, rolling my shoulders. "Everything hurts all the goddamn time. As soon as I feel like I'm making progress, or I'm getting good at something, he pivots and makes me do something new. Then everything hurts all over again."

"You know that's literally his job, right? That's what you pay him for. To kick your ass and you say thank you for the footprint. What are you working on?"

"Landmine rows, seated rows, Tabata boxing for arms and step ups onto the bench with kettle bells for legs until I want to cry."

He nods, an approving grin lighting up his face as we turn onto Center Point Road. "Nothing quite beats lifting heavy shit and putting it back down."

"Okay, Phil." My scoff makes him laugh. "Someday I'm going to out lift you, and then you'll be sorry. I keep telling Phil the only reason I keep showing up is because I can't lift his body weight yet. Someday I'm going to be able to lift his dead body, and that's when he should be really scared."

He scratches his chin as he pulls into the parking lot. "I'll keep that in mind. When you start deadlifting and bench pressing, I'll keep closer tabs on your workouts."

Playfully punching his bicep, I laugh. "You'd better. There'll come a day I can deadlift your ass too."

"Can't wait." He blows me an air kiss as he gets out of the SUV and crosses in front of the hood. When he opens the door, he offers me his hand, and I can't help but smile. Butterflies and bees are both going crazy in my stomach, and I'm regretting not wearing something more... I dunno, something.

He holds my hand as we walk through the parking lot and into the restaurant bar. He only lets go when the hostess brings us to our table, and even then, he takes my hand again as soon as I'm seated.

The bar isn't packed, but it's also not empty. There's a nice ambient undercurrent buzz of chatter while he toes at my boot with his shoe.

The warmth, the connection, his need to be touching me is intoxicating, and I'm struck by a flashback to our first date that smacks me square in the chest.

"What is it, Firecracker?"

Pushing the lump in my throat aside, I try to find my voice. "Just thinking back to the last time we did this." A one shoulder shrug hopefully downplays the emotions swirling in my chest.

"Will you tell me about it once we've ordered?"

I nod, though I'm not sure how to keep the tears at bay.

"Do you mind if I…?" He points at the menu, and I smile.

"Feels like ordering for both of us might be your thing. You did it last time too."

He winks at me. "Can't *not* order something that's called firecracker shrimp, right?" He turns to the server. "Firecracker shrimp, pickle chips, and jacked mac bites please. Then we'll share the tenderloin."

"Extra bun and side?"

"Of course." He almost laughs at her question, which makes me laugh too.

"And what's your sides?"

"Tots for two, please."

None of this sounds bad to me. In fact, it all has my mouth watering, so I stay silent and just let the man work.

"Sure. And drinks?"

We both order pop and water, and with his free hand, Raffi smacks his stomach. "Just wait until you taste this."

I'm quickly learning food is this man's love language. And it's adorable how excited he gets about it.

"What?" He's staring expectantly at me.

"How do you know I'm thinking something?"

"You get this look." He points at my face. "Like you're trying to figure out a puzzle."

"I was wondering what it is about food that gets you so excited. You have a thing about food."

"Doesn't everyone? Some people's food things are unhealthy, some are super healthy, and mine…" He shrugs. "I've loved food since I was a kid. Every picture in my child-hood album involves food in some way. And so it should. There's no greater pleasure than delicious food." So much joy shines through him that it's hard not to smile.

"You shared your sandwiches with me."

The server places our drinks between us, and Raffi's

already got half his water drunk before she's done putting the glasses on the table.

"You mentioned that when we had pie. Are you sure? Sharing food's not normally my jam." He stares at me like I told him the earth is flat.

"You gave me a sandwich from your backpack when we were in lock up together." I'm trying too hard to ignore the hammering in my chest and the zips of electricity from his foot brushing against my calf. The most important thing in the entire universe right now is where his body is touching mine.

He scrunches up his face, pursing his lips. "Doesn't sound like me. I don't share food."

I wag a finger at him. "You did. Even gave me your secret to the perfect PB&J."

He gasps theatrically, a hand flailing to his face. "No way. You must have been special."

My gaze drifts to the floor. He made me feel special and then disappeared for years, so I don't know where we're at with that, or how his statement makes me feel inside.

A knuckle lands under my chin, turning my head so I look at him. "You are special."

That fucking lump is back in my throat. The pad of his thumb sweeps over the apple of my cheek and my eyes drift closed. It's so easy to get caught up in this guy, his charisma, his smile, the warmth of his voice and his fingers.

By the time I've waded through a fraction of the food the server puts in front of me, my ribs hurt from laughing. I've realized why Raffi won't step down from hockey.

It's clear to see in everything he says. He's told me about how Ares got their team mascot, a pig called Bacon, who is such an epic diva. He told me about the team rallying to rescue Taryn's stuff from her cheating ex. She's one of my favorite baristas from Bitches Brew and apparently her ex held all her shit hostage until the team went over and intimidated the shit out of him to give it back.

He makes it sound like the best family in the world to be part of. I don't really blame him for not wanting to let them down or step back at all. His only brother lives in a different country, and he's lonely. He wants to feel needed.

But the more he talks about hockey, the less it seems like it's his dream. From what he tells me, his parents have placed their hopes and dreams of having a superstar hockey player on his shoulders. It's because he loves his team so damn much he's afraid he'll lose his family—blood and found—if he does.

The pressure must be crushing. To have his degree tied to his performance on the ice adds an added layer of complexity I wasn't expecting either. It doesn't feel fair, and yet, he knew when he was signing up that he needed to maintain certain grades to keep his place on the ice, and he needed to play at a certain level to not get benched.

How he's not permanently bent under the weight of expectations on his shoulders is anyone's guess.

"Do you have time? Or do you have to get back?" There's a hope in his voice that mirrors my own. I'm not ready for our date to end.

"What are you thinking?"

He slurps at the bottom of his pop before answering. "Dessert."

CHAPTER 24
Raffi

I'm walking on air as we make our way back to Apollo's SUV in the parking lot. So much so that I take my life in my hands and pull my firecracker flush against my chest and start singing at her.

Under my Skin by Nate Smith is the first song that comes to mind, and I croon it softly while we shuffle back and forth.

"What the hell are you doing?"

She's clearly never been romanced, and that's so far from being okay. She's the mother of my kid. Sure, I've been an unknowingly absent father for the first two years of the kid's life, but that's about to change.

At the end of the day, she carried him, birthed him, and took care of him at great personal cost. She told me over dinner that she changed her degree to go into something that would set her up for a quicker income than what she originally planned to do.

While she was in the bathroom I messaged Apollo and asked him if there are any paid photography gigs going either for the team or any of his family businesses. She'll kill me if she ever finds out I asked, but it's the least I can do.

"I'm dancing with you in the parking lot, Firecracker."

"But someone might see." She glances over her shoulder, and I can't stop the chuckle rumbling through my chest.

"You're fine being fingered next to my car in the parking lot, but heaven forbid someone sees us dancing like this?"

For a hot minute she looks like she might head-butt me but then she puts her head on my shoulder and lets me lead. I'm not sure which is the bigger achievement, that she didn't fight, or that she's letting me lead.

Dancing isn't my strong suit. We're mostly just swaying in the cool night air as I sing low in her ear under the stars.

This might be the happiest I've ever felt in all my life, but since I can't remember the first time we met, I can't say for sure. There's something about holding Victoria in my arms that makes everything feel just right.

When the song finishes, I'm mildly pissed off at Nate Smith for not writing a longer song. I don't want to stop dancing with Victoria, but I kiss her on the forehead and ask her if she's down for dessert.

She paid for dinner. Something that made me feel kinda like shit, but she insisted her mom wanted to treat us both. Apparently her mom's so excited she's going out on a date she handed her cash to cover dinner and told her not to come back before ten.

The fact her mom's so excited to get her out of the house for an evening suggests she doesn't do it often, and while we've talked a little about her, most everything that comes out of her mouth is about Wyatt. She lives and breathes that kid.

Tonight is a treat for her, a night out without parental responsibilities, which tugs at something deep in my chest. She's missed out on so much.

"Where do you want for dessert?"

"Have you tried a Zookie at Zoey's pizza place in Marion?"

She makes yummy noises. "I see your Zookie and raise you a flight of crème brûlée."

Huh. "I'm listening." I walk her back to her side of the car.

"Mom said it's incredible, and we should try it."

Holding both my hands up, I give her my best stern face. "I'd never pick a fight with your mom."

She laughs. "In that case, we're going to ChopHouse Downtown."

It's not even a ten minute drive to the ChopHouse which makes me inexplicably sad. Holding her hand, singing while I drive, or making small talk lights me up inside. It's not enough time with her. I want it all. I want every second with this woman.

We sensibly share a flight of crème brûlée. It's a selection of crème brûlées served on a tray, a trio of cotton candy crème brûlée, jalapeño crème brûlée, and espresso crème brûlée. There's a party on my tongue with every fucking bite. Are there any jobs going in here so I can eat these every day? Sweet mother of God, they're delicious.

"Raffi." Victoria's laughing, spoon poised near her mouth.

"Yeah?"

"People are staring at the sex noises you're making."

"You don't know what my sex noises soun—Oh." I almost drop my spoon at the raised eyebrow and shrewd look on Victoria's face. She knows exactly what I sound like in the bedroom.

She definitely has the advantage right now. If I'm lucky, she's going to let me take her to bed again. Not tonight, but some night. I've dreamt about those red locks being tangled around my fingers since she dumped a drink on my head in the bar.

"Gonna go out on a limb and guess you like it." She points her spoon to the flight between us.

"I'm not sure I've ever had something so delicious on my tongue."

She inhales some cotton candy and coughs, her face going red.

Leaning in, I stroke the inside of her palm. "What is it, Firecracker? Did you taste delicious on my tongue?" No one else can hear me, and there's every chance she's going to dump another drink on my head right now for being so forward, but something about her makes me want to push her limits. Just a little.

Okay, fine, maybe a lot.

"I remember your tongue." Her voice is barely audible in the din of the restaurant, but she's so close to my ear that every word tickles my cheek. Her eyes darken, she licks her lips, and I swear I'm about to combust with how fucking hot she is right now. "I dream about that night regularly." Her chest rises and falls with heavy breaths.

I don't remember what her body is like under those clothes, but it's taking all my strength not to peel them off her. There's nothing I want more than to lie her flat on this table, cover her in crème brûlée and take my time licking it off.

Pretty sure that'd be frowned upon, though.

"You want to tell me about it while I drive you home?"

She shakes her head before tucking her lip between her teeth, saying more with her eyes than I ever thought possible. "Can we go back to your place?"

"The hockey house? People might see you." When she flinches I hurry to finish. "I don't care who the hell sees you with me. I want you to be my girl, and I want a blimp to tell the whole world to fuck all the way off. You're spoken for."

She smiles, but it's shaky.

"If you're not ready to be mine though, that's cool with me. We can take it slowly. My teammates don't have to know. Eloise doesn't have to know. Our parents don't have to know.

It can be just us." I brush her hair behind her ear, stroking her cheek. "Whatever you're ready for, I'm ready for. You set the pace."

She looks me square in the eye and nods. "Okay."

"Okay."

"I want to go back to your place."

Winning the lottery wouldn't feel as good as this. I can't contain my glee as I pick her up and spin her around right there at the table.

"What the lady wants, the lady gets. Let's go."

CHAPTER 25

Victoria

I'd be lying if I said there was no reaction to my arrival at the hockey house. All three de la Peña's are lounging on the couch watching something on TV when we walk in. They don't say a word, but their eyes follow me from the door through the foyer.

Eloise's goalie guy, Ares, the youngest of the three brothers and the one who isn't a twin, tilts his head to the side and nods like something clicked into place for him. He smiles before waving at me, and I offer him a shy wave in return. He moves to stand, but Apollo smacks his chest with an open palm, forcing him to sit back down on his ass. "Don't."

"I was just going to ask if she wanted a drink or something."

"No you weren't." Artemis shakes his head. "Stay."

"I'm not a fucking dog." Ares brushes off Apollo's hand.

Raffi takes my hand, leading me over to the couch. "Guys, this is Tori. We're dating. Don't embarrass me. Tori, these are the de la Peña brothers. None of them live here, yet they can almost always be found here." He tosses the car keys to Apollo. "Thanks, man."

After a quick hello, we stop by the kitchen. A guy I don't know is heating something on the stove.

Raffi doesn't need snacks right now, but he grabs us a couple bottles of water from the fridge, and sticks an apple in each pocket. "For later," he says, but I wouldn't be surprised if he had both of them gone by the time we got to his room.

"Scott, Tori. Tori, Scott." He fistbumps the guys at the stove. "Best friend of the de la Peña twins and all-around nice guy. Not a bad hockey player either."

"I could say a great many things about you right now, Raf. But since we're in polite company, I'll bite my tongue. It's nice to meet you, Tori. If this asshole doesn't treat you right, you come find us, okay?" He cracks his knuckles, but he's grinning at me.

Raffi isn't even blushing. There's no way his friends don't know we're here to have sex, and he's just taking it in his stride, cool as a cucumber.

As we head to Raffi's room, we pass Tate on the stairs. "Hey, jersey girl. Can you give me your friend's number? The one with the Flames shirt?"

Folding my arms, I give him my best mean mug. "That's not how we do things, Mr. Myers. You want her number, you should really ask her for it."

"But I'm playing on the ice while she's in the stands. If I go out looking for her, that's stalking, and stalking's illegal." He laughs. "Unless you're Ares."

I laugh with him. When Ares was trying to convince Eloise to date him, he left packets of hot chocolate wherever she went. It was romantic, low-key stalking, but the guy has a point.

"Fine." I plant my hands on my hips. "I'll ask her if you can have her number. But if you hurt her I'll slice your throat."

The color drains from his face as he attempts to take a step back on the stairs. "Vicious. What's your damage?"

"Shitty, cheating, hockey-playing ex. What's yours?" I jut my chin out at him.

He holds his hands up. "Damn. Okay, you win. But we aren't all shitty, cheating fuckers, okay? I'd never…" He scratches the back of his neck. "I've been cheated on, and it's awful. I'd like to take your friend out for a drink, or dinner, or something, that's all. Okay, fine, maybe give her a shirt that isn't our opposition's too."

I really need to ask what her deal is. That's two games she's worn shirts that aren't the home team's.

"Well, that one's going to be tricky. Eloise and I tried to give her a new shirt, but she wasn't into it."

"Edith's tried too." Apollo crunches into an apple behind us on the stairs, and we all turn to look at him. "You're talking about her friend, Penelope, right? Always wears shirts from the opposing teams? She'll never change. She's totally trolling us." He smirks at Tate. "Good luck with that one, buddy. If Tori won't give you her number, I can ask Edith for you."

"She's the one who was in the crash with you, right?" I'm not great with names, but I'm pretty sure that's who he's talking about. Eloise says she's recovering from surgery on her leg, but she bets she'll be right here with us once she gets better.

Apollo nods.

"She'll respect Girl Code, even from down under." I've chatted to Eloise about Edith, and even though she doesn't know her all that well, she adores her.

"What's a hockey player gotta do to get a beautiful girl's number?" Tate smacks his thighs with both hands, blowing out a sigh of dejection.

"You'll get the girl, bud. You just have to work at it like the rest of us." Apollo pats his chest as he turns to head back downstairs. Did he just come up to chitchat?

"I'll talk to Penelope, see what she says."

Tate's face is turning an adorable shade of embarrassed. "Thanks." He follows Apollo downstairs. "You kids be safe."

There's no chance he knows what he's said, but Raffi cracks up into hysterical laughter, which results in a wicked dose of the hiccups.

"You didn't say anything at all on the stairs," I mention.

His room is sparse—light blue walls, a picture of his parents on the small desk next to the window, and a framed hockey jersey hanging on the wall next to the door to the bathroom.

I climb onto his bed and scooch all the way into the corner.

"I don't need to speak for you with my friends. You can handle yourself." He shrugs, pulling up a swivel office chair next to the bed.

The fact he hasn't assumed I'm going to bone him and jumped right up onto the bed next to me is so fucking hot. He's also not wrong.

I text Penelope, asking if I can give Tate her number. He seems sweet, and pretty determined to work for it, so the least I can do is ask if she's into him.

When I tuck my phone away, Raffi's eyes linger heavily on my face. "You back with me now?"

I barely get to nod before he slides my phone out of my pocket and puts it on his desk. "I really want to kiss you. But I don't want to assume."

Patting the bed beside me, I beckon him over. "No assuming. I most definitely want in your pants. Not sure it's my smartest idea ever. But—"

His finger covers my lips as he climbs onto the navy-blue quilt. "No buts. I know you're scared, but please, can we just see where this goes?"

His words soothe the pain in my chest like aloe on sunburn, and when his thumb brushes the tears from my cheek, I almost fall apart. His lips brush against mine, sending shocks of warmth down my spine.

"Of course we can." He dots kisses on my forehead then my damp cheeks before his lips return to mine.

How can I say no to this man? He's sweet and kind, respectful and funny, and he kisses like he was made just to lie here and kiss me.

I want more, need more. My clothes scratch my burning skin. Why isn't he ripping them off me? Why am I not naked yet?

Dude. I'm all for being respectful but just take off my fucking clothes already.

Fine. If he's going to be all gentlemanly and not rip my clothes from my aching body, I'll take things into my own hands. Literally.

Breaking apart the kiss for half a second, I figure out where the bottom of his shirt is and start tugging it. He's chuckling into my mouth as he keeps kissing me, his hand sliding around the curve of my jaw and into my hair.

"Impatient?" he breathes between kisses. "Can't I just savor this time with you?"

"Not to sound like a raging horn dog, but can we savor without the clothes?"

"What the lady wants..."

I don't feel like a lady right now, I feel like a bitch in heat. It takes a behemoth effort not to dry hump his thigh while we strip off our clothes.

His hands on my bare skin fuel the fire raging inside me. I need him.

Clutching his shoulders, my nails sink into his skin, drawing a guttural moan from him as I drag them down the length of his back. His lips sear a trail down the column of my throat, his fingers slipping into my pussy.

He's in no rush, lazily circling my clit as my hips buck

toward him, frenzied, needy, desperately aching for him to put me out of my misery and let me come.

"What's the rush, Firecracker?"

Staring down at his fingers sliding through my folds, a flash of color catches my attention. Despite the scorching need to climax, I grab his arm, lifting it up to get a closer look.

"What the fuck? When did you get this?"

He looks down at his arm then back to me. "Best I can tell is I got it done the morning after we, you know."

There's a brightly colored firecracker on the inside of his arm. He got this for me? The date on it is the morning after we had our one-night stand. That's so...permanent.

My heart soars, smacking against my ribcage as it tries to escape my body. "Why would you do this? It's so extra."

He brushes his nose against mine. "I'm guessing I got it for the same reason I pursued you the second time even though I couldn't remember you." His damp fingers trail over my hard nipple, sending a shiver through me and pulling a moan from somewhere deep inside.

"You're special, Victoria. I knew it the first time." He tips his head to his tattoo, and we both watch his hand trail over my belly rolls and disappear between my legs. "And I know it this time."

When his fingers pick up speed in earnest, my head tips back against the soft pillow that smells like him. My back arches, my hips roll, and I'm not sure which of us is chasing my orgasm more, but he's resolute. He's not letting go. His tongue has somehow made his way to my nipple and is rolling it around like it's his favorite pastime.

When he pinches my clit, he snaps his teeth on my nipple at the same time, making me shriek.

"Shhhhhhhhhhhhhhhh!" I scold him through his laughter. "They'll hear me."

"What makes you think I don't want them to hear you, Victoria?" His fingers lazily flutter around my clit.

This is it, this is how I die.

Cause of death will read sexual frustration on my death certificate.

Unless I kill him for teasing me first. Then *his* cause of death will *also* read sexual frustration. I'd be pretty justified in his murder too. The judge would agree, no one should tease someone to this extent.

I'm so wet I'm probably soaking his bed, and my whispered pleas are now breathy gasps as my teeth sink into his shoulder to stop myself yelling at him. For all I know, his whole team is congregated at the bedroom door listening to everything we're doing. And I'm not generally a quiet woman. Especially when he's playing me like I'm an instrument created solely for him. No one else knows how to play me, no one else can figure out how to make music from my body, just Raffi.

"Raffi, please." My voice is muffled by the mouthful of shoulder I've sunk my teeth into.

"Since you asked so nicely. Come for me, Firecracker. Let it all go, and come all over my hand like the dirty girl you are."

I want to object, to protest, to fight his instruction. He's not the fucking boss of me. But tell that to my insides. At his command, they've turned to molten lava. I'm shaking all over, sweat slicking my hair to my forehead, and my hips buck as I crest the wave.

Before my orgasm finishes, he's attempting to tear open a condom with his teeth. I want to tell him I'm on birth control, but I was last time too, so he's suiting up whether I like it or not.

If he so much as moves his fingers, I'll rip his face off, so with trembling hands, I help him take the wrapper off and glove his soldier. Hooking his fingers behind my knees, he flips me onto my stomach, gripping my hips and pulling me back to him as he slams his cock inside me.

"Wh-what made you flip me over?" I crane my neck back to look at him. His head's tipped back, eyes closed like he's having a spiritual moment.

When he opens his eyes and meets mine, the desire staring back at me is intense as fuck. "Dunno. Felt right in the moment. Why?" His eyes flash wide. "Do you not like it from behind?" He stops dead, making me whine and wiggle my ass at him.

"Don't stop. It's my favorite." My head drops to the pillow, face down, ass up.

He pulls back, and I can almost feel the warmth of his grin before I can hear it in his voice. "Whatever you need, Firecracker."

My expectation falls short of reality when he doesn't drive into me repeatedly. I shouldn't be surprised to find he's taking this at a leisurely speed too, like he's savoring every second of being inside me.

"Raffi." The pillow muffles my frustrated growl. "If I tell you we can do this again and you can take your time then, will you just fuck me? Please?" Pressing back against him and flexing my walls around his cock makes him groan. "Pretty please?" I flutter my eyelashes at him over my shoulder.

Another wiggle of my ass, another pained groan.

"You're making it really difficult to be a gentleman here, Firecracker."

"I don't want a fucking gentleman, Raffi. I want an animal."

A wicked grin spreads across his face as he shrugs. "What the lady wants..."

CHAPTER 26

Raffi

I wanna bareback this woman so fucking bad.

As much as I'm enjoying every second of pounding her from behind as she moans my name into my pillow, it's not enough.

Not sure how we did it the first time, what position, or how long I lasted, but with every grunt and thrust my balls get heavier, and I charge closer and closer to blowing my load. She already came on my hand, but I'll be fucking damned if this gorgeous redhead doesn't come on my cock before I let go.

Sweat trickles between my shoulder blades as I clench my teeth. I'm going to have to list the presidents in chronological order or something to outlast this woman when she tightens around me so hard I see stars.

Her red mane flows over her back like a waterfall as she turns her head so she can see me as she comes.

"Don't. Stop." Her tits bounce and her ass jiggles as she comes on the most glorious wail I've ever heard.

Between the sounds she's making, the look of untamed need in her eyes, and her vise-like grip on my cock, it's a matter of seconds before I let go. I double over her back, clutching her ass for balance as jets of cum fill this stupid layer of protection between us.

Yeah, I'm pissed about it. I want to own her from the inside. I want to coat her with my cum every damn day to remind her who she belongs to.

She falls onto her back with an ethereal glow and warm smile. "Round two?" She hooks her finger at me, beckoning me down on top of her. There's no stopping me. It's going to take a while to recover from round one. And I fully intend to enjoy the shit out of this woman and make her scream my name while she waits for my dick to be ready for her all over again.

After making light work of the condom and dropping it over the side of the bed, I hook her leg around my waist. If all I ever do again is kiss this woman, I can die a happy man.

I don't care how many rounds she wants, I'm going to give them to her.

I'm walking like I shit my pants as I shuffle to the bathroom. I'm a fit man, but fucking hell. My body is broken from a night in bed with my fiery haired goddess. Sleep was fractured and sparse, between long bouts of passionate lovemaking and outright fucking. Not sure anyone in the house got sleep, but I also don't care.

I expect the toilet flush to wake her up, but when I reappear from washing my hands, Victoria's still out cold. Strands of her beautiful curly hair are splayed across the pillow and over her face. How she can sleep like that is anyone's guess.

She's as naked as the day she was born, leg bent at an angle and creamy skin on display.

"I feel you staring at me." She drapes an arm over her eyes.

"Why are you all the way over there?" She toes at the foot of the bed, but considering the quilt and blankets are a tangled mess on the floor, she comes up short. "It's cold."

Even if she hadn't announced that, her perfectly blush-colored nipples are standing at attention. My dick's operating independently from the rest of my body and thinks it's go-time all over again. But if she's in any way as tender and achy as I am, it's a bad, bad, bad idea.

"Everything hurts." She flaps her hand at me. "Put that thing away—he's done for the day." She peeks out from behind her hair. "He did very well last night, but my vagina is achy, and you broke my clit." She points to her crotch. "Just imagine there's a no entry sign down there. Or caution tape."

As she talks, I kneel on the bed and spread her legs wide. "Want me to kiss you better?"

She props herself up on her elbows, one eyebrow curving as she gives me what has to be the best eye roll to date. "Do you always ask stupid questions?"

Before she can give me a second eye roll, I've pulled her body to me and settled between her thighs to feast on her.

"You're going to have to work for it, you know," she warns.

I grin against her pussy. "I'm good with that."

"Jesus, Raffi. You're making a mess with all your slurping. We're going to have to burn these sheets and start over."

"Victoria?" Jerking my head up from her crotch makes her whimper.

"Yeah?"

"Shut up, lie back, and give me all your juices, bitch."

Her howl of laughter is worth risking my life for. When she grips the front of my hair, I know she's paying attention. Her clit is swollen and super sensitive. Even the slightest graze of my teeth makes her wiggle and shriek. She responds to every flick of my tongue with a hip roll and her fingers tightening in my hair.

My girl loves oral. Which works for me because I love going down on her. And there's no pussy I'd rather eat.

"Mom, this is Raffi Shaw. Wyatt's father."

Standing in Victoria's kitchen, my hand remains outstretched for a long moment before the penny drops. I don't know this woman's name. First. Or last. I don't know Victoria's surname. Fuck.

"Hi, Mrs...uh..." Panic-stricken, I look to Victoria for help but she's doubled over laughing.

"Barnett, Raffi. Our last name is Barnett." Firecracker's mom steps toward me to accept my hand. "I'll try not to be too offended you didn't know my daughter's full name before you kept her out all night." She winks at me, but my heart's beating at three hundred beats per minute.

I hope she doesn't think this is some seedy hookup. I need her to know I'm falling for her daughter, and if I kept my memories from the first time, I'd be all-the-way in love with her already.

"Please, sit." Mrs. Barnett gestures to the table where there is a towering stack of pancakes, a plate of at least two packs of bacon, and all the possible accessories for the pancake stack that dreams are made of.

Brunch with my future mother in law wasn't in my plans for this morning, but I have time before class, and there's no way I'm leaving this mouthwatering feast.

"Hiiiii!" My little buddy comes running at me, fist extended for optimal fist bumpage.

"Hey, lil man." Our fists collide and I make my hand

explode like a firework. He laughs at my sound effects. "You ready for some pancakes?"

He nods up at me, his hair sticking out in just about every direction from what appears to be a very restful sleep. He drops his stuffed animal and holds both hands out to me to be picked up.

Fuck.

Uh. We didn't talk about this. Can I touch him? Is picking him up on the approved list of things I can do in front of Victoria's mom without losing a ball?

Glancing at Victoria, I hesitate. My stomach's going to turn to liquid and leave my body. But she's nodding at me eagerly, her eyes filled with hope. This moment is going to be etched in my soul for the rest of my life.

Scooping him up, I carefully plant him onto his booster seat. "Allergies?" I wouldn't usually think to ask about someone else's allergies, but this isn't just someone else, is it? It's my son. And I never want to do anything that might hurt him, even inadvertently. Plus, Mayrik reminded me to get the low down on all of her grandson's needs.

Victoria shakes her head. One of the guys on our team is allergic to mustard. Weird one, right? But I've been bowled over by how many things the stupid ingredient is in. And it's not clearly marked on labels.

"Alright, bud. What's it gonna be?"

My lil man throws his hands over his head like he's on a freakin' roller coaster. "Pancaaaaaaaakes!"

"Hell yeah!" I fist pump into the air.

"Hell yeah!" He parrots back to me.

Fuck. My bad.

Ignoring the searing looks of *both* Barnett women, I gulp. Note to self, don't cuss in front of the tiny human.

"One or two?"

The kid yells two, and both Victoria and her mom answer "One" at the same time.

One it is. I'm not pissing off these women.

Plopping one onto his plate, I offer him the maple syrup, which I quickly regret. He manages to cover his pjs, his toy on the floor, the table, and drown his poor pancake in half a gallon of syrup.

"Shiiiiiiiitake mushrooms." Rescuing the bottle from him, I ignore the giggles from Victoria and her mom. I'm not going to let this tiny tornado beat me. "Cloth? Wipes?"

Victoria shakes her head. "Just strip him. There's no coming back from that."

I strip him down to his underwear, mop up the surplus syrup with his jammies, and move his flooded plate next to the sink. Grabbing a new plate, I fix him another pancake with controlled syrup dispensing, and ask him what toppings he wants.

When he grabs a handful of bacon, I know without question he's my kid.

Victoria and her mom are already seated, piling their plates with food.

"Pass the juice please, Tori?" Mrs. B says.

The nickname catches me by surprise. Should I be calling her Tori too? I thought she liked her full name, but hearing the short version roll off her mom's tongue makes me wonder.

"Is it okay if I help out?" I want to be helpful, I want to learn how to do things Victoria has done for the past two years of Wyatt's life without relief.

At her nod, my heart swells, excitement charging my every breath. When I've sliced up Wyatt's pancake into toddler-sized bites, filled his sippy cup with juice, and made sure there's no stray syrup dripping onto the floor for the third time, I grab a plate.

Both Victoria and Mrs. B have conservatively filled plates.

I'm torn between being polite and eating as much as I actually want.

"Raffi?" Victoria points her fork at my empty plate.

"Yeah?"

"Eat what you want."

My unsure glance over at her mom is met with a reassuring nod, so I load that sucker up and go to pancake heaven.

Partway through my pancake-gasm, Wyatt taps my hand to get my attention. When he catches my eye, he presses all four fingers to his thumb on each hand and gives me the sign for "more"' then rubs his tummy to say "please."

What the hell? He knows how to sign?

"Don't get too excited. He only learned a few words at baby classes. Only a couple stuck. More and please are the two he uses a lot." Victoria reads my confusion like we've been together our whole lives.

Victoria's mom purses her lips, confusion flitting across her face.

"My niece is deaf, so my whole family speaks American Sign Language. It's actually what I'm studying in school. A bachelor's degree in ASL and English interpretation. I'd love to be an interpreter someday. Is he allowed more?"

Victoria nods.

It's mundane. We're sitting around the table eating a meal together. Wyatt's asking me for more pancakes and laughing when I make yummy noises with each bite I take. For most people, it wouldn't be a big deal, but it hits home just how much I could have missed out on if I never happened upon Victoria in the bar.

Even if I had gotten my memory back, how would I have ever been able to find Victoria with only a fake name to go on? Would I have gotten all of my memories back? There's no guarantee I'd have remembered she was in my phone as Firecracker.

Grief lumps up the pancake stuck in my throat. I'm between a rock and a hard place. I need to stay on the ice to keep my place in school, but if I get hurt again, Victoria will never forgive me, and if I forget about her... Fuck. It doesn't bear thinking about.

Now that I've met this kid and re-met his mother, pieces of my heart have fallen into place, and I don't ever want to be without them.

The tiny hand touches mine again, making me clear my throat and thoughts.

"You need some more, little guy?"

He shakes his head. "Sad?"

"Who, me?"

Damn this kid's observant. Though considering how close I am to sobbing into my syrup, it's probably easy to spot.

"No, kiddo. I'm not sad. I'm happy."

His face scrunches up, the cogs clearly turning in his brain.

"Sometimes happiness looks a bit like sadness." It's hard to explain to a nearly-three-year-old what I'm feeling, but I've gotta try. "I'm glad I found your mom, that's all. She's special."

He nods and turns his attention back to his depleting pile of bacon, as though my explanation was enough.

The stares of Victoria and her mom linger on my face. Should I look up at them? Or give them space? I don't want them to think I'm putting this on for the sake of a performance, but if I avoid their looks will they know I'm genuine?

Overthinking isn't my strong suit, and my head's starting to hurt. I cram another mouthful of food into my face before daring to look up.

Piercing jade eyes meet mine across the table. Emotion wells in Victoria's eyes with unshed tears. The urge to hold her is almost overpowering. I hate that I made her cry, even once, let alone the number of times she probably cried herself to sleep in the years we were apart.

I never want to upset her again. But every time I step out onto the ice, she's going to be worried.

It's a situation I never could have imagined, and one I have no idea how to solve.

CHAPTER 27

Victoria

Watching the father of my child interact with his son is the most precious thing I've ever seen. Mom squeezed my hand when Raffi had his moment a couple days ago over brunch. He's been busy with practice, the gym, and hockey since then, but he's kept in touch via video chat and text messages.

He's the most romantic person I've ever known. Like something straight out of a romance novel. And he's constantly exhausted. He woke Wyatt up the other night with his snoring, and it was through the speaker of my phone.

As I step into the rink, my stomach churns. Not sure how Apollo de la Peña found out I have some basic photography skills, but here we are. My sneaking suspicion is that my—crap on a stick, Raffi is my boyfriend—might have suggested the team should get some new headshots taken, but he denies it. They all do.

The smell of sweat seems to be stitched into the fabric of this place. There's a general funk. I'm sure it's cleaned regularly, but there's just a lingering odor that seems like it's part of the building.

"Tori." Apollo holds out his hand. He's fully kitted out and ready for practice. We decided to have them all freshly showered and wearing their uniforms but not post-game sweaty messes.

Getting set up takes a few minutes, and by the time I'm done, there's a line of hockey players all standing ready for their moment. Apollo goes first, but that feels like cheating. Even my toddler with a flip phone could take a good picture of the de la Peñas. There's no bad angle when it comes to that family.

Artemis and Ares go next—with their striking jaw lines and dark hair, the family resemblance is undeniable. How are so many players on this team so good looking? The ratio is off. Does that mean there's a team out there that's just full of ugly dudes? Because these guys...they're hot as hell.

"Hey, Firecracker." Raffi strides toward me. He grabs me in a hug, smelling of whatever that musky cologne he wears is, and it makes me want to chuck my panties at him.

"Hey, yourself, hotshot."

"It's taking all my strength not to kiss you right now."

I shake my head then get a couple shots of his grinning face. "I'm working." I point my camera at Apollo. "Your friend and captain over there is paying me an extortionate amount of money to take pictures of all his friends. No kissing allowed."

Raffi makes duck lips, so obviously I snap another picture. "Was that negotiated in the contract? No kissing the subjects of your photography?"

Despite knowing he lives for my eye rolls, I can't help myself. He can be an idiot sometimes.

"If I say yes will you move out of the way so I can take Scott's picture?"

"Maybe."

"You know you already have headshots, right?" Their

existing headshots aren't bad. Some of them have a black eye or missing tooth, but from what I understand, that's just the nature of the game.

And it's not even the external injuries we need to be worried about.

Apollo shrugs. "We wanted to go in a different direction."

Uh-huh. I bet that direction started with Raffi fucking Shaw asking his friend for a favor for the mother of his child.

"Can you stay and take some action shots of warm up? And come back for a game to get some game night shots?" Apollo is way more enthusiastic than I'd expect. Does he *really* enjoy getting his picture taken? Or is he simply creating opportunities for me to be in Raffi's space.

From the twinkle in his eye, Apollo's new name should be Cupid.

"What, no black tie event you want some candids taken at?" The sarcasm drips from my voice, but the team captain's face lights up like I turned on a light switch.

"Oh. Maybe."

My stomach swoops. "I was kidding."

"Don't joke about things with the de la Peñas, Firecracker. They host those kinds of parties all the time."

"Been a while though." Ares pipes up from wherever he's been quietly lurking. Traitor. "We're overdue."

"Dad's company does annual headshots too." Artemis chimes in from behind Ares.

They're all in fucking cahoots. Meddling pricks.

Beautiful meddling pricks. I won't need to do much to these photos when I get them onto the computer.

This situation is escalating. I'm not going to turn down business, but this feels awfully like charity, and I'm going to have to make sure they're not creating opportunities to give me money just for shits and giggles.

They at least need to see my work first.

"She doesn't look amused." Ares is pretty observant. I'm guessing my resting bitch face is in full force right now.

"I don't want charity."

Apollo snorts. Artemis pulls out his phone and opens a browser to the very rudimentary website I threw together. "You need to improve your website, Tori. It doesn't do what it should to showcase your talent. And you need more portfolio pictures loaded so people can see the work you do."

"You've looked at my website?"

Apollo nods. "I know we have a reputation for being lavish, but we don't throw away cash. If you were a shitty photographer, we wouldn't hire you."

"No matter who wants in your pants." Ares grunts as Apollo elbows him in the gut. "Fuck. Ouch. It's true though." Ares rubs at his stomach.

"It is true. You have an eye for a good shot, and we have photography needs." Artemis is so matter of fact.

"Plus, we like keeping it in the family if we can." Apollo tips his head to Raffi.

I can't tell if they're epic bullshitters or savvy businessmen. There's a pretty good chance they're both. What, if anything, has Raffi told them? Do they know he has a child? Do they know he forgot I ever existed?

Either way, they seem like genuinely nice guys, and if they're paying a photographer for work anyway, there's no reason it shouldn't be me. They're right—I'm damn good at what I do, even if it's not what I set out to do when I first came to college.

Apollo claps his hands. "All right, get your asses on the ice before Coach has my head."

Raffi kisses my cheek before grabbing his stick and helmet and skating out into the rink for practice. I've never seen a hockey practice before. As I walk around the arena snapping pictures of the players, the coaching staff, the equipment, I'm in awe. I can't believe how much the coach rides their asses.

These guys are incredible athletes, pushing their bodies, and probably spirits, to the breaking point. I don't know how any of them can walk by the time the session is done. And they have to train independently at the gym and play games on top of it.

It's grueling.

I can barely lift six sets of one hundred pound hexagonal deadlifts with Phil at the gym, while these guys are literally skating circles around me. It's incredible.

But it's also unsustainable. Why would they put their body to such extreme physical trauma? How many of them will go on to be pro hockey players? How many play because they love it?

So many questions swim around my brain as Raffi makes his way over to me. "You hanging around?"

"Do you have plans?" I feel like a bashful teen asking a boy out for the first time. My skin prickles with heat as I wait for his answer.

"We have book club today, but I have time for a coffee if you'd like."

"And food." I point at him. There's no way he's trained that hard and doesn't need food. This guy eats twenty four seven. He could have just eaten and still would find room for a snack.

"Always. My girl gets me."

I want to kiss him, but I don't want to embarrass him in front of his teammates and friends. And honestly I'm not sure I can handle the globs of sweat trickling down his face and dropping from his nose and chin.

"Go shower. You smell."

"And they say romance is dead."

"No chance of me being romantic when you smell like that."

"Fair point." He gives me a casual wink before heading into the locker room and I snap a few shots of the Zambonis as they come out to resurface the ice.

Would Wyatt like skating? Is it something you're born with an affinity for? I'd absolutely fall on my ass, but if my kid's dad is as graceful as a fucking ballet dancer on the ice does that mean Wyatt would have wicked skating skills too?

Waiting out in front of the rink, I scroll through the photos on my camera. The screen is small so I don't see the entire picture, but I've caught a couple of close up sincere shots of the guys during practice. Their smiles are genuine, their loyalty and trust clear in how they look at each other. And I can't help but laugh at Apollo and Artemis giving Ares a noogie after making a great save.

The warmth from the team radiates from my tiny screen. It's so wholesome, and when they're not all stern-stare concentrating, they're smiling and laughing with each other. I'd love to submit these photos for a human interest story on team dynamics. I had no idea what it was like until I stepped into their space. It's easy to see why Raffi loves these people.

"That's a good one."

Ares's voice scares the fuck out of me. I almost drop the camera but clutch it harder instead, my knuckles turning white.

"It's easy when you have a handsome subject though, no?" he says.

I don't know whether to roll my eyes, smack him, or message Eloise to tell her to control her boy toy. Either way, the goalie laughs at my reaction.

"How is he?"

Oh. He's here for a purpose. What the hell do I do with that?

"Raffi?"

"Sí."

"I...uh..."

"It's not a trick question, Tori. I'm concerned about him. He's pushing himself a lot." His voice hangs at the end of the sentence like he's unsure about something.

"You know we just started dating, right?"

Ares nods. "Bet you'd notice a behavior shift, if he was having more headaches or whatever."

Can't argue with that. "I'm worried about him. I'm not going to lie—it's scary. I had to leave the game last time. Waiting for him to take a hit..." A lump grows in my throat.

A warm hand covers mine as I cradle my camera. "I get it. It can be a dangerous sport. But odds are in his favor generally. Most games we all come out fine, or no one would play."

That's debatable. Sometimes it seems like Raffi would play it even if his skates were on fire.

Pushing the lump down with a hard swallow, I lean closer to him. "He won't step down from playing."

Ares doesn't flinch or react, he doesn't gasp, or smack me —if someone suggested I step down from doing something I love, I'd want to hit them. Instead, his face shifts, sympathy filling his eyes. "It's hard when it's something you love, even when it's hurting you. It's like a drug."

The youngest of the de la Peña brothers has a relationship with drugs and alcohol that is no secret.

"You can't force him to leave." Ares's face is stern.

"He has to play." I nibble on my lip, already having said too much.

He tilts his head in question, but before words come out of his mouth, a warm hand meets my lower back, and Raffi kisses my temple. "You ready?"

I give a last lingering look to a curious Ares before nodding. "Absolutely. Let's go."

CHAPTER 28

Raffi

"I forgot my book." Jackson Gilbert drops onto a chair next to me in Apollo's apartment. Jackson always forgets his freakin' book.

"I didn't." Scott waves his like it's the most precious thing he owns. "For a change." His copy has multi-colored tabs sticking out of it. He likes to annotate his books. Each tab means something different, quotes he likes, I dunno what else. There are a bunch of colors and damn near every page has a tab.

Justin and August show up to our monthly Get Lit meetings even though they graduated already. When they can at least. Making a book club meeting in their hometown isn't always top of their list of post-grad priorities, but it keeps them connected to the team. No matter what goes on in our lives, we all make time for book club.

I make time for the snacks, but book club happens while I eat.

All three de la Peña brothers are here too, so's Tate and a couple of the rookies. They're here to suss out what we do. Either that or they think it's all about the porn.

For the first time ever, we've opened our ranks, and there are outsiders staring back at me around the table. Austin Morgan, a friend of the de la Peña twins, is in town from Minnesota. He used to play for one of our opponents, the Minnesota Snow Pirates. He's here with two of his former teammates, Lincoln Scott and Finn O'Brien.

They're good guys—hard workers, not assholes during games, and always ready to put their hands in their pockets for a good cause. We may be enemies on the ice, but outside the rink, they're actually not that bad.

Though I'm not sure they can be trusted to take Get Lit as seriously as it should be. We don't fuck around with our romance. But the guys say it's just a one off. Maybe they'll take it back to their own team.

When a knock sounds on the door, everyone looks at each other. Aren't we all already here? Another quick headcount tells me we're full. Plus, the snack table's buckling under all the food, and there are no more seats, or space, around this table.

Apollo swings the door open and three Flint Flames—two former, one current—stand staring back at him. All the way from Michigan, huh? I smell a rat.

"I brought snacks." Jeremy Lewis lifts two grocery bags and grins. He walks past Apollo like he owns the place and heads straight to the food table.

"Who invited them?" Tate's voice is low but carries because everyone else is silent as fuck. It's common knowledge that AJ Williams's hit on me in my rookie year didn't help my concussion problems. He's standing with Jake Talbot, who we're playing on the ice tomorrow night.

"No one." Jeremy turns to face the room. "I saw it on the socials." He points at one of the rookies, who slinks down in his chair.

Fucking idiot. If anyone else shows up, that kid's going to be doing the worst chores for a month. And then some.

Jeremy surveys the table we're all sitting around. "Thought it was a party, not a book club though." He jerks his head to his buddies, standing like spare tires in the doorway. They're both red in the face. AJ's holding a crate of beer, and Jake's eyeballing the hall leading back to the elevator like he might take off and leave his friends.

Former players from the league like Jeremy and AJ getting together on a whim? Unlikely. What the hell is going on here? To my knowledge no one's getting married, and there haven't been any deaths in the extended hockey fam. We don't have an NHL team so they can't be here for a game, unless they're passing through to Minnesota, but why would the Snow Pirates come here to go back to Minny?

AJ and Tate stand in the doorway. AJ's been staring at me since the damn thing opened like he's waiting for some permission so I stand up and walk over toward him. There's a collective breath sucked in around us, like people aren't sure what I'm going to do. But I forgave him long ago for the accident. It wasn't a dirty hit, it was just bad luck and that could have happened to any of us.

"You're letting the heat out." I hold out my hands to take the beer from him and usher him inside. When I've ditched it in the kitchen, I turn to find him behind me, hand outstretched.

"Raffi, how are things?" His eyes narrow like he's assessing me.

A quick glance back into the living room makes every pair of eyeballs snap away from the two of us like a perfectly choreographed comedy moment.

"They're...okay." I rub at the back of my neck before breaking open the pack of beer to stack it in the fridge.

His raised eyebrow says he doesn't believe me. Like Ares's

drug problem, AJ's battle with depression and bipolar disorder isn't a secret in our world. He kept it to himself at first, but once he'd gotten it under control, he started speaking out about it more and more.

With a heavy sigh, I close the fridge and drop my voice. "Depends on the day. Headaches aren't as frequent, but when they hit, I'm down and out. They hurt like Satan himself is stabbing my eyeballs with hot pokers."

His face softens. "Doesn't sound good, Raff. We should talk about it." He peeks into the room where our friends are pretending not to eavesdrop on our conversation. "Not here. But soon."

I agree and return to the table via the mountain of snacks to pick up a plate. That bougie bastard Jeremy Lewis has brought some of the fanciest food I've seen. Who the fuck brings Brussels sprouts to a book club?

Not that I'm complaining. Fucking love Brussels with a balsamic drizzle and whatever the hell else he's got in this bowl.

"Don't knock it till ya try it." The man in question bumps his hip against mine as he peruses the rest of the table with an already full plate.

"Is that how you pulled the wife?"

I load extra sprouts on my plate next to a watermelon salad O'Brien tells me is a recipe which came from the Morrison household in Minnesota. It's got feta and some green leaf shit in it.

"What book is it this month?" How Jeremy has managed to balance so much food on his plate is anyone's guess.

"Pippa Grant's *The Gossip and the Grump*." It's Lincoln Scott from the Minnesota Snow Pirates who answers, a spoonful of potato salad poised mid-way to his mouth as he picks up one of the twins' copies and waves it.

Ares clears his throat. "This is serious shit too. I don't

know many of you out of towners, but if you fuck with my book club, you're out." He jerks a thumb at the door.

It's hard not to laugh. When Justin started this book club, many of us joined to support him, or out of curiosity, but now it's part of our life. Reading our monthly books gives us space to decompress, and talking about them around a table gives us time to be together that isn't at the gym, class, or on the ice.

By the time we get into the discussion about Sabrina and Grey, Pippa Grant's inclusivity and diversity—including a character called Zen with they/them pronouns—and the way she includes a fun pet or animal in each book, Jeremy is in.

He's moved himself away from the main discussion with Apollo's copy of the book and a giant plate of food and is reading in one of the seats in the living room. Finn's right there in the armchair next to him. The two poke their heads up every now and then to chat about something on the page and it's the most wholesome thing I've seen in a while.

By the end of the night, some of our visitors have picked up some of Pippa's backlist, namely her hockey romances. Jake has sent a group chat to the Flames asking if anyone wants to start a book club, and damn near everyone's leaving with a box of food. Because while a bunch of college athletes would usually devour every damn thing in sight so nothing is left to take home, we've been beaten by this spread.

Austin sits at the table with the de la Peñas, while Linc and Finn leave with our rookies. Jake heads back for curfew, taking Tate's copy of the book with him. He tried to take Scott's, but learned pretty damn quickly that he doesn't let anyone borrow his perfectly annotated copies.

AJ beckons me into the living room as people start leaving. Jeremy's asleep on the couch cuddling Bacon, our team's potbellied pig mascot. And Ares's cat, Puck, is curled up behind his knees.

Book club is an all-family affair.

"Wanna talk about it?"

A shake of my head seems to have been expected when AJ nods in reply. "I never did either, at first."

"It's like talking about hockey in anything but a good light is frowned upon. It's all good, all the time. You know?"

AJ takes a slow drink from his non-alcoholic beer. "It's a scary thing to do, speak up when things aren't going well. But once you do, it feels better. Like whatever was blocking the back of your throat and weighing down your shoulders is gone."

He levels me with a sympathetic stare. "Why do you play?"

My mouth falls open to reply, but no words come out.

He holds up his hand. "I don't want to hear why you feel you should play, Raffi. I don't want whatever you've conditioned your brain to believe. Hell, I don't even need the answer. But don't lie to yourself. The hesitation just now... You might try to fool me, but you can't fool yourself."

Heat coats my skin as embarrassment curdles in my stomach. I hate being so transparent, so obvious. He's right, though. I was going to give him the "I play because I love hockey," answer, even if it's not the entire truth.

He stares out Apollo's penthouse window into the darkness. "Raffi, life's too short to do something that doesn't hold your whole heart. If you're not playing because it's the thing you think about from the second you open your eyes to the moment your head hits the pillow, then you can reevaluate."

Without looking at him, I say the words that have been festering in my chest since Tori confirmed my suspicions. "I have a son."

I steal a glance at his profile. His brows flinch, but that's it.

"He's two. I didn't know about him because I lost my memory of his mom."

His body sags next to me. "That's not good, Raf. You've

taken some heavy hits since then too. And you're slowing down on the ice."

Telling it like it is stings like fuck when the words land. He's not wrong. No amount of time at the gym with Phil or extra ice time is making it easier to keep up.

"Not enough to get benched, but I follow your stats. You're approaching a crossroads."

"I have to play." My voice is quiet. I don't want to wake up his friend on the couch or draw attention to anything more than a casual conversation happening in the living room. I don't want my teammates to lose their faith in me.

"Why?"

All my reasons, the real ones, burn my tongue, but I can't share them. My parents' hopes and dreams, the fact I'm the only one in college, if I don't play I'll lose my scholarship, my place in school.

It's all heavy as fuck. "I have reasons." It's weak, but it's all I have in the space I'm in. Is that an excuse? Maybe. If I say it out loud that'll make it all true.

Am I scared my team will turn on me? Or rally for me? The answer is yes no matter which way you cut it.

"You should share them with your team." Jer stretches on the couch, arms above his head somehow managing not to disrupt either animal curled around him. "They're your family, Raffi. When you win, they win."

"Do they know about your kid?" AJ's staring out the window, his voice quiet enough I'm not sure Jer heard him.

"No."

"Why not?"

A shrug is all I got. "I'm afraid his mom won't let me spend time with him? I dunno." I rake my hands through my hair. "I'm scared I'll suck as a dad? I'm scared they'll judge me? I don't know why I haven't told them. Maybe they'll think he's a distraction, or will blame him for the slip in my game."

"That's a lot to unpack." Jeremy offers me his plate that, unsurprisingly, has food on it, but I decline. "Any grown-ass hockey player who blames a toddler for even one loss on the ice is a fucking coward and needs to not take up any of your time."

AJ nods at his friend's verbal assault.

"Is it possible you're starting to think about how your career might impact him? Watching his dad on the ice? The potential to get hurt?"

Maybe. If I wasn't before, I am now.

"Is that why you stopped playing?"

Jeremy shakes his head. "Stopped playing because my knee was acting its age. Didn't have any more gas left in the tank."

"I stopped because I wasn't good enough." AJ's frank statement hangs between the three of us, but I don't believe it. "I'd never have made it in the NHL. Pressure is too high, and I was too broken to make it mentally. Then I got proper treatment, medicated, married and had my twins." His tone changes, grows warmer, lined with an emotion I can't place. Pride?

"It's not easy, but it was worth the decision at my crossroads."

"Mine too." Jeremy crunches something with a grin. "What's left for you if you take out the hockey?" He holds his free hand up. "Not saying you should or need to quit, but if you take out the thing you're grinding for day in and day out, what else you got?"

These guys have a way of cutting through the background noise and getting straight to the hard stuff.

"What do you want to do with your life?" AJ asks.

"I want to be an American Sign Language interpreter. I want to help people who can't hear communicate with the world."

"Fuck." Jer thumps his chest with a fist.

"A noble goal." AJ smacks Jeremy's back like he's helping a kid cough something up.

"Can you do that without hockey?"

My body goes cold. I'm good at ASL, sure, but I need the degree, the qualification. Otherwise I'm just another schmuck who learned a language off the internet. And while that's possible, and more than acceptable, I need the piece of paper no one can take away from me.

"I'm on a hockey scholarship." The words linger in the air on my whisper, sympathy heavy in both men's eyes as they listen to the woes of a damn near stranger in my captain's living room.

"Sounds like you've just got to hunker down and ride it out." Jer looks like he's sucking on a lemon as he says the words.

"I'll figure it out."

AJ pats my shoulder. "I bet you will, but please be careful." His concern is probably edged with guilt for the hit he landed on me that tipped over one of the dominoes, but it also feels genuine.

"Hey, I was meaning to ask. Why are you all in town? Feels like a weird series of events must have happened to bring you all to little old Cedar Rapids."

"One of our old coaches is retiring from Iowa State."

"Booooooooooo." Can't help it, it's built into my whole system to boo them as soon as someone says their name. "You all played for him?"

AJ nods. "Great coach. He coached Austin, Linc, and Obi on different teams. But we played together." He points between himself and Jer. "About fifty of us are all in town for the ceremony and dinner."

"He doesn't know it, either. It's going to be fun." Jeremy eats something else from his plate. It's possible I've found someone who can eat even more than I do. "Glad we gatecrashed book club though. That was fun. Think we can get Sorcha and Freya to make a book club with us?"

AJ shakes his head. "We have more chance of getting our kids to do it than our wives."

"Could be fun. Kids book club could be tricky with multiple ages though."

Both guys look at me for a moment before Jer smacks my chest. "Been a dad for ten minutes and already he's bringing the logic."

Shaking my head, I chuckle. "I'm the snack guy. I bring the snacks, not logic."

"We better make a move." AJ turns to head back into the kitchen with Jer and me on his heels.

Ares stands in the doorway, arms crossed, an unreadable look on his face, eyes dark.

Shit.

How much of that did he hear?

CHAPTER 29

Victoria

Sunday mornings are usually my favorite but my stomach's in knots as I stare at the clock. I might be changing my mind about Raffi coming by to take Wyatt and me out for some family time.

We're heading to the Fun Station, a giant indoor playground Wyatt loves going to and hates leaving, and I have no clue how it's going to go. It was Raffi's idea—he wants to spend the day together. Like, the whole day. He's bringing Panera bagels for breakfast, we're going to the play area for the morning, and after lunch we're going to visit the gardens at the Brucemore estate. They haven't recovered after the derecho storm that swept through Cedar Rapids in 2020.

It destroyed more than seventy percent of the mature tree canopy, including more than fifty, century-old trees. Many of the historical landscape features will have to be restored—a process that will take decades.

I used to go sometimes, not often enough that my entrance fee would help them earn what they need to keep making improvements, but I tried to take beautiful photos to post online hoping to help promote them to new visitors.

It's a beautiful place. I haven't been there in such a long time, and my fingers are already itching to take some pretty pictures. There's nothing more satisfying than the crunch of fall leaves underfoot as you walk around in nature.

Wyatt loves making snow angels in leaves, but I haven't taken him to Brucemore since he was a couple months old. There's no way he remembers any of it. I'd never dare take him into the mansion—no one needs Hurricane Wyatt to go in among those artifacts and whip up a frenzy. But the gardens are gorgeous and expansive.

If indoor play followed by outdoor play isn't enough to tire out the little crotch goblin, we've met our match.

They decorate the mansion for holidays, and while Thanksgiving and Christmas are both coming up pretty freakin' quickly, part of me is loath to believe I'll be with Raffi even next week, let alone for major holidays.

Gotta get through this first family "date" first, right?

Wyatt's running circles around the dining table brandishing a plastic sword. He's swinging a shield too, but I have no clue who he's running from.

A sharp knock at the door makes me start, even though I'm expecting it. Palms clammy, heart racing, I open it and learn that casual Raffi might be my favorite. He's in sweats and a Raccoons t-shirt, clearly ready to crawl through tunnels and zip down slides with the toddler.

He kisses me on the cheek. "You look great."

My face heats. It's only jeans and a sweater, some boots and day two curls, but he makes me feel like I'm dressed to go to the most formal occasion on the planet. The way his approval skims my curves makes me want to strip and do him right here on the kitchen table.

"Raffiiiiiiiiiiii!" My pint-sized terror comes flying toward him, sword and shield held high as he screams. "Why are you here?"

His directness is adorable and also a bit rude, but Raffi doesn't miss a beat. He hands me the bag of bagels. "I was thinking about taking your mom out to the Fun Station. Would she like that?"

Wyatt's face falls as his mouth drops open. "No! Take me! Mama doesn't like it."

"You sure?" Raffi picks him up and spins him around. "You don't think me and your mom would have fun going down the slides?"

Wyatt shakes his head emphatically. "No. Meeeeee! Take meeeee!"

Raffi laughs. "Okay, what do you say we go get your shoes on while your mom gets to eat a hot breakfast?"

Wyatt nods, grabs Raffi by the hand, and drags him toward his bedroom. Mom comes trudging down the hall, slippers protruding from the bottom of a fluffy green nightgown.

"What was all the fuss about?"

I open the bag Raffi handed me, and cheesy warm air smacks me right in the face "Raffi brought breakfast." Guessing each bagel is the same, I offer them to Mom. "Want one?"

She takes one and unwraps it with a groan.

"He then told Wyatt he was taking me to the Fun Station, and Wyatt lost his shit because he wanted to come too."

Mom both laughs and burns her tongue at the same time. She's always been a sucker for a breakfast bagel.

When I take the first bite of melty cheesy goodness, it blows my mind. The combination of egg and sausage is chef's kiss. If Raffi doesn't hurry back I'm going to eat his as well. Except, the bag has four more bagels inside.

I shouldn't be surprised since Raffi most definitely loves his food. The guy's constantly eating, and yet never gains a single pound in weight. Jerkface.

Why is it so many guys can eat whatever the hell they want, but when I so much as look at a calorie it takes up residence in my butt cheeks?

Speaking of my butt, my phone vibrates in my ass pocket. There's a message from the bestie on the screen.

> Eloise: Are you panicking? Please don't panic. Raffi's a nice guy, and he's not going to leave you again.

> Tori: It's not Raffi I'm worried about. What if he decides he doesn't like me?

The bagel lies heavy in my stomach. Why are we like this to ourselves? We tell our friends and our kids they're the best thing in the world and mean it, but when it comes to self-talk we often don't truly believe all the good things we say. Or anyone else says about us for that matter.

We can be such assholes to ourselves. I'm a fucking delight. I know this. But add in a boy I want to really like me, and I'm questioning everything about myself.

The fuck is that all about?

> Eloise: Of course he likes you. What's not to like? You're a delight aren't you?

I can't help the grin spreading across my face. It's like she's in my head right now.

> Tori: I'm an absolute fucking delight.

> Eloise: Then what are you worried about? Worst case the two of you don't work together as a couple and you figure out coparenting, best case you get something way cooler…

> Tori: …

I don't know that I want to figure out coparenting. Coparenting means splitting time with my kid. It means sharing holidays I've had all to myself since Wyatt was born. It means not being with him when he's sick sometimes, or him hurting himself when he's with Raffi and his family.

Shit.

Digging the heel of my hand into my chest doesn't cure the ache spreading under my skin. I'm not ready for that. Not at all. Don't know that I ever will be. Can I still be a good mom and let him go?

Ugh. The bagel swells as it travels down my body into my stomach, making me queasy.

> Eloise: I don't need to finish the sentence.
> But since you're being obtuse.

> Eloise: You could fall in love and be a
> family.

> Eloise: I felt like that needed to be said in a
> message by itself.

> Eloise: Stop worrying about what he might
> find wrong with you, and just be yourself
> and enjoy spending time together.

Easy for her to say. I'm not sure if I'm more concerned he's going to dislike me or love Wyatt, but the anxiety is rising to uncomfortable levels in my body.

> Eloise: It's easy for me to say, but I also
> know you, Tori. You're a great person and a
> great mom. Stop worrying about what one
> guy thinks of you and just have fun.

Well. When she puts it like that I feel kinda foolish for letting it get to me.

Tori: Yes, mom. I'll do my best.

Eloise: Fear is healthy. But getting so
caught up over what might happen that you
don't enjoy the now isn't cool. You've got
this.

I hate when she brings the best friend logic.

Raffi comes back into the room before I can shoot off a reply to Ellie Bellie. I'll catch up with her after our day out. Maybe Mom can watch Wyatt so I can take her out for hot chocolate to make up for being a whiny bitch.

Wyatt is snuggled against Raffi's chest, already wearing a coat and shoes. What voodoo did Raffi work on our kid to get him to agree to not only one of those things, but both?

A pang of something strikes my chest, but I don't have time to analyze it.

"Good bagel?"

I take a huge, unsexy bite. A string of cheese lands causally on my chin and Raffi plucks it from my skin and feeds it to me.

"Me, mama! I'm hungry."

I hand my number one guy the rest of my bagel before cracking another one out of the bag.

"Am I driving?" I ask.

Raffi shakes his head. "I borrowed Apollo's SUV again. I got this."

The relief that unfurls in my neck muscles is palpable. I fucking hate driving. If I could get around without ever having to drive again, I would.

"Why didn't you bring your own car?"

Pretty sure he told me once that he has his dad's old car.

"It's a piece of shi—silliness. I don't want to drive you around in something that could easily break down on the side of the highway. Apollo insisted."

The rumors around the de la Peña family are persistent. There isn't a day that goes by when one of them isn't the butt of college gossip. But the more I get to know them, and know of them, the more it's clear they're just really good people.

"He sounds like a nice guy."

"Best captain I've ever played under. They're a tight group of brothers, but they never make the rest of us feel like we aren't part of the family too, you know?"

I shove the rest of my bagel in my mouth then we pick up the thirty five bags that come with having a small child. Wyatt doesn't want Raffi to put him down while he eats, so the two of them walk to the car munching on breakfast.

The resemblance between them is almost comical. The way they look at each other, their mannerisms. Wyatt's already working his dad's lopsided smile like he knows it's going to get him places.

"You got everything?" Mom stands at the door while we load the car.

"I think so. Do you need us to bring anything back?"

She shakes her head. "Just have fun, okay? Oh! Do you have your camera?"

Shit. Almost forgot. I pause before I run back inside, but Raffi gives me a reassuring smile. "It's all good. I can watch him for thirty seconds."

He's trying to comfort me, but instead makes me feel like an idiot. I don't truly believe anything sinister is going to happen in the time it takes me to get my camera, but I can't help the tug in my gut. It's there damn near every time I leave my kid.

Mom gives me a quick hug as I hurry back to the car with my camera. "You kids have fun."

Raffi double checks Wyatt's seatbelt before getting in the car and letting me do a final check. I'm sure it's good, but there's no harm in being super safe when it comes to car seat safety. He's still rear-facing, and will be until he's fifty. Height limit be damned.

Ugh. Fine. Maybe not quite thirty-five but as close as I can get. The idea of him riding up front in the passenger seat makes me break out in a cold sweat.

"Ready?" Raffi unwraps another bagel and sits it on his lap.

"Ready!" Wyatt screams from the backseat.

I give one final wave out the window to Mom as we pull away from the sidewalk and will my flapping stomach to simmer the fuck down. It's just indoor play and a walk around some gardens. No big deal.

So why does it feel like it's a big fucking deal?

CHAPTER 30

Raffi

This is the most fun I've had in as long as I can remember. There's something freeing about channeling your inner kid and just letting go.

Can't remember the last time I was in a maze, but from the delighted shrieks of my son as I chase him through the squishy foam play area, it won't be my last.

We've been here for an hour. For the first forty minutes, Victoria joined us inside the play frame. She doesn't like to be too far from Wyatt, that much is clear, and I can't really blame her. She's been a single mom for his entire life, since that stick showed two lines, and as such, she's got a tight grip on the reins.

Even now, I encouraged her to chill out with a snack and a coffee but her gaze is heavy on my skin. I bet she's had to abandon any number of fresh, steaming hot cups of coffee over the years, and even though it's play maze coffee, I figure it counts.

If someone had told me to take a load off and go have a snack, I'd grab the chance with both hands. And I'm not a single parent. But Victoria, something won't let her disconnect. She said she has stuff to read on her phone, a reading app, but every time I glance her way, her eyes are on me, not the screen.

I'm not mad about it. I don't begrudge her wanting to make sure Wyatt is safe. She knows me as a hockey playing douche who got her knocked up and ran away. But over time I'm sure she'll see I can be trusted to hang out with Wyatt a little more. Sure, I have a lot of stuff to learn, but I bought a book on parenting and even started reading it. I'm not normally a fan of non-fiction stuff, but this is a subject I most definitely need guidance on.

Wyatt tugs my hand, guiding me back toward the slide. We've become fast friends, and I love it. He's such a fun dude, and while the parenting book prepared me for something called a "Threenager" I haven't witnessed demon mode yet.

When we reach the bottom of the slide, before we even manage to get to our feet, an older kid barrels across the foam padded floor, crashing into Wyatt who tips backward and lands flat. The shrill wail can be heard three zip codes over as thick tears spill down his cheeks.

The temptation to get up and chase the older kid and kick his ass is tempting. But I'm pretty sure that's a no-no. Right? Grown-ass adults can't just beat on little kids for being careless and knocking their kid over. Yeah. Sounds right.

Instead, I bend and pick Wyatt up, giving him a once over to make sure he's good. No blood, no signs of a bump or bruising, it must have just been the shock of being knocked on his ass that made him cry. I can relate, sometimes when my legs go out from under me on the ice without warning, I want to cry too. It's not a fun feeling.

Victoria appears at our side in seconds, like she watched the whole thing. She holds her hands out to Wyatt but he tucks his head into the crease of my neck and clings tighter. She can't hide the hurt that lingers in her features, the sad eyes, the downturned lips, but she offers me a reassuring pat on the arm.

"You're doing great."

Not sure if she's happy or sad that I'm doing great as there's a pang of disappointment hanging on her words that feels awfully like she wants me to fail. I'm sure she doesn't. She's probably just scared of me spending time with Wyatt and not wanting to include her.

"Hey." I cup her face with my free hand, acutely aware we're in a kid's play area and kissing the shit out of her at the bottom of the slide is probably uncool, too. Yet the urge is like fire in my veins. "You're a package deal for me, you know?"

Tears well in her eyes, but she doesn't seem convinced as she nibbles on her lip.

"I mean it. I want things to work out between you and me as much as I want to be a good..." I pause, he's right here, and I don't want to say the D word in front of him yet. "I want to be there for Wyatt. I'm falling for you, Victoria. I'm not here to take him from you, or to make you feel less of a mom, or whatever fears are floating around in that smart brain of yours. Consider me back up, a relief pitcher after some long, hard innings by yourself. I want to be a good role model, sure, but I also want to be a good partner to his mom."

I mean every fucking word of it, too.

The smile on her face is shaky, vulnerable, and tells me I'm not too far wrong with my guess that she doesn't want to be pushed out of her kid's life in any way. Which is fine for me, because that's not what I want either.

Standing up from a foam mat with a spider monkey kid clinging to your person takes more core control than I apparently have. Turns out, Dad muscles and hockey player covered in heavy hockey equipment muscles are totally different. It's wobbly, takes a few attempts, and results in Victoria snorting with laughter, but we get there in the end. Maybe it's 'cause I'm not wearing skates.

Wyatt refuses to let go. Victoria says he doesn't take midday naps anymore, but this mini firecracker is tired.

"Should we go for a drive? See if we can get him to take a n-a-p?"

She smiles again. "Ever the hopeful optimist, eh? We can try."

Before I can take a step forward, a stab of pain hits behind my eyes. I don't have time for a migraine, but that's not how these things work. Hopefully it'll stay a low-key headache until we can get back to the house.

Fruitless optimism again. There's precisely zero chance of me making it beyond the fucking parking lot without this blowing up inside my brain. My vision blurs. Can I make it out to the car?

Maybe. But certainly not worth the risk while carrying my son in my arms.

The temptation is to hide what I'm feeling from Victoria. But if this thing between us is going to work out, I need her to be able to trust me, and for that to happen, I have to be transparent in all things.

"Tori?"

Either the use of her nickname or my tone makes her head snap toward me. "What's wrong?"

"Can you take Wyatt for me, please?" The pulsating pain in my head gets stronger. The screaming kids, the harsh bright lights. This is literally the worst possible place to have a stupid headache right now.

My eyes can't focus as she guides me to the door. She's got her camera bag, Wyatt's bag, and Wyatt, but she's somehow ushering me to safety, her hand on my lower back. She's saying something to me, but the sound of her voice is distorted. All I know is that she's not yelling, or maybe she is and that's why there's a drummer in my skull banging on my brain.

"Keys." Her voice is sharp. We're somehow at Apollo's SUV, Wyatt's in his seat and Victoria has no bags hanging off her. Man, she works fast.

The world sways as I grip the side of the car. She's patting down my pockets, and while I want to help, all I can do is grit my teeth and hope the nausea welling in my stomach passes quickly, if nothing else.

She finds the keys and helps me into the car, starts the engine, and before we're out of the parking lot, I close my eyes and let the darkness win.

CHAPTER 31

Victoria

I've never suffered from migraines, neither has Mom, but when Raffi turned to me in the Fun Station, pale, wincing, and disoriented, my gut told me that's what it was. He was out cold before I even backed the car out of the space. He woke up when I roused him, so I figured we didn't need a detour to the hospital, but the thought crossed my mind.

There was no way Mom and I could get Raffi out of the car and into the house, so I had no choice but to call for backup. Eloise is pacing the sidewalk outside my house when I pull up. Ares and both his brothers are waiting to help.

They asked if it would be better to drive to the hockey house and put Raffi in his own bed, but I told them no. I don't want him waking up and thinking I just dropped him off at the first sign of trouble. I don't want him thinking I left him.

I've lived that and wouldn't wish it on anyone.

Not to mention that I really want to take care of him.

Between the six of us, we get a pretty out-of-it Raffi into bed. Apollo found migraine meds in Raffi's bathroom, so we manage to get those and small sips of water into him before he lies down again.

I make my room as dark and quiet as I can, and Wyatt can have all the screen time he wants so he doesn't make Raffi's headache worse by running around screaming with a sword again. Artemis suggests a cold compress, so I make that as well.

The internet says to try caffeine but he's too out of it right now to drink a cup of coffee. Eloise has gone to the store to find some ginger candies for him to eat when he wakes up. They're apparently good for the nausea if that's one of his symptoms.

He hasn't lost consciousness, but he's pretty messed up. Apollo insists on calling a doctor to come and check him out. Not the team doctor, though—the consensus among the guys is they needed to keep this in the family, and not potentially get Raffi in trouble with the team.

The doctor hooks him up to an IV for meds and hydration and says he'll be back later to remove it or replace it depending on how Raffi is.

I don't know what kind of doctor he is, or how much his house call costs, but the de la Peña brothers tell me it's covered and not to worry about it.

While Raffi sleeps, Mom makes everyone coffee, and Ares orders food on an app that's at my door before Eloise is back from the store. She arrives to everyone opening bags and Artemis and Mom getting plates from the kitchen.

"How is he?" She rubs my back before placing the ginger candies on the counter.

"Resting, hooked up to an IV. Doctor said he'll be back later to check on him." I can't help glancing at the brothers who seem to be having a full-scale conversation between themselves just with their eyes.

"Is this the first time this has happened?" Ares takes a bite of his shawarma.

I nod and say, "At least in front of me. It's probably not his first headache." I don't know how to thank these men. Not only for the simple things like loaning us a car or calling a doctor, but for showing up for Raffi when he needs them. That kind of friendship is next level. And considering how things went with Jazz, well, I know how precious it is. As someone who recently believed all hockey players are dicks, I've had to eat humble pie. Turns out, only *some* hockey players are dicks.

Eloise's hand covers mine as she sits next to me. "He's going to be okay." She sounds far surer than I feel.

"We'll make sure of it," Artemis says confidently, but the shaky feeling in my stomach doesn't go away.

There's a heavy silence hanging over all of us, and I can't help staring toward my bedroom. How often does this happen? How does he manage alone? If he hasn't told the brothers sitting across the table from me, does he tell anyone else? So many questions, so few answers.

"Do I call his parents?"

Eloise shakes her head. "I don't think so. They might freak out. He might get mad. Maybe just wait for him to wake up first?"

She's right. The relationship I have with Mom isn't the same kind everyone else has with their parents. If I call his parents and they flip out, I don't want him to be upset with me. And what if he hasn't even told them about Wyatt and me? That would just bring more stress onto his plate.

He'll tell them when he's ready.

"The kid's his, isn't he?" It's Ares who speaks, but I snap my wide eyes to Eloise.

"You didn't tell him?"

She shrugs. "It's not my story to tell, Tori. Friends don't tell friend's secrets, even to their boyfriends."

I can't fight the urge to hug her right now. "Thank you."

"Of course. In fairness, he never asked either. Don't give me too much credit. He's pretty good at figuring out when I'm side-stepping the truth." Her cheeks are red as she glances across the table to her beau.

Theirs is a somewhat unusual pairing, but they work so well together it makes my heart happy for her.

"He's like a mini Raffi," Apollo confirms, dragging a piece of pita through the fresh hummus quickly disappearing on the table.

"He is." It doesn't take long for me to give the guys a brief rundown of my history with Raffi. By the end of it, I can't tell if they look like they might laugh or cry. I can relate. That's how I felt when the pregnancy tests all told me I was pregnant, for real, and had no way of reaching the father.

"Shit." Ares blows air through his teeth before glancing at Mom. "Sorry."

She pats his hand. "That's probably one of the least offensive words these walls have heard." She snorts before giving me a pointed look.

"That's tragic." Apollo has stopped eating the hummus, which is a damn shame because it's mouthwateringly delicious, but also works for me because it means I can swoop in and finish the tub.

"It all worked out in the end." Mom sounds so sure Raffi is my forever. Now that I've found him, that's it.

My heart swells in agreement, but my brain says it's early still.

After the guys leave, I check on Sleeping Raffi. Disney probably wouldn't have made the same money if they'd had a snoozing hockey player instead of a princess, but it makes me giggle.

Apollo said he'd tell their coach Raffi had a wicked case of the shits and that's why he won't be at morning skate tomorrow. And thankfully, they don't have a game until way later in the week, so he won't be in trouble for having to sit out a game.

At least I don't think so. If he misses practices during the week will his coach bench him for not showing up? I'm sure there is a complex system of rules at work, but I don't know any of them, and it didn't occur to me to ask his friends before they left.

Eloise stays. She's going to take Apollo's car back later, and if we need it again for something, we'll figure it out later. Apollo didn't seem too worried that his teammate keeps using his car. Eloise said it's because he has a couple.

Jeez. The wealth is strong with this one.

She sets up camp on the couch and lets Wyatt pick the movie, so the three of us snuggle and watch *Ruby Gillman: Teenage Kraken* for the eleventy billionth time. By the time it's over, Eloise offers to hang out with Wyatt as he smushes together multiple colors of Play Doh like a sociopath while I check in on Raffi. She's the best.

"What time is it?" Raffi's voice is hoarse and croaky when I enter the room.

"You don't need to worry about the time. How are you feeling?"

"Like I've been hit by a tank." He keeps his voice low and quiet, so I mimic it.

"I brought you a drink." I circle the bed and hold out the glass with a straw. It's room temperature because I didn't want icy water to make things worse for him.

When he tries to move, his arm catches on the IV. "What the hell?"

Settling on the edge of the bed, I brush his cheek. He's clammy. The only light in the room is a sliver from the hall so I can't see his face, but he sounds like shit.

"It hit you pretty hard. We needed to bring in a doctor."

He gulps down the drink. "Who's we?"

"Ares, Apollo, and Artemis came by to help get you out of the car and into bed."

"Your bed?" There's a levity to his voice. If there was more light, I imagine he'd be wiggling his eyebrows at me. The urge to smack him makes my fingers twitch.

"Yes, dummy. My bed. I wasn't sending you back to that house of animals. Who'd take care of you?"

"Tate's a pretty good nurse, but he doesn't have your rack." He reaches a hand out and slides it in mine.

"Why didn't you tell anyone you were getting such bad migraines?"

"They aren't all like this."

"One is one too many, Raffi. How often do these happen?"

"Not that regularly. I keep on top of it. Maintaining a daily routine can sometimes help stave them off. Guessing I didn't hydrate enough yesterday. Usually I get a warning though. Not today. I'm sorry for scaring you." He strokes my hand.

"I can handle it."

"You shouldn't have to."

"Neither should you." There's sternness in my voice. I'm trying hard not to judge. The more time I spend with his teammates, the more I get him wanting to stay in their circle.

"What did the guys say?" He shifts up in the bed a little with a grunt.

"Well, they called a fancy doctor who'll be back later to change or remove your IV. They brought your meds, carried you to my bed, and helped me get you settled. I'm going to guess they love you a lot."

There's a smile in his voice when he speaks. "I love them, too."

"They're worried about you. We all are. Apollo is going to cover for you at practice tomorrow morning so you can rest.

There's no way any of us are letting you skate, so don't even argue."

He chuckles, and it makes the bed vibrate. "I like when you're bossy and have mom voice."

"I'm always bossy with mom voice."

"Not like this."

"You want another cold compress for your head?"

"Mmhmm. Please." His words are slurred like he's falling back to sleep. The doctor said rest is the best thing.

When I move to stand, he grabs my arm. "Come back though please? Will you cuddle?"

As he talks to me, it occurs to me there's not much I wouldn't do for this man. "Of course I'll cuddle. As long as it doesn't disturb you."

He grunts. "I like when you disturb me, Firecracker. Hurry back."

It's not long before I've replaced the compress on his eyes and snuggled into bed next to him. My head rests on his chest, his arm around me as he kisses me. "I really am falling for you, Victoria Barnett. You need to start accepting it." His voice is thick with sleep, but filled with determination.

As my eyes flutter closed I admit to myself I fell for him a looooong time ago. It's past time to let him back into my heart.

CHAPTER 32

Raffi

It's game night. I've spent all week long doing all the things I should do. Eating right, sleeping right, and hydrating so much that I slosh when I walk. I eased back into training at the gym, Phil made sure of it. I even tried to hit up one of Lauren's classes, and she tattled on me to Phil.

I'd be mad, but they're looking out for me, and I appreciate that. My tendency to push myself too far will end up biting me in the ass if I don't take the right steps to recover.

Warm up felt good. My legs are strong from all the squats at the gym, and my mind is focused. Victoria is in the stands, and while we decided not to bring Wyatt for a while yet, she brought his favorite stuffed animal to the rink, and he's sitting in my locker for good luck.

I'm not sure who's sweeter, mini firecracker or mom firecracker.

Victoria stayed with me all night Sunday and all day Monday. She didn't let me leave her bed for anything other than a trip to the bathroom. She forbade me from watching TV, listening to music, or even reading books. It was full rest.

We talked a lot, in hushed voices, and Wyatt crashed into bed with us to read some stories while I dozed next to them.

Something about being in their space makes me feel whole, balanced, like I'm right where I'm supposed to be.

When the starting buzzer echoes around the rink, adrenaline fills me from the skates up. We win the opening faceoff and my buddy Tate sends me a great cross-ice pass that I chip forward to Apollo who's lying in wait by the goal. A quick wrist-flick and the Wolves' goaltender doesn't know what's hit him when the puck sails under the crossbar and lands in the net.

The crowd goes wild as we go up one to nothing against the visitors within the first twenty seconds of play. I clocked where my firecracker was sitting during warmups, so I give her a wink. She looks green, like she might puke, but she gives me a shaky smile all the same. I love that bright red lipstick on her.

I haven't asked her if she's looked up video footage of the hits I've taken over the years, but from the anxiety that radiates from her at every game, I bet she has.

An early goal is the momentum we need, and excitement sizzles in the air. It's our quickest goal so far this season, and knowing I had a hand in it makes me all the more determined to push hard. As a hockey player, our first shifts have to be good ones. Starts are huge. Hitting the ice with a lot of energy isn't always easy to do, but the team is focused. We're not letting the wolves win in our barn.

A quick interception from the faceoff ends up with the puck on the Wolves' bench. The puck comes back into our zone, and within seconds the ref's hand goes up calling a penalty against Artemis for slashing.

Going a man down this early in the game wasn't on our bingo card either, but we'll figure it out. Sure, our best defender and penalty killer is sitting out the penalty kill, but we've got this. It was an easy call for the official, but that doesn't stop the crowd booing him as he reports the penalty.

The Wolves power play kicks off with two huge shots on goal, but Ares isn't accepting goals tonight. His face is serene, his concentration on point, and his back to back blocker saves are straight up impressive as fuck.

It's a huge kill, but we pull it off. Sweat streams down the faces of our penalty kill special team.

When he returns to the ice, Artemis lays out one of the Wolves with a perfect open-ice check much to the enjoyment of the crowd. It's a physical game, big hits across the board, but we're really stepping up our presence on the ice. It's a great way to frustrate teams and get under their skin. Anxiety slithers under my skin at the prospect of taking a heavy hit. The physical nature of the game in general makes it a possibility every time we ice, but tonight it's playing on my mind more than usual.

We dump it in deep on the forecheck but the Wolves turn it over and head into our zone. Ares holds them off for the rest of the period, and goals in the final ten minutes from Apollo and a deflection from Jackson's stick bring us across the line with a three-to-nothing win.

It's a glorious shut out for Ares, well deserved. He stopped forty three shots and didn't end up with a penalty when the Wolves basically dry humped him and got away with it. In truth, I felt like a passenger for most of the second and some of the third, coasting even, but we pull out the win despite my being 'off.'

By the end of the game, Victoria has some color back in her cheeks. I'm fucking exhausted from overthinking every move, every play, every goddamn shift on the ice. But if I don't play hockey, what would I do?

Should I talk to Mom and Dad about stepping down? The weight of their potential disappointment at not having a superstar hockey playing son is crushing. They've never said it outright, they probably know it would ruin me, but whether or not they voice their concerns is irrelevant. I can't let them down. It's all they've talked about for years.

And the team probably wouldn't take it well, either. Rationally speaking, people graduate every year. People get injured. But this isn't anyone else, it's me, and it feels so far from rational that we aren't even in the same time zone.

Victoria made a good point in bed the other day when I convinced her to just lie with me for a while. She said if it was any other player on the team who was in my shoes, I'd tell them—without a beat of hesitation—to listen to the doctors and do what they needed to do to stay safe.

But with me, I just keep pushing through because it's what I should do.

She said "should" is a dangerous word, and she's right. I'm just not sure how to get out from under its crippling pressure.

As I step into the showers post-game, I resolve to look into alternative options to finish out my degree without my scholarship. The guys might play in a rec league or something so I can still get my ice fix every now and then.

I don't need to make a decision right now. But the fear in Victoria's eyes as she watches me skate onto the ice would probably be the exact fear in Mom's eyes if she knew the extent of the potential damage playing could do.

Victoria yelled at me for not telling my parents just how bad things are, too. She thinks that if they knew the risks they might not be so set on me making it to the National Hockey League. I mean, she makes a solid point, but I'm sure they'd be disappointed.

It's hard to know for sure until I actually talk to them.

"You getting dressed or are you gonna sit and stare at the wall?" Water sluices down Tate's bare chest, dripping onto the floor. "You okay?"

"Hm? Oh. Yeah. I'm good. Just tired."

"Two points, good game." He offers his fist for a bump. "Saw Tori out there. She coming around?"

"Nah, man. She's firmly in team 'it's too fucking dangerous.'"

He nods before plonking next to me on the bench. "What do the doctors say?"

Dunno. They'd probably agree with Victoria if I'd been to see them every time I've had an "episode" but I didn't want to get benched soooo...

"Oh, Raf. Please tell me you've been telling the doctors about your symptoms."

My body's on fire with shame even though I'm in nothing but a towel.

"Fuck. Man. Stop being a dumbass, and go talk to someone." He pats my shoulder. "I'm not a snitch, but you really should trust the team doctors to know what's best for you. If that's not playing..." He shrugs. "Gotta do what you gotta do."

That's easy for him to say. He's not the one who might have to hang up his skates from playing. Or worse, drop out of college.

"I know." He nudges me. "It's not a nice prospect. A life without hockey. Phew." He whistles. "I can't imagine it. But know what's worse than a life without hockey?"

I look him dead in the eye. "What's that?"

"A world without you." He bumps my shoulder.

"That's what Victoria says."

"Your girl's a smart one. Think about it. And go talk to a fucking doctor." With that, he flashes his ass at me and gets his shit dry.

Victoria is waiting for me when I leave the rink. "Good game."

It's so sweet of her to be supportive when she probably

wanted to puke for the entire game.

"Are they all going to be out for a while? Or are they going back to the hockey house?" She twists a curl around her finger, her face turning a shade of pink I fucking love on her. My girl's horny. We haven't done anything since before my migraine last weekend, and at the mere suggestion of getting some, my dick's paying full attention.

"Why d'you ask, Firecracker? You want some quality time?"

She tilts her head, her eyes skimming the lines of my game night suit. "I want some quality orgasms."

Fucking love that she doesn't hesitate to state her mind. She knows what she needs, and if she doesn't get it, she'll go somewhere else. Which is hot as hell. A girl with a healthy sex drive is the most delicious thing in the whole world. I'll meet her where she is, every damn day.

"You need a release, eh?"

She licks her lips, staring directly at my crotch. "You're not getting out of the parking lot without blowing your load in my mouth."

Fuck. Her filthy mouth nearly has my knees buckling. Gripping her jaw, I make sure she can't look anywhere but in my eyes. "You're so hot when you're dirty."

She snickers. "I'm always dirty."

"Exactly. Let's go."

We don't say goodbye to anyone as we leave, but she's already texting someone as we make our way out into the parking lot. When I catch her eye she purses her lips. "Girls have to tell each other when they're leaving, and that they're safe. Penises don't typically have those kinds of restrictions."

She's right—the guys wouldn't think twice about me heading home without them, nor me them. It's a whole different world for women. I come to a complete stop right in the middle of the road. "Does Eloise have a ride?"

Victoria's smile lights up the whole street. "She's good. Ares has that touch-her-and-die thing going on. But I appreciate the awareness for my gender." She pats me on the shoulder before we continue our way to the car.

I'll have to teach my son about consent when he's older. I'll have to teach him a whole bunch of shit. Fuck. That's some next level responsibility.

"Jesus, your brain's loud, Raffi. What the hell are you chewing over?"

"Just the parenting challenges of raising a boy."

She laughs. "Can we shift your thoughts for now?" She unlocks her car and tugs the back door open.

"To what?"

"Sit the fuck down, open your pants, and let me suck you off till you come."

Fucking hell. What is my life? This. Fucking. Woman.

I'm not going to argue with her, or wait for her to tell me again. I'm also not going to object. She'll get her O. In fact, she'll get many, but after that game, and the adrenaline charging through my body, a release is just what I need.

She climbs into the car with a wicked grin on her face. That bright red lipstick is about to get smeared all over my cock, and I can't wait.

"Sit back and close your eyes, Raffi. Let me take care of you."

CHAPTER 33

Victoria

Most women don't like giving head. I can count on one hand the number of my friends who like having dick in their mouths. Okay, wait, I can count my friends on one hand so that's not exactly a fair sample. But it's commonly held knowledge that women hate blowies. That's why dudes created "Steak and a blow job day," so they're almost guaranteed a blow job once a year from their significant other.

I'm not one of those women.

I fucking love giving head.

Having that much power literally on the tip of my tongue is intoxicating. The ability to turn a guy into a babbling, writhing, mindless being with my gag reflex is one of my favorite things to do.

Raffi's head is tipped back against the window in the back seat, his eyes closed just like I told him. I like that he doesn't fight. He'll give me my happy ending at some point, I know that without question. He's not a selfish lover. But when I want to take care of him, he's absolutely down for it.

And right now, I need to take care of him. Even if the

throbbing between my thighs is driving me insane. I'm aching to touch myself, relieve some of the pressure, but I'm so focused on giving him what he needs all I can do is rub my thighs together and enjoy in disappointment, the frustration, and the anticipation of Raffi ravaging me when I'm done sucking him off.

Game night hits differently.

Maybe it's the hot suits. Maybe it's the heady smell of a win in your own arena. Maybe it's the heightened hormones flying around the ice with the puck—adrenaline, testosterone, perhaps a healthy dose of serotonin and dopamine.

Either way, there's a buzz from my guy that makes me want to fuck like a wild animal in the middle of a freakin' forest.

I feel it sometimes at the gym after a workout. I'm tired, hot, sweat's dripping down my ass crack and under my tits, and all I want to do is tear my clothes off and ride Raffi's dick until we both come. Repeatedly.

Whatever witchcraft it is has me sucking Raffi's cock straight to the back of my throat as soon as he opens his pants to let me.

A rough groan falls from his lips as he pulls my hair back from my face. "Such a hungry firecracker." The last word catches in the back of his throat as I trail my tongue all the way to his tip. "Mmmm." His hips lift from the seat of the car with a squeak of the leather.

It's started to rain, huge droplets are pelting the car and windows, obscuring the view outside. Or, more specifically, of anyone who might be passing after the game.

Curling my tongue around the head of his cock makes him damn near purr, and I can't help but grin. His reactions make me so fucking wet. He twists my hair around his fist, but lets me set the pace, toying with his dick as I lick and suck him.

Precum slides out from his slit, and I collect it on my

tongue, smacking my lips together after I swallow. Warmth flickers low in my belly. I can't wait for him to fall apart in my mouth.

The rain falls heavier, the windows steaming up with our breaths. Raffi's chest rises and falls, little puffs visible with every exhale.

I take his length down my throat far enough to gag, coughing against his head, but that won't stop me. Tears well in my eyes as he thrusts in my mouth.

"You're so pretty with my cock in your mouth, Firecracker." He coos at me, letting go of the clump of hair around his hand and threading his fingers into my curls.

Dropping my jaw, I let him take the lead. His desperation to come as his thrusts get faster and jerkier has me chuckling as his cock thumps the back of my throat again, making me cough.

My desperation to please makes tears well in my eyes. I deliberately wore mascara that would run when I cry. Will he like the mess on my cheeks from my eyes watering? We're about to find out. I can't wait for him to feel how soaked my panties are from taking care of him like this.

He pushes deeper, and my jaw aches from hanging open. His hand curls around my throat, cupping the burn of his cock being so far down my throat.

"You can take it, pretty girl." His words are loud enough to hear over my gagging. Tears stream down my face and drool drips from my chin.

One of us is going to give in first, and it sure as hell isn't going to be me. I'm not stopping until he squirts into my mouth.

Blinking back tears, I wrap both hands around the base of his cock and pump in time to his hip thrusts. When he's close, I slide a hand between his thighs and cradle his balls. A soft squeeze is all he needs to tip him over the edge. I'm rewarded with thick, hot jets of cum spraying all over my mouth and down my throat.

I can't stop myself from fingering my clit a little, the boiling heat between my legs too much to ignore.

His whole body is tense, muscles hard and firm, as a string of expletives tumble from his mouth. I don't have a ton of experience with guys, but the amount of cum spurting from his cock seems like a lot.

When his muscles relax, and his biting grip softens on my scalp, he withdraws his dick from my mouth. There's a trickle of cum making its way down his softening shaft. I don't want to waste a drop, so I pick it up with the tip of my tongue, making sure I lap a few times at his sensitive head.

He shivers, making me grin again and his thumb touches my face. There isn't much light in the car, but a nearby street-light shines enough light to see the satisfied haze settling over him.

"So fucking hot with those marks on your face, Firecracker."

I let out a satisfied hum around his cock before letting it go and planting a tiny kiss on the tip. "I'm glad you like the mess."

"Love it." He grips the back of my head, fists my hair and pulls me closer. His tongue starts at my chin and drags down the length of my cheek before he smacks his lips together. "Your tears are fucking delicious."

I've never been so turned on. My nipples are pressing against my bra, and the heat between my thighs is enough to start a fire. My pulse throbs everywhere, all at once. I don't want to take my fingers off my clit, my wanton, needy, dripping pussy isn't happy when I stop. My legs tremble, but I wedge myself on his leg and keep rocking, chasing my own release.

His smile is warm. "The only time I'll make you cry from

now on is when my cock's down your throat, and I'm here to dry your tears with my tongue."

Sweet baby J.

This dirty man and his dirty mouth.

"They taste like hard work." He licks the other side. "Dedication." Another sweep of his tongue tickling my cheek. "Determination." Another lick before he places his mouth close to my ear. "Are you a dirty cum slut, Firecracker?"

In any other situation, any other person on the planet, I'd punch his face for calling me any kind of slut. But right here and now, in the back seat of my car while my hips glide up and down his outstretched leg in a desperate bid for friction, I can't deny how turned on I am by his words.

Sinking my teeth into my bottom lip, I nod. He strokes my cheek with the tenderest of touches. "Are you *my* dirty cum slut, Firecracker?"

The soft whimper of need that leaves my body barely comes close to the raging fire in my veins and the scream brewing in my body. I slip my hands under his jacket and grip handfuls of fabric as torment drives me to hungrily ride his leg.

"So needy. So perfect." He moves his leg, the blissful collision of his shin against my aching pussy providing a split second of relief before molten hot feral desperation charges through my body, making my nipples tingle. "So amazing." The tender swipe of his fingers across my face makes my insides melt, and his words wash over me like stepping into a stream of warm water.

"Raffi."

His mouth is on mine before I can get anything other than his name out from between my lips. "My cum tastes so good on your tongue, Victoria."

The more he talks, the more I need. It's not graceful, the way I'm bucking my hips against his dress pants. He's going to need to dry clean this fucking suit before long. My pussy's throbbing, aching, begging for Raffi to make me come, but he simply kisses my forehead, tucks away his already hard cock, then holds out his hand for my key.

"I'll make you come, but not here. Your place or mine?"

"Why are you driving?" My hips are rolling, head tipped back as I chase the release I won't get from dry humping his leg. If I try harder can I get there through my leggings?

"You're shaking. I'm not sure we'd make it in one piece if you drove."He's not entirely wrong. "Are you okay? Do you need anything?" How can someone with such a filthy mouth on him be so goddamn sugar sweet?

Somehow, I pry myself off him and compose myself enough to slide into the passenger seat. Raffi looks like a model as he sits in the driver side, while I look like some sort of under-bridge troll. My curls are wild, my face is streaked with mascara, and my cheeks are pink.

Raffi starts the car, plants his hand on my thigh and turns to me with a smirk. "Play with yourself on the drive home, Firecracker. Stay ready for me."

CHAPTER 34

Raffi

Is there any sweeter sound than the voice of a gorgeous woman pleading with you to let her come?

If there is I haven't heard it. The sopping wet sound of her pussy while I drill into her is a close second, but hearing my name fall from her desperate lips sends goosebumps all over my body.

Halfway to the hockey house, she changed her mind. So we're on our way to her place. And by the time we pull into her driveway, my firecracker is a needy fucking mess.

"Let me taste you, Victoria."

As she pulls her hand from her pants, her whimpers make my already hard dick throb. Her salty sweet juice drips from her fingers onto my tongue in an explosion of flavor.

I take it back. Her pleas are sweet, but her arousal is even sweeter.

"Raffi, please..." Her breathy begging makes my world spin.

Moving her hand from my lips, I plant her palm on my cock. "See what you do to me, Firecracker? So fucking hard for you. Again."

Another moan as her head falls back on the seat. She's writhing where she sits, her ass brushing back and forth on the seat like it might give her the relief she needs. We both know it won't.

"Ooooh, pretty girl. You won't get what you need from that seat." I can't help the chuckle that escapes. I'm living for her desperation right now. Only because it mirrors my own. The scent of sex is heavy in the car, but if I stop to give us both what we need, we won't see a bed tonight.

And for as much as I love my feisty redhead, there's something particularly enjoyable about when she softens. When she's pliable and needy, her walls are down and her vulnerabilities on display.

It's only for me, only ever for me.

Because she's mine, and we both know it.

Both Wyatt and Victoria's mom are in their bedrooms. Hopefully Mrs. B sleeps like the dead because I'm not sure my girl can hold her tongue. She's already half naked before I get the door closed behind me.

"You okay, Victoria?"

Her scowl is adorable, and when she flips me off I cross the space and bite the tip of her finger. She grabs my hand, trying to shove it between her thighs. The warmth is tempting to sink into, but I want to enjoy this hunger for just a little longer. I've never been about the chase, but with the ache building in my balls, and my girl being whipped into a starved frenzy, I can't help but want to stretch this moment out.

When she purses her lips, squares her shoulders, and plants her fists on her hips, I know I'm in for a ball crushing. Can't fucking wait. Few things are more beautiful than my firecracker in full glory.

The corners of my mouth twitch with the urge to smirk, but I bite the inside of my cheek, the pinch of pain keeping my excitement under wraps for now.

She doesn't say a word. No tirade or challenges to my manhood. No threat. Nothing. She simply guides me to her room, flicks the lamp switch on her bedroom table so there's extra light, falls back on her bed, spreads her legs and lips and fingers herself.

Kicking off my shoes, I almost eat dirt, stumbling when I see how pretty and pink her pussy is. Her arousal glistens under the light of her lamp as she hums with pleasure, her fingers strumming her clit.

I make short work of my clothes as she drives herself closer to the edge. Her body's wiggling, feet scrambling for traction on the sheets while she whimpers and moans into her fist.

I can't help pumping my cock and just watching her. Calling her a goddess is almost an affront. She's ethereal, hair spilling over the bed in perfect waves, tits beckoning me with her perfect rosy nipples. I almost come. My dick's rod-straight and rock hard as my hand glides up the shaft, turning over the head, and trailing tightly back down.

My building orgasm is stronger than my patience, but I'll be damned if I come twice before Victoria explodes all over my fucking face.

Never in a million years.

"Sit on my face." I point at her before waving my hand to indicate she should move and give me space to lie down.

"It won't work. I'm too big."

Fuck that noise. Tugging her ankle, I make myself some space on the bed and lie flat on my back. "Sit. On. My. Face."

"I'll crush you, Raffi. It sounds good in theory, but I don't want to hurt you."

"The only way you'll hurt me is if you don't sit on my fucking face right this fucking second, Victoria."

She crawls up the bed toward my head, grips the headboard, and swings a leg over my head so her knees bracket me in.

She lowers herself over me, but there's no way she's giving me her full weight. She's holding out, and I don't like it one little bit.

"Victoria? Sit on my goddamn face. If you have to focus on holding yourself up you're not going to be focused on spraying my face with your cum. Please? I'm begging you, just plant your pussy on my tongue and ride it until you come."

She lets go a bit more, but she's still holding herself up. Bracing both hands on her hips, I tug her ass down and lap at her pussy. If she won't do as I ask her to, I'll make it so she can't maintain balance. I'll make her legs and arms shake so hard the only thing holding her upright will be her knees against the side of my head.

The time edging in the car and on the bed have only served to make her arousal thicker, creamier, even sweeter. It's as though I can taste her desperation nestled right here in her pussy.

Her clit flicks off the tip of my tongue as she moans, throwing her head back. It's something I love about her in the bedroom, that moment when she tosses her head back and her hair spills over her shoulders and tits.

She rolls her hips, cautiously kissing my tongue with her pussy. But I need more. Pressing my tongue against her clit, I drag it back and forth. She crams a fist against her mouth, dropping a hand from the headboard. Her weight settles on me more, but she's not fully relaxed.

Settling her where I need her, I let my hands wander as I lick and bite and suck and tease at her clit like she's my favorite toy to play with, and I'm not stopping until she breaks. I'm in no real hurry though, happy enough to take my time. But when my fingers reach her nipples, she's already arching her back, panting, whispering pleas to let her come.

Humming against her pussy just makes her want it more. Her juices are running down my face, my chin, my throat, and coating my lips and tongue. The more I lap, the more she gives me. When I pinch her nipples, hard, she grabs a pillow from behind my head and shoves her face into it with a breathy howl.

"So...close..."

It's adorable that she thinks I can't read her like a well-worn copy of my favorite book. She's cresting the wave when I squeeze her nipples even harder, and my tongue kicks into frenzy gear, flicking against her clit with renewed energy.

She's waited for this, worked for it, almost damn near killed me for it, and I'm more excited about her orgasm than she is. When her fingers ditch the pillow and slip into my hair, scratching nails biting into my scalp, she's finally let go of her inhibitions.

When she rolls her hips so deep her entire pussy grinds on my face, she's given into her base desire to just fucking come.

She explodes on my face, giving me the most delicious orgasm I've ever tasted, and it doesn't stop. She drips cum onto my nose, my mouth, and by now she's covered the tops of my shoulders and the bed with her arousal.

Her moans don't stop, so neither does my tongue or her riding my face. If she isn't finished, neither am I. Within a minute or so, her first orgasm crashes into a second as she bucks herself against my face, thrusting against me with such wild abandon her hair flaps around her face, clinging to her sweat sheened skin.

She collapses on the bed with a thump against the quilt. "I made a mess." She's starfished out on the bed, her hand covering my soaking wet face.

"Wouldn't have it any other way."

CHAPTER 35

Victoria

There's an inherent intuition as a mother when you wake up and it's past the time your child usually gets you out of bed. It's like we've been implanted with a chip. As soon as our eyes open, something goes, "This is not the natural order of things."

So when I wake up, roll over to a cold and empty space beside me, and there's not a sound to be heard, panic grips my entire body. It's almost nine on Sunday morning. I can't remember the last time Wyatt let me sleep past six any day of the week, never mind a Sunday.

I fell asleep before I had a chance to put any clothes on, so I yank sweats and an oversized Rainbow Brite shirt from my drawer before damn near tripping over my own feet to search the house.

Mom's sitting at the breakfast bar cradling a cup of coffee. She flaps her hand at me in a "chill the fuck out" bid, then hooks a thumb toward the living room and puts a finger on her lips.

Tiptoeing into the living room, I hold my breath. But

nothing could have prepared me for the overwhelming adorableness right there on my couch.

Raffi and Wyatt are snuggled under a blanket, Wyatt curled in the crook of Raffi's arm with a bowl of goldfish crackers on his lap. Blippi is on the TV which is how I know Raffi's all in. No way in hell Wyatt gets to watch Blippi with me on a Sunday morning. Trolls is my current favorite.

The closer I get, the more obvious it becomes that Wyatt is out cold, and my hot, grown-ass-adult hockey playing boyfriend is sitting glued to my kid's favorite TV show. It's not even that he can't reach the remote, it's right next to him on the arm. He's just invested in Blippi's travels to a hockey rink.

On screen, Blippi's riding around in a Zamboni living his best life. On the couch, Raffi's cramming my son's goldfish crackers in his face, living *his* best life, too. I turn to find my camera. This moment is one Raffi's going to want to remember for the rest of his life. I do, too.

When he finally notices me, I'm leaning against the doorframe, a half drunk cup of coffee in hand, and the panic that had seized me when I woke up is long gone.

"Morning, beautiful."

I almost laugh out loud. There's no way I look beautiful right now. I'm not wearing a bra, my giant boobs are practically at my belly button, there's a hole in the knee of my pj pants, and my hair... Oof. God knows what that looks like considering the amount of sexing we did overnight. It probably looks like I stuck my finger in an outlet.

But I can't help but smile.

"Wanna watch Blippi?"

With a shake of my head, some wayward fuzzy curls fall into my face. "I'd rather cleave my nipples off and feed them to a bear."

He rolls his lips, silent laughter shaking his body. "I was thinking."

"Did it hurt?" I make my way around the room and plop down on the arm chair sitting a couple of feet from his side of the couch.

He nods. "Almost always."

Wyatt stirs in his arms, letting out a soft snore. He doesn't generally nap this early in the day, or at all much these days—he decided he just doesn't need them—but this is the most adorable thing I've seen. And I birthed a cute kid.

"Mom invited me over for Sunday dinner."

I know where this is going before it even leaves his mouth. He wants to take Wyatt to meet his parents. I knew it was going to happen at some time, I just wasn't ready for it to happen now. I guess I could follow them, and sit around the corner from his parents' house in case something goes wrong.

I need to slow my roll. That's stalking. And creepy. And from everything I've seen between Raffi and Wyatt, there are few things Raffi couldn't handle as his dad. Even if something happened, Raffi's parents raised Raffi, and they'd know what to do in case of an emergency.

So why does my stomach feel like the choppy ocean on a rainy day?

He slips his hand over mine. "I'd like to bring you and Wyatt to meet them. If you're not ready, that's cool. But Dad carves a mean joint of meat, and Mom has already bought one of every toy she has found since the day she knew Wyatt existed. They're ready. But if you're not, then that's the end of the discussion."

He always knows what to say, right at the moment I need to hear it. Tears well in my eyes. Not because he's being considerate and patient, but because he included me. He wants to introduce me to his family. It hits just how much I mean to him, which, considering the fact I thought for three years he abandoned me because there was something wrong with me, well, it chokes me up.

"What is it, Firecracker?"

"You want me to meet your mom."

"And dad. Of course I do. I've met your mom. You know it's the natural progression of relationships, right?"

A tearful laugh bubbles out of my mouth. All I need now is to snot in front of him, and I'll complete my swamp witch get-up. "Yeah, but, I dunno. I just. For so long I thought there was something wrong with me."

His other hand cups the one already holding mine and he pulls my hand to his mouth to kiss my knuckles one at a time. "It was never you, Victoria. Not ever. And if I have to spend every day convincing you of that until you believe me, I will."

His knuckles graze my cheek, catching my tears as they trickle down my face. "You know how special you are?"

Not? Ugh. I hate that's my first reaction to his question, but it's how I feel. I wouldn't say it out loud. If Wyatt heard me talking smack about myself, I'd get a talking to. Even at two years old he knows we only talk positively about ourselves.

"I fell for you once. Hit my head and lost my memory. And fell for you all over again." He leans forward, careful not to upset Wyatt where he's starting to stir. "I might never get my memory back of our first time meeting. But I don't need it, because I already love you all over again. Falling in love with the same woman twice? Especially when she dumps a drink on your head? That's pretty special, because *you're* pretty special."

This hot-mess-mom-express is ugly crying now. Thick, heavy tears stream off my chin and onto my shirt. Raffi's smile is soft, and a sniff from the direction of the kitchen tells me Mom's as emotional about it all as I am.

"I don't love you because you're the mother of our son, Victoria. I love you because you're unapologetically you. You're quietly vulnerable, but only for me. You're strong, and kind, and you're the best fucking mother on the planet. Sorry Mrs. B."

Mom giggles but doesn't reply.

"I want you to meet my parents not because you're Wyatt's mom, but because you're the woman who has stolen my heart twice. And I don't ever want it back."

Wow. I get why this guy writes songs. He should write a romance novel.

"You might want a shower first, though. While I love..." He waves his hand in front of my face. "You may want to..." He looks around. "Wash the cum out of your hair before you see my mom," he whispers then winks at me, making me snort-laugh. "Go shower. I'm going to make a Play Doh castle with our kid and try to convince him I didn't eat any of his goldfish crackers while he was drooling on my shirt."

Getting cum out of curls isn't something I'm used to having to do, but eventually the crusty mess gets washed away in the shower. By the time I'm dressed and ready to go, my boys are too. Nerves shred my stomach, but we climb in the car and Raffi sets off toward his childhood home.

Guess it's time to meet the in-laws.

"Tori, it's so nice to finally meet you." Raffi's mom makes it sound like we've been together for years and years and we never got around to hanging out. I thought it had been weeks, but when I did the math on the ride here after Raffi's declaration of the L-word, it's more like a couple months. Doesn't feel like it at all, it feels like no time has passed at all.

Mom says it takes a moment to fall in love, so I don't feel quite so foolish about my emotions. But can a love born from lightning striking twice in the same place last forever?

Guess time will tell.

"Mrs. Shaw, it's a pleasure."

She scrunches her face up. "Please. It's Ani and Travis. No

Mr. and Mrs. in this house." She opens her arms, but waits for me to nod before pulling me into a hug. As Raffi's dad does the same, Raffi places Wyatt on the floor.

"Mayrik, Dad, this is my..." He swallows, his eyes glassy, and his chest heaving with effort as he sucks in slow breaths. "This is Wyatt." His voice breaks on our son's name, cracking something in my chest. He could have called himself Wyatt's father, I wouldn't have been mad, but I appreciate him taking a little more time to use the term in front of the little man. Just in case things don't work out, or in case it makes me uncomfortable, either way.

Both Raffi's parents crouch down to Wyatt's level, smiles warm, respecting his distance. It must be so hard for them not to rush him, pick him up, and squish him until he squirms, but they're patient and quiet. Their efforts to not overwhelm him aren't lost on me, and it occurs to me Raffi might have prepped them not to go full grandparent all at once.

Wyatt hasn't called Raffi daddy yet, he might never, and Raffi's okay with that. But he knows Raffi is his dad, we told him this morning before we came to Raffi's parents' house. I'm not sure he fully understands yet. We're letting Wyatt decide what to do with that information and not encouraging him or leading him one way or the other.

"Hi, Wyatt," Ani looks like she might explode with excitement, but she keeps herself under wraps. "I'm Ani." She flicks her gaze up at me like she's seeking validation she's doing okay, so I give her a reassuring nod. "And this is Travis."

When Wyatt doesn't move, I crouch down next to him, patting his back in slow circles. "These are Raffi's parents. Ani is Raffi's mama, and Travis is Raffi's daddy."

He looks at Raffi, then back at his grandparents. "Like nana?"

I nod at him. "Just like nana." I turn to Ani. "Did you think of what you'd like for him to call you?"

Ani's face lights up like I just gave her a lifetime supply of her favorite candy. "Grandma and pawpaw? Is that okay?" Her uncertainty, the insecurity in her voice, makes me want to hug her. "Or Mayrik, like Raffi calls me? Too complicated? I don't want to overwhelm him."

"Of course. Wyatt, can you say Mayrik and pawpaw?"

He parrots it back to me while I point between Ani and Travis. When they stand, they maintain distance.

"He's not allergic to anything, right?"

I shake my head.

"Can I give him a juice box?" She's speaking in a hushed whisper, but Wyatt's little face turns to me with gleeful hope in his eyes.

"He's at his grandparents' house." I shrug, giving her a smile. "I fully expect you to give him all kinds of things he might not ordinarily have."

The glint in her eye sparkles as she beams at me.

"It's the nature of grandparents, right?"

She nods, biting on her bottom lip.

"Thank you for asking, though."

"I have chocolate." She's stage whispering, but this time it feels more for Wyatt's benefit.

Travis winks. "Wyatt might not like chocolate, Mayrik."

Her face brightens at the word Mayrik. The joy our child is already bringing to these people warms my heart. It grows even stronger when he takes Ani's outstretched hand and walks with her into the kitchen.

Tiny traitor, sold out for the promise of some chocolate and a juice box. I can't deny there's a pang of something sharp in my chest as he walks away from me.

Raffi pulls me to his chest, planting a kiss on my forehead. He doesn't call me ridiculous, or say I'm overreacting. He doesn't laugh, he just stands stoic, quietly supportive, as my toddler follows his grandparents into the kitchen to embrace the impending sugar high.

I hate hockey.

The more I watch it, the more I hate it.

The ball of dread lying heavy in my stomach isn't helping. Every time Raffi steps onto the ice, cold tendrils of fear curl around my spine. There's a headache brewing behind my eyes from clenching my teeth so hard.

I snapped at Raffi before he left for the game. He spoke with the team doctors this morning, they ran some tests and declared him fit to play.

In my official medical opinion, from years and years of endless studying in medical school and working with athletes forever, I think it's a bullshit call.

Fine. I'm a no one with no medical know-how. But this isn't a smart plan. At all. My gut says Raffi needs to step down before he hurts himself.

Listening to his mom last weekend, it's easy to see why he pushes himself. She gushes about how successful he is on the ice. Everything comes back to the game in their house. I'm not sure if it's deliberate, if they think *he* wants it so badly and they believe they're encouraging him, or if *they* want it for him.

Either way, they need to sit down and have a frank conversation about the likelihood that Raffi won't end up playing pro hockey. I mean, there's a chance, but from what I've gathered from his teammates and researching on the internet, the NHL is unlikely to come calling. His medical history has rendered him a liability, even if he was the best player ever to skate on the ice.

I could be wrong. I'm not an expert on hockey any more than I'm an expert on medicine.

Wyatt leans forward on Penelope's lap to smack on the glass. He doesn't understand much, and he hopefully can't hear anything with those ear defenders on, but he's wearing a shirt with Raffi's number on the back.

Raffi hasn't seen it yet because he didn't come our way during warm ups. But as the arena gets ready for the first period, he skates our direction, tapping the plexi to get Wyatt's attention.

"Raffiiiii!" Wyatt's voice pierces the air as he waves frantically at his dad. Raffi winks at him before turning his attention to me.

I whisper to Wyatt to show Raffi the sign we've been working on. It's the American Sign Language sign for "I love you," and we've both been working on it for a week or so.

Raffi rolls his lips and blinks quickly like he's trying not to cry. I love how sensitive he is.

Holding up one finger for him to pause, I pluck Wyatt from Penelope's knee and rotate him so Raffi can see what his shirt says.

When he tilts his head to the side, his smile spreading, I hand Wyatt back, and turn to show him that his name is on my shoulders and his number is on my back.

I may not like his choice to continue icing, but we're a family, and we support each other.

He covers his chest with his gloves.

I mouth "I love you."

He grins with a wink and mouths "I know. I love you more."

I jerk my chin at the ice over his shoulder. "Go gettum, hot shot."

He salutes me, offers his glove at the glass for Wyatt to fist bump, then skates off.

Eloise nudges me from my right. "You're adorable when you're mushy."

"I'm never mushy." The words barely come out around the lump in my throat. For years all I wanted was for Wyatt to have a father, for someone to love me in spite of the fact I was a single mom.

Now that I have what I yearned for, it's hard to believe it's going to last.

Fear is a fucker.

We're playing the Cincinnati Vipers. If I didn't already know that, all I'd have to do is look at Penelope's boobs. She's wearing the away team's shirt once again. I can't help but laugh.

From the opening puck drop, the Vipers are, I don't know what the technical term is, but they're assholes. It's a much more physical game than I'm used to. So, naturally, my heart's lodged firmly in my throat.

Raffi's concentration is clear. He's fully focused on the game. As he chases the puck, a Viper collides with him.

My stomach lurches as his head cracks against the boards and he crumples onto the ice.

Time stops.

An audible gasp ripples around the crowd.

Someone shouts a really loud "fuck."

No one breathes, or moves, or speaks as he lies motionless on the ice.

Eloise's hand slides into mine, squeezing in quiet comfort.

There's a blur of movement on the ice as Ares leaves his crease and zips across the rink to where emergency services are already surrounding Raffi's motionless body.

People in the seats around us whisper in concern. In my periphery, spectators stare at their phones and chatter grows louder by the second but I can't pull my eyes off the father of my child.

To my left, Penelope has turned Wyatt to face her, she's bouncing him on her lap and blowing raspberries on his neck so he doesn't see the commotion on the ice.

It's only when Eloise stands up to put her arm around me I realize I've made my way to my feet.

When they bring the stretcher out, my knees buckle, blood chilling in my veins. Eloise holds me, not letting me fall. Or bolt onto the ice. I'm not sure.

When they load him onto the stretcher, my heart shreds into tiny pieces. I can't lose him again.

I can't lose him again. My whole body shakes uncontrollably as both teams on the ice stand watching with the rest of us.

When they push him toward the tunnel, tears stream down my face.

What's the protocol for player injuries? Do they call his parents? Will he need to be taken to the hospital? Should I try to find my way "backstage"? Is that allowed? Should I call mom to come take Wyatt?

She's working. Her phone will be off. There's no way she can come for him.

Apollo skates across the ice toward me. His mouth moves, but no sound meets my ears. I try to nod. His sympathetic eyes do little to thaw the abject panic spreading throughout my body.

Eloise is patting my pants. When she pulls out my phone, she holds it up to my face and it unlocks. "Your mom?"

"She's at work. I don't know who can take him."

Penelope offers, but she has no car seat, or toys, or anything vaguely child friendly in her house.

"Tori? Tori? Your phone is ringing. It's an unknown number, should I answer it?"

My gaze shoots back to the place on the ice where Raffi was lying. The ice has been cleared, and the officials are all gathered in a huddle.

Eloise is talking to someone on my phone. "Tori?" Her voice is sharp, forcing me to look at her. "It's Raffi's mom. Can she maybe take Wyatt while I take you wherever you need to be? Would she be okay with you going to the hospital and not her?"

They have toys, they've even got a bed for him in the room that was formerly a home gym. It's now an homage to everything Wyatt loves. Blippi, Number Blocks, and Paw Patrol.

They're a safe space.

The urge to haul my kid to the hospital is persistent. But it wouldn't be fair to him. He's already rubbing his eyes and resting his head on Penelope's shoulder.

"Okay." My tongue feels too big for my mouth. It's dry. And words are hard. I don't know if Raffi's mom would even consider not being by her son's side so that I can, it's a bit... presumptuous.

Eloise says something else to me, but I can't hear her. I pick Wyatt up from Penelope's arms and make my way down the row to the exit.

No idea if the girls are behind me, but they'll find me if they aren't. Eloise comes with me to wait outside for Raffi's parents. If Wyatt loses his shit at the thought of going with them, that'll make my decision for me. I'll just take him with me.

Do they have a car seat?

Penelope goes to find whoever Jim is and ask where I need

to go to see Raffi. But as we wait, an ambulance whizzes past, a blur of red and white lights and sirens. I almost drop Wyatt, but Eloise catches him before I crumple to my knees on the sidewalk.

I don't know how long it takes for Ani and Travis to arrive, but Travis's arms loop under mine and pull me to my feet.

"Do you want one of us to come with you?" Ani is waiting for me to lead. If it was Wyatt in hospital, wild horses couldn't keep me away from his bedside. My heart swells that her unspoken words suggest there's no where else I want to be than at her son's bed side, and in order for that to happen, she's content to sit with her grandson. It sends a sliver of warmth back through my body.

His parents are next of kin. I have no rights at the hospital. I don't know his medical history. They have more right to be there than I do.

Wyatt has already looped his arms around Ani's neck. It's good, what I wanted. But damn if part of me wasn't holding out for my kid to need his mama so I could snuggle the crap out of him in the waiting room of the hospital.

I try to find my voice, but nothing comes out but a choked sob.

"I'll drop Ani and Wyatt home and circle back." Travis is the voice of reason through the clouds blocking my brain.

"I'll keep you posted if that's okay?" Eloise introduces herself to my boyfriend's mom, offering to be her helpful self and swaps numbers while Ani puts Wyatt in the rear-facing car seat in the back of their SUV.

Travis offers me a smile I've seen on both his son and grandson's faces. "Raffi told us what seat you have, and we got one too. It's new, too, not off one of those buy and sell places. You can't ever tell if a seat has been in an accident before or not." He nods somberly. "Microfractures."

If my body was responding to me, I'd probably laugh. It's so sweet of them to be so invested in Wyatt the way they are. But right now, I've got nothing.

They drive away as my tears continue to fall. Somehow Eloise gets me into Penelope's car. She turns the heat up to high before she pulls away from the sidewalk, slipping her hand into the free one on my thigh as I stare blindly out the window.

"It's going to be fine. He's going to be okay." I'm not sure who needs the reassurance more, me, or Eloise herself as she chants in the back seat.

As we pull into the parking lot of the hospital, my whole body trembles despite the heat. He has to be okay. I need him. Wyatt needs him. He's going to be just fine.

Right?

CHAPTER 37

Victoria

On our way into the emergency room, it occurs to me they won't let me see Raffi because I'm not family. Why didn't I beg Travis to come with me?

We check in with the reception desk, then take a seat in the waiting room. Eloise is staring at her phone, tears trickling down her cheeks, her shoulders shaking.

"What happened?" Penelope moves to comfort her. I would, I should, but right now I can't. My legs jitter and bounce as my stomach roils and twists.

Eloise shakes her head, sending a pointed glance my direction.

"It's okay. Whatever it is." It can't be worse than what I'm currently living through.

"It's about a hockey injury."

If I wasn't already chilled to the bone, I'm sure a chill would roll through me. "It's fine." I'm not sure it is, but I don't want her to feel like she can't talk in front of me.

"A hockey player in the UK has just been pronounced dead. There was a freak accident on the ice. A player's skate slashed a player from the opposing team's throat." She's sobbing quietly as she struggles to get the words out. "He essentially bled out on the ice, in front of the fans of the game. Both teams formed a circle around him, and they brought out shields."

She's reading from her phone. "There's a video circulating of the incident, but I can't." She drops her phone into her lap. "I don't want to see it."

This isn't what I need to hear right now. It's terrifying enough that Raffi is in the hospital. And it's not like I need any additional evidence to prove to me that he should quit playing hockey. But my stomach sinks, and my heart squeezes.

I can't even imagine how much of a bizarre confluence of events it is for a hockey player to pass away at a game, but it doesn't fill me with confidence about my boyfriend. The one I currently know little about as I sit in the waiting room.

Twisting my hands on my thighs doesn't help. Neither does pacing.

The girls talk in hushed voices about the fallen player in the UK league. He was originally from Minnesota, a former NHL player with the Pittsburgh Penguins, Adam Johnson. If it didn't already feel like I had belts strapped across my chest, it would probably be even harder to breathe. I don't have words for how tragic it is. Is there somewhere local to lay flowers, or sign a book of condolences, or somewhere to donate money? I feel so fucking helpless. I need to do something. But what?

Head hanging in my hands, body bent forward, I wait. It's all I can do. When someone knows something, they'll come and find me.

At some point, I stretch out over a few seats and fall asleep.

Sometime later, someone's rousing me from my nap. Apollo de la Peña's concerned eyes are heavy on my face. "You hanging in there?"

I nod, but my insides have disintegrated, my outsides are trembling, and I'm going to cry again any second.

"I spoke to the doctors." Travis's voice comes from behind Apollo. He must have arrived after I fell asleep. "He's okay. Still out cold. Couple stitches on his forehead, concussion is likely." He winces. "But he should recover."

Tears are pouring down my face as I sniffle through his words. "Th-thanks for letting me know."

Apollo pulls me against his chest and strokes my back. "Shhhhh. There, there. It's all going to be okay. He's going to wake up and recover. Okay?"

Despite his words, I can't nod. Until Raffi wakes up, the results of his CT and MRI scans come back, and he talks to me with his own mouth, in his own words, the only thought consuming my every thought is that he might wake up and forget we ever existed.

Again.

Okay, two thoughts. He could also die.

"We're all here for you, Tori. We're a family, and we've got you." Apollo doesn't let me go for a long time. Until I'm cried out all over again, and there's more snot on his shirt than I have left in my body.

When I eventually pull back, I take in his face. He's pale, dark rings under his eyes. It was only a few weeks ago that he was in this very hospital after a car accident almost killed his best friend.

How is he so strong, so enduring that he can be in this space so soon after one traumatic incident, for another?

He searches my face. "If he forgets again, we'll help him remember. Okay?"

What if his brain swells really badly?

What if there are secondary issues? Like clots, or stroke? Is he at higher risk of those things? Probably.

What if he wakes up and wants to skate again? I rub at my chest as a hiccupping sob comes out of my mouth.

"Apollo." The anguish in my voice draws attention from

across the waiting room. "What if he doesn't stop playing? What if he doesn't wake up? What if...? What if he dies?"

I fall apart on the captain's shoulder all over again. He's probably still a bit achy from his own shit, worried about his best friend, and here he is in the hospital that probably brings back awful and recent memories, for a member of his team.

If my heart wasn't already spoken for, I might shoot my shot.

Apollo doesn't run away screaming at my breakdown. He just sits next to me, holding me against him. Does he realize he's holding me together right now? If he lets go, will I fall to pieces? Feels like it.

Eloise gives me an update about Wyatt, she shows me a picture of Ani snuggled up in bed cuddling Wyatt and reading him The Gruffalo. It's one of his favorite books, and that they even have a copy shows me just how much attention Raffi has been paying.

Another rub of my chest doesn't shift the pain, and no amount of kneading the muscles in the back of my neck make them any softer.

When Apollo gets up to go and talk to someone, Artemis takes his place, curling his fingers into mine. When Eloise is finished messaging Raffi's mom with an update, she curls her fingers into my other hand.

We sit in silence, and when Apollo returns with a scowl wrinkling his model face, the weight in my stomach sinks even deeper. "Oh, no."

"Come with me," Apollo holds out his hand.

I shake my head, a fresh wave of tears spilling down my cheeks. How can I have tears left in my body?

"If he's dead just tell all of us." I gesture around the room with my hand attached to his twin brother's. "Everyone deserves to know." I sniff, then wipe my nose with my arm. To his credit, Artemis doesn't react to the fact his arm was dangerously close to my boogers. These guys are romance movie level stand up guys.

"He's not dead, amiga. Please? Come with me. You can sit with Raffi while he sleeps."

My feet carry me to his side before I consciously choose to even stand up from the chair. "You got them to agree to it?"

He nodded. "If something happens and they need to treat him you're going to have to leave, okay?"

It's not even a question. Of course I'll leave if they need me to. I just want to be by his side.

"Bien. Let's go."

My feet squeak to a stop on the linoleum floor as it hits me I might not be ready to see him like this. Apollo's warm hand wraps around my waist, guiding me forward until we get to Raffi's room.

He gives me a squeeze. "You ready?"

Swallowing hard, I can't stop my body from shaking again. I'm not, but I need to be, so I wrap my hand around the handle, twist, and push it open.

CHAPTER 38

Raffi

Hospitals stink. Not even of something whiffy like potpourri, but of bleach, or whatever the cleaning solution is they use to make the whole building smell of chemicals.

Could be worse, could smell like blood. I'll take small mercies where I find them right now.

I know where I am before I open my eyes.

There's a familiar ba-dum-bum-bum throbbing in my brain and pulsing pain in my head. Something went down last night on the ice. Last thing I remember was skating out for the first period.

Flashes of Wyatt signing he loved me, my name across Victoria's shirt, and the game intro skate flash in my brain. Relief settles into my chest. I might be hurt, but at least I remember who my people are, where I am, and what happened.

Better than last time, at least.

Someone's holding my hand, their warmth radiating into me as they sit in silence, just holding onto me.

Forcing my eyes open, it all takes a moment for the

banging in my head to simmer down to an acceptable level. After a few blinks, I take in the room. Victoria's holding my hand on one side. Apollo sits on a chair in the far corner of the room, and Mom's got the chair to my left.

It's bright out, but the room only has one small window and the blinds are pulled. When my gaze lands back onto Victoria, she offers me a tired smile. Her hair's pulled into a ponytail, her skin seems paler than usual, and her bloodshot eyes have dark lines under them that suggest she probably hasn't had much sleep.

Fuck.

"Hey, Firecracker." My voice is croaky, dry, hard to force out.

"Hey yourself." Her chin trembles as she blinks back tears. "You remember." The last bit's barely a whisper.

"I do. You okay?"

She arches a brow so high I'm afraid it might jump off her face, but that eye roll. I damn near get a hard on right here in my hospital bed. Her face says "Of course I'm not okay, you idiot." And I love her for it.

"Cap." I nod across the room to Apollo.

"Hey, Raffi, how you feeling?"

I close my eyes briefly. "Like my face collided with a wall."

He nods, his movements slow like exhaustion is pulling him down. "Close enough. I'm going to step out and tell the nurse and the guys you're awake. Okay?"

Victoria answers for me. "Thanks, Apollo." Gratitude sparkles in her eyes.

When he leaves, I turn to Mom. "Have you been here all night?"

She shakes her head. "No, sweetheart. We had Wyatt last night." She grins so wide it's hard not to smile with her. "Tori's mom took him this morning so we could come and sit with you. Dad's out in the waiting room with your teammates."

As though she summoned him, Dad walks through the door. He drags Apollo's chair across the room and plants it next to Mayrik before picking up her hand.

"By all accounts you've been keeping the severity of things from us, Raphael." Mom's eyes bore into me from her seat.

Victoria shifts her weight. "I should take a walk."

Subtle as ever, but I'm not going to get through this conversation without her right here by my side. Clasping her hand, I shake my head. "Stay. Please."

She flits her gaze to my parents before settling back into her seat. "Okay. But you know I'm not going to keep my mouth shut."

"It's one of the many reasons why I love you."

She smiles a tearful smile, sniffing. "Just one."

Dad leans forward and pats my hand. "Why have you been keeping things from us? What's going on?"

My head's thumping, but before I can say a word to my parents, a doctor and nurse come in to run some checks and ask some questions. Apollo brings in a fresh jug of water, a cup with a bendy straw, and another cup filled with ice chips.

When they all leave again, I take a long, slow drink before rolling onto my side. "I didn't want to disappoint you." My voice breaks as I speak, splinters of grief finding their way into my words. I really didn't want to disappoint my parents.

"But playing pro hockey isn't something that's likely to happen for me." It's the most painful thing I've ever admitted to myself, but it's also true. No team's going to want to touch me. I'm a ticking time bomb. The more hits I take, the more concussions I get, it's just a matter of time before it starts to truly impact my game on the ice.

"I tried to soldier on, push through, but once the school year's up, I need to be done."

Victoria bursts to her feet with a grunt of displeasure.

"What is it, Firecracker?"

She shakes her head, rolling her lips like words are fizzling on her tongue, and she's trying to keep them all inside.

"That sounds like a good plan, Raffi." Mom sniffs.

Victoria smacks her thigh.

"We have only ever wanted you happy and healthy. If hockey isn't bringing you joy, or if it's risking your life and health, then of course you should stop playing." Mom strokes the back of my hand. "I'm sorry you ever thought we were pressuring you to do something more, something you might not have wanted to do." She gives a shaky glance to Dad. "I thought playing in the NHL is what you wanted, it's what you've always wanted to do since you were a little boy."

She must be reading between the lines, I've never told her that I felt pressure from them. I guess moms always know.

"Mayrik's right, Raffi. If you'd spoken up sooner, or if we'd known the extent of the symptoms you were experiencing, we'd have steered you in another direction. Why didn't you tell us?"

"We can't afford college without my scholarship. I need to play to finish my degree."

Their faces fall.

"We'd have found another way. Student loans, a bank loan, something. Something easier than risking yourself every time you step out on the ice." Mayrik's voice is softer, her eyes sad.

"I can't stand here and listen to you talk about going back on the ice for the rest of the season, Raffi." Victoria's voice quivers with either fear, sadness, or rage, I'm not sure which.

"There are only a few months of both school and the season left, Victoria. It'll be over soon." As the words come out of my mouth I hear how I'm justifying risking my life to the mother of my son and the woman I want to marry. It's not going to land well.

As expected, it doesn't. Her jaw drops, closes, and drops again, then she swings her arms like she's dealing with a complete idiot.

"It *will* be over fucking soon if you smack your head again and end up dead." She waves a hand at me. "And before you tell me it's unlikely, or it never happens, it happened last night. While your face was bouncing off the plexi glass in our rink, a player in the UK passed away from an injury sustained on the ice." Tears trickle down her face as her words gain speed.

"I will support you in many things, Raffi. But I can't watch you step onto the ice ever again." She presses her chest like it's causing her physical pain before jabbing a finger at my parents. "Tell them about the migraines. About the debilitating headaches that leave you lying in dark rooms. Do they know about the memory loss? That you forgot the first time we met because you got injured in a game?"

She flexes her hand like she's unsure about whether she's done gesticulating, or rubbing her chest. "I get wanting to be part of something bigger than yourself. Hell, I've spent time with your teammates and even I could be tempted to skate with them because they're just that kind of group. But Raffi, something you don't realize about those guys sitting out in those chairs is that they love you regardless of whether you play hockey or not."

Victoria isn't even pausing for breath at this point. Nothing is going to stand in her way. "They want you alive just as much as I do, and if that means not lacing up with you for practices and games, given the choice, they'd choose your wellbeing, every single day of the week and twice on Sundays."

She sniffs, wiping tears from her face with an aggressive hand flap like she's mad at herself for crying. "They'll still be your friends if you don't play. Just like your parents would love you if you don't go pro. Just like we could figure something else out to enable you to finish out your degree."

"But, I…"

She holds a hand up to me, her eyes narrowing in warning. "Excuses. All excuses. You keep forcing yourself to play hockey because you're afraid of what you are, of what life would be like without it. Maybe? I dunno. But there's a very real risk that with it, you could end up dead, then you'll be no use to anyone. Not least of all, our son."

She slow-shakes her head, disappointment oozing from the simple action. "You have so much more to give in life than just numbers on a scoreboard, Raffi. Know your goddamn worth. You want to be an ASL teacher, be one. You want to translate, do it. You want to start a charity for either ASL or victims of concussion, or mental health in hockey, do that, too. Hell, do it all, you're capable of so many things, but you don't seem to look beyond the blinders of the ice, of your responsibility, of not letting down your teammates and your parents. But all the while, letting down the most important person of them all, yourself."

By the time she's done, her chest is heaving and she's breathless. Her tears have left damp marks on her shirt. Both my parents are crying, and Apollo has made his way back into the room.

"She's right, Raffi. We don't want to leave our sticks out for you like they're doing across the hockey community today for the fallen player in the UK."

Victoria's face squishes in confusion. "What?"

"In the hockey community, it's a tradition to place a hockey stick outside your front door to show respect for a player who won't be returning home." Apollo's voice is thick with pain as he speaks. I don't know what happened, or who he's talking about, but it's clearly having an impact on him.

Victoria is still confused, looking at me with pursed lips.

"The thought is that wherever their spirit is heading next, they might need a stick."

Mom sniffs again, as Victoria wobbles on her feet. Thankfully Apollo catches her and guides her back to her chair.

"That's so sad."

Apollo nods, his face grim. "Is that really why you force yourself onto the ice for every game? Because you don't want to disappoint your parents, and you don't want to take out a student loan for the rest of your tuition?"

My face is hot. Everyone's staring at me, but I can't deny that it's true. "I looked into financing. I could get a loan, but the repayments, the interest...it would cripple me for years. There's no way my parents can take on that level of stress."

My friend, my leader, my captain shakes his head before sitting at the edge of the bed. "Why didn't you say something sooner?" He doesn't wait for me to answer. "Pride? We're your family, hermano. We could have helped. We still can."

"Already did." Before I can object, there's a new voice in the conversation. Ares leans against the doorframe, arms folded, looking every bit as pale and exhausted as his older brother.

"Already did what, Ares?" I pinch the bridge of my nose, hoping it makes the pounding stop for just a minute. This is an important conversation. I need to figure things out, *we* need to figure things out, but my brain is turning to goo inside my skull.

"I paid for your tuition last week when I figured out you were being an enormous cabrón."

Victoria leans toward Apollo. "What does that mean?"

"Technically it means male goat."

It's the first time she's smiled since I opened my eyes, and the knot in my chest relaxes just a touch.

"And I made sure you can stay in the hockey house for the duration of the year." He doesn't even look smug when he says all of this. The intensity on his face suggests he's angry, but the emotion in his voice tells me he just wants to keep me safe. And it's all I can do not to cry.

"You did?"

He nods. "Took longer than it should have or could have because my girlfriend wouldn't gossip or tell me anything, and I had to do some digging myself."

Victoria gives a smirk of approval before saying, "That's my girl, Ellie Bellie," under her breath.

"But I handled it. Pollo is right, though, we could have handled it much sooner if you'd just been honest about it and gotten over yourself."

"I wanted to play." The words tumble from my lips on a tired sigh. "I really did. I do. Being on the ice is hard to compete with."

Ares and Apollo offer sympathetic nods. They get it.

"But lately, it just hasn't felt the same. Since I found out I lost my memories, almost lost my family." I can't bear to look at Victoria right now, her cheeks glisten in my periphery, and I need to hold it together to finish this discussion with my friends and teammates. "I just couldn't see a way out."

"That's when you talk to us, it's what we're here for." Dad's voice is thick with emotion.

"Or us. We've got you, too." Ares's voice is firm and emphatic.

"And if you want to do any of those things Tori just listed for you, you come to us, okay? If there's one thing my siblings and I have in common is that we like to spend our inheritance on worthy causes and people we can trust not to piss it away." He winces. "Sorry, Mrs. Shaw."

Mom giggles. "It's okay, Apollo. I've heard worse."

My teammates stand up and pat my legs like a weird choreographed dance move. "We'll talk more later, okay? But for now, no more worrying, rest and recovery. We'll figure it all out, together." Apollo's words hit heavily as he and Ares leave the room.

Mom looks like I've killed her puppy, Victoria's sobbing again, and my head hurts like fuck.

"We've always taught you to come to us with anything, Raffi." Dad's just as crushed as Mom looks. "There's always a way to fix things, there's always a choice, you're never trapped."

Nodding, tears trickle down the sides of my nose. "I just didn't want to have to be a college drop out when the whole family's so proud that I'm the first one to go. I didn't want to leave hockey when everyone was so excited to have a superstar in the family."

"Oh, Raphael, you silly boy." Mom leans forward and cups my face. "We still have a superstar in the family. No matter what you do, no matter what you've done or will do, you always make us proud, always will. You're never a disappointment to us."

The weight of responsibility lifting from my shoulders is tangible. Hearing my parents say they'll love me no matter what I do is a balm to my insecurities, and part of me can't help but feel like an idiot for not talking about it all sooner.

But it's out there now, and the next step is to figure out which way my path should go.

R affi's home.

He's under doctor's orders to rest, which I'm enforcing, but he's not thrilled about it. The de la Peña's have put a TV in his room. From my vantage point in the doorway, my boyfriend, my son, a grumpy black cat and a rather adorable potbellied pig are all snuggled up together in Raffi's bed watching Octonauts.

Apollo and Scott are on a beanbag in the corner, Ares is lying lengthways across the foot of the bed, Jackson and Artemis are sharing the loveseat on the other side of the bed, and Tate is on the floor with a pillow crammed behind his back against the wall.

Why they didn't just take up residence in the living room and crowd around the bigger TV is anybody's guess. But there's something wholesome and ovary-exploding about a bunch of grown athletes snuggling with their pet pig and my kid to watch cartoons.

Snacks and drinks are strewn around the room. Raffi and Wyatt are sharing the biggest bowl of popcorn I've ever seen. And at least three of the team are drinking beer.

It's the weirdest situation I can recall. But it's also the sweetest. The guys have rallied around Raffi, he told them he's not going to be playing hockey anymore, and while they were sad, there was also an air of relief around the team. Deep down, they all wanted him to step down to protect him.

Despite the grief of losing a member of their extended hockey family hanging heavily in the air, Ares is more relaxed than I've seen him lately. Raffi swears he'll pay the brothers back for their kindness, but they won't hear of it. They just want him happy and safe. It's breathed some relief into my veins that he woke up this morning firm about giving up college hockey. For a moment, I'd feared he'd get out of the hospital, away from the doctors, and decide to go back.

Something's shifted in him. It's like the guilt, or responsibility has been lifted from his shoulders, and he's able to see clearer.

His parents came over this morning. Ani baked enough food for the whole team. It's as though Raffi's guilt has moved to his mom. Her excitement over him doing something more, *being* something more blinded her to the fact he was keeping secrets from her. Now that she knows the truth, she feels like crap.

Mom's coming to pick Wyatt up in a couple hours, then I get to snuggle my man, listen to his heartbeat, and let him kiss away my tears of relief that he isn't dead.

He's not allowed to do anything physical for a couple weeks. He insists that doesn't include sex, but I'm not willing to take any chances, at least not yet.

"Wanna watch something downstairs?" Eloise's small voice interrupts my staring. She's the best best friend I could have hoped for, and she has no idea just how amazing she is.

"I absolutely do." Keeping my voice down, I leave Raffi's room and head down to the living room with my bestie. "What you want to watch?"

We pick an old episode of Brooklyn 99 as the episodes are short, funny, and we can chit chat if we feel like it.

"He seems to have made his decision." Eloise's voice is quiet. "Did you give him an ultimatum?"

I shake my head. "Didn't have to. This last hit scared him. That, or it knocked sense into him. I can't tell. Either way, he's done playing hockey." My jaw unclenches a little just by saying the words out loud.

"Sounds like something finally got through to him." She doesn't say anything else, but her pointed stare suggests that something may have been me.

I hope so. If he makes a habit of listening to my opinion in our relationship, we can't go wrong.

"Isn't Wyatt's birthday coming up?"

Ugh. My stomach sinks. "Not till June. I have some time, but I feel like a terrible mom. I haven't done anything for it. At all. I need to get my shit together."

She casts a glance toward the stairs. "It's as though you've had other things on your mind or something."

I toss a throw pillow at her. What kind of hockey players have throw pillows? Bougie ones, that's who.

She laughs and lobs it back. "We'll figure something out. Try not to stress about it."

"I'm a mom, Eloise. Stress is my status quo."

CHAPTER 40

Raffi

I'm going stir crazy.

I'm not allowed to work out yet, and Victoria won't let me do anything physical in the bedroom. And while I love her appetite for giving head and taking care of me, I just want to fuck my girl senseless.

Is that so much to ask?

Apparently so.

She's been amazing over the past couple weeks. She's all but moved me into her house with her mom and Wyatt so she can take care of me. But, the truth is, she wants me to be close to her and Wyatt as much as I've needed taking care of.

Waking up in the morning, often by being smacked in the face with an eReader or tablet of some kind by the most adorable miniature version of myself is one of my favorite things.

I'm teaching him to make the best PB&Js in the world, while his mom casts a wary side eye our direction. Granted, a soon-to-be threenager wielding a butter knife is probably not the smartest idea I've ever had. But I've got him.

Living here, even temporarily, I've become familiar with

the Barnett family's routine. They eat every meal they possibly can together. And when Victoria isn't at class, or working on a shoot, she's with our son.

They're practically joined at the hip.

Mrs. B works every hour of every day, and then some. She probably has one of those time turner things Hermione Granger has in *Harry Potter*. How does Victoria's mom have the energy to cook and clean? I've been helping out where I can, but after putting their dishes away in all the wrong places, I got relegated from emptying the dishwasher, to loading it.

And when I turned all their cream towels a light shade of pink because I neglected to pull out Wyatt's bright red Paw Patrol tee from the laundry, I got told to leave that the hell alone, too.

I'm not even trying to cause trouble. I want to be helpful. These women have been nothing shy of amazing to me, and as much as I love food, my cooking skills need some work. Apparently there are only so many times you can say thank you with grilled cheese.

Who knew?

Wyatt is slashing his plastic child-friendly knife his nana switched out for the metal one when he threw it across the kitchen and almost broke a vase. He's hacking a piece of bread into pieces instead of carefully spreading grape jelly on top of it, but he's having fun, that's all that matters. Or at least, it's all that matters in this moment.

His birthday party is coming up. We gently guided him in the direction of a Paw Patrol party. Decorations are much easier to come by than for some of the international cartoons he loves. For a beat we thought we were going to have to pay international shipping for Peppa Pig or Bluey decorations, but he relented. Ryder and the pup-squad will do just fine.

Penelope is baking the cake—apparently baking is her jam, and I can't wait to taste test just how good she is. We have more Paw Patrol decorations than I know what to do with, and most of my teammates are coming.

My parents have already bought him a ride-on tractor thing he picked out in the toy store, and they're so freakin' excited to be coming to their grandson's birthday party, they've told everyone who'll listen.

It's adorable.

"Are you actually going to eat any of that?" Victoria bumps my hip with hers. "Or are you just letting our kid chop an entire loaf of bread into duck-sized chunks?

"Haven't decided. He's so gleeful chopping the bread, I might go get him a second loaf."

She narrows her eyes at me in what I've learned is her signature mom face. It's both adorable and terrifying all in one go. "I will unalive you."

"He could help. He's really great with a knife."

She shakes her head, flinging out one of her all-time-best eye rolls. "That's dark, Raffi."

"No one would ever suspect him either. He's just too cute."

She claps her hands. "Okay, buddy. Are we finished making sandwiches?"

Wyatt looks up at me, and I answer with a shrug. If Victoria tells me I'm done at something, I'm fucking done. But this kid of mine has no such sense of preservation. He shakes his head. "More." He waves his knife around like it's a wand, a huge glob of jelly dropping onto the counter.

If there was a trapdoor under my feet, I'd make it open so I could flee. Unfortunately for me, the architects of this particular house didn't factor in an escape route from the Mrs.

"Wyatt Jefferson Shaw."

He tips his head like she said it wrong. He's adjusting to the fact she's using my name as his surname now. We both are. His birth certificate has her last name, because she didn't know mine. She's applied to have it changed, and despite the ball ache and red tape, she's determined to set the official record straight.

Makes me so fucking happy.

"Yes, mama?"

"We're done with the sandwiches."

He scowls, scrunching up his face. "Not done."

She plants her hands on her hips. "Am I going to have to intervene here, little man?"

If I gave her the stink eye he's currently giving her, I'd inevitably end up with a slap upside the head. My son's got balls, that much is true.

"Wyatt bud?"

He turns his attention to me.

"How does goldfish and Mario sound?" I'm bartering with a tiny version of myself. This is my life now.

He shakes his head.

"Fire?" He calls the movie Elemental 'fire.'

That should bring him around. He glances at the knife in his hand and puts it on the counter.

"Kraken?" Come on kid, work with me here. My skin's starting to prickle with sweat. Don't let me down in front of your mom, please? Let me earn some brownie points here.

He climbs down from the stool. "Tur-rrrrrrrrrrrtleeeeeeeeeeeeeeeees!" He takes off at high speed.

"If he gets jelly on the couch, Mom is going to sever your dick with a cleaver." Victoria's got her camera out on the table, there are prints from the past few weeks scattered on the table.

"You're so good, Firecracker."

She blushes. "It's not what I thought I'd do, but I'm good at it."

There's no bragging in her voice, just facts. Good is an understatement, but when I correct her she gets all squirmy.

"What did you think you were going to do?"

She shakes her head before collecting all the prints into a stack. I spy at least three I want to buy, frame, and gift to my friends. "Don't put those away, I want some of those for the guys. They're so good."

She smiles, rolls her eyes, and puts the prints in a box. "I might even let you." She winks at me.

"What did you think you were going to do?"

She levels me with That Look. "Taking your life into your hands by not dropping it, Shaw."

"Maybe." I slide my hands around her waist, pulling her close to me. If we're chest to chest and she takes a swing she'll struggle to land a hit.

"What's that smirk for?"

"If you're standing a couple feet away and decide to clobber me you'll have better range to make it hurt."

She giggles before dotting kisses along my jaw. "If I wanted to hurt you, I could. Even from here." She lifts her knee like she's sending a warning shot. "But I don't. We've both been hurt enough." She kisses me. It's soft, tender, and so full of emotion a lump forms in my throat. "It's us against the world."

"Damn straight." I brush my nose against her. "Tell me what you wanted to do."

She's suddenly very interested in my chin. "When we met I wanted to be a paralegal. When I got pregnant... It's a lot. Raising a kid alone, even with Mom, I just couldn't. So I changed to something more hands-on, more instant in terms of income, something flexible I could do while raising Wyatt."

Regret coats her every word.

"But..."

She sighs. "But I sometimes wonder what if, you know? What if I really loved being a paralegal? What if I went a step further and studied to be a lawyer? What if? What if...? So many what ifs."

"Why don't you pivot? Study law instead?"

She laughs. "Raffi, I'm Wyatt's mom. I can't do a billion years in college, and be there for him in the way I need to. It's just not possible." She pulls away to turn, but I grab her and bring her back to me.

"We're going to talk about this, over and over until you realize you're not an island anymore. You *are* Wyatt's mom, that's true. And you're the best mom he could ever want or need. But you're not alone. You have support, you just need to lean on it. You have me, my parents, and we have a whole hockey team of friends bewitched by our son. Can you think of one damn thing my teammates wouldn't move heaven and earth for if Wyatt needed it?"

She snorts. "*Now* you're okay leaning on your teammates? You've had quite the change of heart, mister." Her brow arches, meaning I've lost any ground I had on this one.

"Don't make the same mistake I did."

Her brow flinches.

"Don't be stubborn, either."

The corner of her lips twitch.

"Please. Think about it. If becoming a paralegal, or at least dipping your toe to see if it's really what you want, is something you want to do, we'll make it happen." I plant a kiss on her forehead. "If we've learned anything lately it's that life's too short for what ifs. We've gotta find our bravery, and make shit happen."

Sucking in a deep breath, I press on. "Being a mom is a huge part of you, I get that. But that's not everything you are."

"Your whole life revolves around Wyatt, Victoria. And I understand why. But what about you?"

Her head cants like she has no idea what language I'm speaking.

"Exactly. You've lost yourself." Another kiss. "Might be time to find yourself again."

"I-I wouldn't even know where to start."

When I give her a squeeze, she softens against me. "Oh. I dunno. Applying for a place and a student loan to study to be a paralegal might be a good place to start."

"Let me think about it."

In mom-speak that means no. Even I know that one.

"I'm not going to let you let this fade away into obscurity just because you're afraid."

Victoria straight up growls. "I'm not afraid."

Check. Mate. "Prove it."

CHAPTER 41

Victoria

I t's a Friday night, and we're both at the gym. Together. For a pump class.

Lauren and Phil are on the stage, benches, bars, and plates ready. The place is packed, there's not a spare space on the floor, and Raffi's bouncing on the balls of his feet. Once pump is over, we're doing a combat class. Back to back thirty minute classes.

Mom's staying at her new boyfriend's house, and I love that for her. Wyatt's at Raffi's parents'. And with an empty house we could be doing anything in right now, we're at the fucking gym.

Who am I?

My PCOS symptoms have gotten better since I started taking Metformin and working out at the gym. And while the scales aren't showing any movement yet, I'm definitely losing inches and building muscle. I needed to buy new jeans a few days ago because I've dropped a size.

I'm not hyper-fixating on calorie counting, or pushing myself to go to the gym every day. I'm eating better, sleeping right, drinking water, and exercising a few times a week. I feel better, but for the first time in as long as I can remember, the numbers don't matter to me.

Raffi has been cleared to return to exercise. We're both training with Phil a couple times a week, and attending group classes, sometimes together, sometimes not. Raffi, overachiever that he is, also comes to the free training times to get his sweat on.

My guy's a beast, whether he's skating or not.

When the fans switch on, I know it's going to be a moist one. Music pounding, purple lights bright, and a disco ball hanging in the middle of the gym, we're ready to lift.

Halfway through the warm-up track, Raffi presses himself against my back. "You're so hot when you squat, Firecracker."

A shiver slowly snakes down my spine as I pop my ass back just a little. Yeah. He's hard.

Trying to stay focused for the rest of the class is almost impossible. Having a loaded metal bar across your shoulders while you're working out or lifting weights over your head is hard enough when you don't have coordination. Add in your boyfriend's raging hard on for you and the dirty, dirty things he wants to do to you, and, well, it's distracting as fuck.

Just over an hour later, we head to the parking lot.

"I'm going to smother you in your sleep," I mutter.

He loops his arms around me as I cross the lot to the car. "I love you too, Firecracker." He kisses the sensitive spot just underneath my ear, and it makes me whimper.

"We're in public, Raffi. Phil won't let us come back if we fornicate outside his gym."

"What Phil doesn't know, won't hurt him. Can you say fornicate again?"

I barely make it to the passenger seat unscathed. Raffi is a feral, sweaty mess, and he's rock hard. After he starts the car and pulls out of the lot, he sticks his hand between my thighs.

"Raffi." His name falls from my lips as the heat of his hand meets my already hot crotch.

"What's the matter, Victoria?"

My hips buck against the seatbelt. What is it about exercise that makes you horny?

I should be tired. I'm a sticky hot mess, and there's nothing about me that currently looks sexy, but I'm ready to strip down and ride my guy like a prized bronco.

Squeezing my nipples through my tank and sports bra as he grinds his heel against my crotch makes me mewl. I can't take it anymore. Plucking his hand from the inside of my thigh, I toss him a wicked grin before shoving it down the inside of my leggings and panties.

"Hungry, pretty girl?"

"Finger me already, or I'll do it my goddamn self."

"Oh, fuck no you won't. I was on the bench for long enough. You don't get to take this away from me." His fingers slide between my lips and find my clit with ease. "Ooooh. So wet, Firecracker. So deliciously wet for me."

His fingers barely graze my clit as we inch closer to the house. If he doesn't hurry the fuck up I'm going to finish myself off right here on the front seat.

I'm not sure whether the car is even off or not before I'm unbuckling my belt and hauling ass into the garage. But before I can get to the door, he's splayed me face-down on the hood and he's sliding my leggings down my thighs until they're in a pool around my feet.

"Can't wait, can you?"

Arching my back only makes him chuckle.

"Such a hungry girl. What do you need?"

"Raffi, please." The frustration brewing in every muscle makes a scratchy growl in my throat when I speak.

"Please, what?"

I'm going to murder him. Actual murder. "Please, fill me."

He shoves his cock inside me with a grunt. The intimacy of him being bare isn't lost on me. I'm on birth control, and neither of us are sleeping with anyone but each other. "There. All full. Feel better?" The sarcastic fucker doesn't move. He just stands there, balls deep in my pussy.

"You know that's not what I meant." I'm whiny, and I don't care.

"Oh?" He pulls out. "What *do* you mean?"

"Raffi." My snarl echoes around the walls of the garage.

"Say it." He rams his dick back inside me.

"I want you to fill me with your cum. Happy?"

"Why?" This man is on track to die if he doesn't hurry the fuck up and get to the good bit.

"Why what?"

"Why do you want me to fill you?" He kicks my legs apart enough to get just a little deeper with his dick.

My back arches more, hips rolling to meet him, but he holds me steady, pinned against the hood of the car. "I like your cum."

"Because..."

The desperation, the heat building between my legs, the pressure in my nipples as they press against the car are all too much. "Because I'm a dirty cum slut."

The rumbling hum of approval from him warms my extremities, but he's not done tormenting me. He plucks me off the hood, holding me against him by my tits, dick firmly buried inside me, face in the crook of my neck.

"You forgot the most important word, Firecracker. You're not just *a* dirty cum slut, you're *my* dirty cum slut. And I fucking love filling you with my cum." He drops me back onto the car and drills into me from behind.

By the time we collapse into bed, we've fucked on the car, the washing machine, the stairs, and in the shower. But we're still not done. The ache in my muscles doesn't stop me from wanting him inside me all the damn time. But he's insisted on a time out.

He's eating crackers and cheese sitting upright next to me in bed. "You're too quiet. Want some?" He offers me his plate, and I steal an apple slice.

"I have something to tell you," I say.

His eyebrows jump. "Me too."

"You first."

He taps my nose with a piece of apple. "Nope. You started, you go first."

My hands are clammy again, like I did another pump class. "I start the business program in the fall."

He almost drops his plate as he whoops and cheers. He sets the plate on the bedside table, drags me out of bed and spins me in circles as he gushes about how proud of me he is.

"What if I hate it?"

"What if you don't?"

"But...what if I hate it?"

"Then you'll know and there won't be a 'what if' anymore."

I hate when he brings the logic. "Your turn."

"I started the paperwork to create a charitable organization to help people like me. Athletes with concussion problems." His face starts to get red.

"You didn't!"

"I did. It takes a while. I wanted to start the admin stuff now before we ramp up into finals."

"What's it going to be called?"

"Hard Knocks."

A laugh bursts out of me. "I love it. I'm so proud of you, too. Guess we're both doing scary, new things."

He nods, brushing my hair out of my face and guiding me

down onto my back, lying on top of me. "No one else I'd rather ride into the fire with." He kisses me, teasing my lips apart with his tongue. "It's us against the world, Firecracker."

Epilogue

RAFFI

Why am I so nervous?

It's a kid's birthday party, for fuck's sake. *My* kid's birthday party. It should be easy. It's low key, all I have to do is show up and eat snacks. Literally my favorite thing in all the world to do.

Maybe because while this is Wyatt's third birthday party, it's only my first. There's a big part of me that feels like I failed him by missing out on his early years. Guilt weighs heavily on me for not being there for his mom, or him.

Have I earned the right to show up to parties and eat snacks?

I'm having second thoughts.

Not about the party, but about the costume.

There are giant chalk paw prints from the sidewalk, up the drive, and along the path leading to the door. Eloise and Victoria did those at the butt crack of dawn this morning. When I tried to help, I was ushered away.

Instead, I helped Mrs. B figure out the inside. Well, once we got the balloon arch assembled outside the front door. Just inside, there's a table with firemen hats and party favors—Firemen Dalmatian stuffies.

In the dining area, the tables are lined with hilariously titled snacks around a fire hydrant centerpiece. "Pupcorn" popcorn, "puppy chow" Chex mix, paw print cupcakes, dog bone Rice Krispies treats, paw-tato chips, cheese "ruffs," Zuma's water bowls—blue jello cups— cookies, all manner of candy.

It's gonna be a great party.

The grill's been lit out back for burgers and dogs, and the coolers are stocked.

Sure, beer isn't the most common beverage for a kid's birthday party, but as long as Wyatt doesn't get drunk, we're good.

"Ready?"

When Victoria nods, her Skye costume bobs. We both went big for this one and Wyatt freakin' loves it. I don't care what all my friends think about the fact I'm dressed as an over-sized dog, my kid—dressed as Ryder—is over the moon.

Eloise appears offering us bottles of water. She's dressed as Everest which tracks. Eloise is the kindest soul I've ever met. She would walk through fire if Wyatt asked her to, and he asked her to dress up as Everest.

Penelope is dressed as Mayor Goodway, complete with a Chickaletta chicken toy tucked under her arm. She came to drop the cake off fully kitted out in costume. Victoria's friends are amazing.

When the doorbell rings, my stomach drops, and I brace myself for the ribbing.

My parents are the first to arrive. They've met Mrs. B a couple times so they're basically old friends. They haul their gift into the house and place it next to the gift table before making a huge to-do over the birthday boy who eats it up.

When the bell rings again, my muscles tighten. It's my friends. While I've seen them at school and home, I haven't seen them as much as I'd like, or as much as I used to. I miss them.

I tug the door open, not expecting the assault on my retinas that's waiting for me. Apollo steps in first, dressed as Chase, he's pushing his girlfriend, Edith, in a wheelchair. She's had a rough go of things, so seeing her out and about dressed as the pup Rex, who rocks a wheelchair too, warms my heart.

Behind them, Ares is sporting a Marshall costume. Artemis is Rocky, Scott's Rubble, and Tate brings up the rear dressed as Mayor Humdinger.

Pretty sure I'm having a heart attack right now. That, or my heart's growing so big in my chest there isn't enough room for it. Each of my friends have a gift and a smile.

"Did you tell them to dress up?" Victoria nudges me out of my stupor, and I shake my head.

"They just did it themselves?" Her voice is low. Eloise is giggling, probably at how ridiculous Ares looks dressed as a cartoon character.

This might be the single best day of my life. My team has rallied around me once again, proving that we ride together, always, no matter what.

"I don't even know what to say." Gratitude and warmth are bubbling at the back of my throat as tears fill my eyes.

"Where's the snacks?" Tate's not shy about letting me know he's hungry.

Scott twists his body to tug his pants out from between his butt cheeks. "Fucking costume's a size too small. But I wasn't gonna be the only one without." He flexes his knees doing a half-squat before tugging the fabric around his balls.

Victoria's jaw hangs open, and she blinks a few times before speaking. "I need my camera." She darts away to grab her camera while the guys shake my hand and head to the gift table.

"This is fu—uh—reaking epic." Ares casts a wary glance at the grandparents on the sofa making Wyatt giggle before gesturing to the decorations. "When do the rest of the kids arrive?"

"Any time now." I offer him a beer, but Victoria clucks her tongue.

"No beer yet. Photos first, then beer."

"Yes, ma'am." Artemis gives a quick salute.

"You heard the lady. Pups assemble." Apollo is already moving to where Victoria is pointing.

When she has us all situated, she starts snapping. The girls join, and when Mom steps in to take the camera from Victoria, she swoops Wyatt off Dad's knee and we get some pictures of all of us before some of just us, my family, my future wife and my son.

Apollo assumes responsibility for Victoria's camera and encourages the grandparents to step in for pictures. Mrs. B and Phil, our personal trainer from the gym, join first. Apparently they've been dating for a few months but Victoria's mom didn't want to say anything until she knew whether it would go anywhere.

My parents are up next, we do all kinds of picture combinations until the doorbell chimes and Wyatt's little friends start to trickle in.

Within the hour, the house is a mess, my teammates have posed for an untold number of pictures with random kids they don't know, and not one single beer has been consumed.

By six, the kids have all left, and it's just our closest friends and family remaining. Artemis has ordered pizza, Apollo and Ares are on trash duty, and Scott and Tate are bagging up all the extra candy, and slicing up the cake so the team can take pieces home with them. That's additional pieces to the slices everyone's claimed for after our pizza party dinner.

Wyatt had a quick nap, but he's found his second wind. He's sitting on Jackson's knee, smacking stickers into a Ninja Turtles sticker book. Jackson has a sticker on his cheek and another on his nose, but he's taking it like a champ.

After pizza clean-up, the little guy goes around the room hugging and kissing everyone, saying thank you and good night to each and every person. I'm not sure who's more touched, my friends, or me. I've almost cried about thirty five times today. It's all just so amazing.

When Phil comes in from outside announcing the fire pit is lit, Eloise announces she's grabbing s'mores ingredients, and Victoria heads into our room.

A few minutes later, she presents me with my guitar, and we follow everyone outside.

It's not cold, but Mrs. B has a basket of blankets in case anyone needs any. She's thought of everything.

Edith is draped over Apollo in a chair, her head snuggled into his shoulder. Ares and Eloise are in a similar position. The guys are sitting wherever they can find space, the cooler has been cracked open, and a number of people are toasting marshmallows in the fire.

"Don't eat all the s'more or you won't get invited back next year." I point at my circle of friends. "Any requests?"

"Ed Sheeran."

"Taylor Swift."

"Fleetwood Mac."

"Stephen Kellogg."

The diverse requests come thick and fast, and I already regret asking.

As I ignore every request so far and strum the first few notes of California Dreaming by the Mamas and Papas—an oldie, but goodie—Victoria settles on the ground next to my feet, all wrapped up in an enormous blanket.

Her phone chimes between songs with an alert that there's someone at the door. She turns it to Artemis who's sitting to her left. "Isn't that your sister?" She's already on her feet racing to the door, probably so Athena—if that's who it is—doesn't wake our sleeping kiddo.

Less than a minute later, Victoria comes back out of the house, Athena de la Peña striding close behind. "Is this true?" Athena holds out her phone to Artemis who jumps to his feet.

Whatever's on the screen, even sitting outside in the firelight, causes Artemis's face to visibly pale. "Does he know?"

"Quién? Papá?" She rolls her eyes—she might beat out Victoria for having the most expressive eyes I've ever seen— "Síííííííííííí." She flicks him right between the eyes. "Pendejo. Check your phone."

Apollo and Ares are looking at the screen now too, and all three brothers pull their phones out. It's clear from their flaring nostrils and stiff postures that whatever is going on is bad, really, really bad.

"Shit." Artemis turns his phone to his sister. "Twenty two missed calls and…" He scrolls the screen. "More text messages than I can count."

Apollo pats his brother's shoulder. "We'll figure it out. There's nothing he can do about it, right?"

Artemis shrugs. "I'll need to call the legal team."

"I'm sorry, Raffi. We really need to leave." Ares speaks for the group. They give Victoria a quick hug, then me, and try to reassure us they're okay before hurrying away.

"What the hell was that about?" Tate voices the question on everyone's mind.

It takes a good thirty minutes and texts from all three brothers to the group chat to insist it's nothing "that bad," before any of us relax and open another beer. But soon we're back for another round of s'mores, and kicking back with some tunes.

I have no idea if I believe in heaven, but if I did, it would look like exactly this. My family, my friends, tasty food, and great music.

(SIX MONTHS LATER)

It's cold as fuck.

I don't know why my darling boyfriend thought it would be a good idea to launch his foundation and have a fundraiser the week before Christmas, but it's cold as fuck.

I've never seen Raffi so nervous, or so fucking handsome. This is next level. He's fighting with a bow-tie in our bedroom mirror.

In the past six months, he's moved out of the hockey house and in here with Mom, Wyatt, and me, he's stopped playing hockey, and he's busted his ass at school.

From a student who was scraping by in his classes while balancing his hockey schedule, he's now bossing it. He's in his senior year, and he's doing himself, and everyone who knows him proud.

"Are you going to stop staring at me and help, Firecracker?" His grumbling frustration makes me swallow down a laugh. I'm not gloating and being smug until he admits he was wrong, and I was right.

"But you insisted on ordering a self-tie bow-tie, Raffi." I shrug. "You said you had it under control."

He growls, folding the fabric for the fourth time. "Clearly, I don't have anything under control right now, Victoria."

"What's that? You were wrong?" I cup my hand around my ear and lean into the room from the doorway.

He turns from the mirror, pointing his flaccid tie at me. "You—" He cuts himself off, jaw dropping comically. "Holy fuck. Wh-I—" He scratches the back of his neck before pointing at me again. "You—Fucking hell, Victoria." He swallows, hard, and takes three strides toward me.

Guess he likes the dress.

Bracing my palm on his forehead, I wag my index finger at him. "Down boy. We don't have time, and I'm not having you mess up my hair before we even get to the venue."

He steps back, as always, respecting my "not now," and beams back at me. "That means I can find a dark corner at the fundraiser and have my way with you." He directs his attention to his crotch. "We can wait an hour."

"No. I take it back. After the fundraiser you can ruin me. Not before, or during. After."

His expression shifts, threatening to fall, but his smile holds. "No take-backsies." He's so fucking pleased with himself. It's something we've been teaching Wyatt lately. Once you say something or give something to someone, you can't take it back.

"When it involves five hundred of the country's most prominent rich people in the sportsverse, I'm definitely holding this boundary."

His eyes roam the emerald satin fabric of my dress. "How did you find time to go shopping for this? It's absolutely fucking stunning." He trails his hand around the thick straps that cross around my waist and follow them around the back to where they tie. "Oh, my, Jesus Christ. There's no way. Nope. I'm not agreeing to keep my hands off you when you're in a backless dress, Victoria."

Men. I roll my eyes. "It's not backless, Raffi. It's got straps, see?" I gesture at the thick satin straps crisscrossing over my back. "It crosses back over at the front and ties in a pretty bow."

The cogs in his brain turn as he follows the path of the fabric. "So, if I untie this bow, it'll make your whole dress fall down in front."

"Raffi Shaw, I will beat you to death with your old hockey stick."

He chuckles, the sound vibrating in my core. "Might be worth it. Just figuring out how it all works, you know, for *after* the fundraiser."

Crossing the room, I shake my head at him with a "tsk." I pull open the top drawer of the dresser.

"You should leave the underwear where it is, Firecracker. We don't need it." There's a smile lacing his words, and if I turn around, he'll be licking his lips, or have that wolfish grin on his face that usually has me bent over and screaming his name in ten seconds.

We don't have ten seconds, though. Our friends will be here any moment, and I'd rather not put on a show for them.

Pulling out what I was looking for, I spin to face him. "I had this made for you to match my dress. It's already tied, but if you're insisting you're good with the self-tie..." I shrug.

"Gimme the friggin' tie, woman."

"Say I was right first, man."

He sighs. "You know you were right. Why do I have to say it?" He's whining like a child, and not even the ding of the doorbell is getting him out of admitting it.

"Because if you don't, you're not getting laid tonight." I don't give a fuck about the bowtie, or that he was wrong, or whether or not he admits he was wrong, I just live for the playful banter between us.

"I love you." He steps toward me, and I step back.

"I love you, too." I even add the sign for "I love you."

"You were right. I was wrong. Will you fuck me later?"

"And they say romance is dead, Raffi."

He's licking his lips. "Just a taste?"

"You two better not be doing dirty things in there." Apollo's voice echoes down the hall.

"Yeah, I have a sensitive disposition. My ears couldn't handle such noises." Ares is most definitely not a sensitive soul, but the thought makes me giggle.

"Ignore them, take your time." Eloise, always the voice of reason and patience.

"Raffi, you told us not to let you be late." Artemis's voice carries a note of caution.

I'm definitely not performing in front of anyone, so I turn and head out to our waiting friends. The guys decided we needed Escalades—plural—to come and pick us up. Apollo, Artemis, Ares, and Tate are all waiting in my living room, looking dapper in their tuxes.

The girls and I coordinated the colored bow ties to match our dresses. Eloise has freshly dyed bright pink hair, and she's in a cotton candy colored, knee-length tulle skirt, with the most delicate, intricate, lace bodice. It has a plunging neckline, leaving a triangle of skin to show down to her belly button. She looks incredible.

Penelope is wearing a Snow Pirates blue, A-line, V-neck floor length gown, with long sleeves. The ruched chiffon wouldn't work for me, but man, she looks like a runway model. Tate hasn't taken his eyes off her since we walked into the room.

With Edith out of town, Apollo's plus one is his sister Athena. She has a lacy dark purple one-shoulder number. It's an opulent evening dress with a thigh split so high I'd be terrified to sit down in it, but she looks incredible.

I have no idea who Artemis is bringing, but we'll find out

at the gala. His date is meeting him there, I guess she didn't want the fuss of, well, all of us showing up at her door. Don't blame her, we're a lot.

Eloise rushes across the room to me. "You look amazing." She air kisses my cheek.

I hate having attention on me, so I brush her off. "You saw pictures."

She shakes her head. "Didn't do you justice. You look fantastic."

"She's right." Apollo chimes in. "I know you're not supposed to comment on a woman's weight, but your trips to the gym are showing. You look great."

My face is on fire. Mom's quietly milling around the room taking pictures with my SLR camera and Wyatt, who was supposed to be in bed by now, is chatting to Ares, probably telling him about his new lightsaber that one Ms. Mayrik Grandma bought him two weeks before fucking Christmas. Raffi's parents are here too, and so's Phil. We have a full house.

Something's got the hairs on my neck standing at attention, but it's probably nerves about the fundraiser. I'm desperate for it to go well for Raffi.

"How's school going, Tori? We haven't seen much of you since you started law school." Artemis, not letting the attention fall from me, speaks loudly enough for everyone to hear.

When it came time to submit my applications and decide on what I wanted to do—really wanted to do—a paralegal wasn't it. So I decided to give law school a shot. Turns out, it's hard as fuck, but it's lighting up my soul in a way nothing else has. Not even the birth of my son. Which is saying a lot.

"It's hard. Exhausting. I'm running on caffeine and living in the library, but I'm loving every second of it."

He nods, like that's the answer he expected. "I'm serious about having a job for you when you graduate. My company is always looking for smart lawyers. Nothing seedy." He winks at me.

"We'll see where I end up specializing. If I want to practice criminal law then I won't fit in with your company, Artemis."

He relents with a shrug. "Keep your options open."

It's nice knowing Raffi's hockey family doesn't stop at the guys. With every woman these men fall in love with, another woman joins the circle. They have our backs every bit as much as they have each other's.

"We should be leaving." I turn around, but Raffi is nowhere to be seen.

When I look back, Mom has the camera pointed at me, and it takes a beat to figure out why. Raffi's on his knee, with Wyatt standing right in front of him, holding out a small black velvet box.

"Mama, Daddy bought you a ring."

Mom's crying so hard, Eloise has to take the camera from her, and a couple of our friends giggle. Now it makes sense that they insisted on meeting here early before going to the party.

"Victoria Barnett, I forgot you once, but I loved you twice. Share my peanut butter jelly sandwiches with me, work out with me at the gym, and let me kick your ass at Ms. Pacman. Forever. There's no one else in the whole universe I want to do even the most mundane things with. Be my wife, Firecracker, there's no one else but you."

I've never been more grateful for waterproof mascara. Tears stream down my face. Wyatt grabs my leg, squeezing hard. "Mama," he whispers. "You're supposed to say yes now, right, Daddy?" His head turns back to Raffi, who's now holding the box with the sparkling ring in it.

"If she wants to, kiddo. Can't rush forever." The hope in his eyes, the hesitance in his smile, even though his heart knows my answer, he's nervous.

"Of course I'll marry you," I choke out between sniffles.

"Good, cause my back up option is out of town today." Raffi winks at me before launching from his knee to kissing me like it was the first time all over again.

Our friends erupt into applause, and Apollo cracks open a bottle of champagne with a loud pop, and the cork pings off the ceiling. He winces. "Sorry, Mrs. B."

Phil catches the cork and tucks it into his pocket. "All good." He curls his arm around Mom's shoulder, she's still sobbing.

When Raffi slides the ring onto my finger, he wipes away a tear of his own. "I love you so much, Firecracker. I can't wait to spend forever with you." He offers me his hand. "Wanna go and make a bunch of rich people give us a shit ton of money?"

"Damn straight."

"Damn straight!" Parrots the three year old from between our legs.

The ride to the venue feels different, *I* feel different. Being engaged doesn't change anything between us, from the moment I met him he's had my heart, even if I didn't realize it. The diamond glistens as we drive into the city.

"You're very quiet, Firecracker. It's freaking me out."

A quick jab in the ribs makes him chuckle.

"Just thinking."

"Does it hurt?"

Another rib jab. He rubs it this time. "What is it?"

"I guess I'm just waiting for the other shoe to drop."

"If you look for walls, Victoria, you'll find them."

It's such a simple statement, but so very true.

After a couple minutes in traffic, we arrive at the Double-Tree. So glad we're staying here tonight because I heard they have warm, ooey gooey cookies at check in. Straight to the top of my favorite hotels list. I haven't traveled much, but I know most hotels don't serve cookies!

A doorman with a top hat opens the door. Press are out front, taking pictures of people arriving on the red carpet.

Wow.

A red carpet.

When Apollo said they'd help plan the evening I should have guessed they'd bring the bougie.

Once we get inside, people are milling around everywhere. There's a heavy scent of wealth in the air, but I try not to let that knock me off balance. I'm here for my boyfriend—ha, my fiancé—to raise money for a cause dear to both our hearts. And after we've served our obligatory schmoozing time, I'm going to fuck him senseless.

If you're not ready to be done with Raffi and Tori's story, click here to join my mailing list and get their exclusive bonus scene!

Grab more stories from your favourite UCR Raccoons now:

Penelope and Tate in Dropping the Mitts

Snowflakes and Slapshots (Whole team)

Home for the Hockey-Days (Whole team)

Also by Lasairiona McMaster

Two for Interference - Minnesota Snow Pirates book 1

Minnesota Snow Pirates books 1-3 Boxset

Freezing the Puck - Cedar Rapids Raccoons book 1

Two for Tacos - A Snow Pirates Novella

www.Lasairiona.com

Author Note

Before anyone from my OG/Original readership comes from me, yes, I changed up some of the details from my previous published series (Lisa Millar, AJ Williams, and Jeremy Lewis). Why? Because I'm going to be re-writing them, and I've never been happy with the character names. I chose them on a whim before I got into my career, and I'm going to be bringing them back in the future, more in line with my brand. So just roll with it, mmmkay?

What a freakin' roller coaster this book was. I didn't get to write much over the summer of 2023. My personal life was really kicking me in the teeth, and I just couldn't find the right balance between mom, responsibilities, and writing.

It was all just a bit too much.

Which meant when I hit October, everything caught up to me. Because when you try to outrun your responsibilities and problems, they are always faster.

Turned out, I had five weeks to write this book and get it to my editor, which wasn't the most fun thing in the world to face. I don't binge-write books. I tend to be a slow-and-steady author, churning out a solid, consistent, daily total that I can manage.

This was savage.

It was fast paced. Racing a deadline is not something I ever want to do again, and I'm not too proud to admit, it got a little dicey there for a minute. Every time the universe threw something at me, I almost curled into the fetal position and just gave up. But for real, of all the months for the universe to crap on me, this wasn't the one.

Except it was.

During the five weeks I wrote this book, my laptop broke, my phone broke, my washing machine broke, I was sick for ten days, my son had the worst case of strep he's ever had (and he gets an annual dose, so this one really was a doozy,) I was waiting for news that my friend with end-stage cancer had passed, and I had some health issues going on to boot.

On top of all that, these characters just wanted to fly free and tell their story. They were chatty, they deviated from my outline a couple times, but they swore to me they knew what needed to happen. So, I just held on for dear life and hoped they knew what the hell they were doing.

Five days before I typed "The End" on this book, a tragic accident occurred on the ice at a rival's barn here in the UK resulting in the death of former Grand Rapids born, NHL star, and Nottingham Panther, Adam Johnson.

Despite not playing on my home team, his death hit me hard—like so many others across the world. There were tears, gut-punching grief, and I couldn't face sitting at the computer to write about my beloved Raffi getting injured on the ice when Adam had literally just passed away.

Needless to say, this book has been a process. With each release comes its own share of challenges, but this one seemed to have more external factors at play than usual, and it left me wondering if that meant to push through, or just throw my hands up.

I pushed through, and in some ways, Raffi and Tori are my favorite. Yes, I say this with every book, but there's just something warm and wholesome about this second chance romance that hits just so.

I know many/most amnesia books have the hero getting his memory back, but in the real world, things don't always unfold that way. And while I originally had it that way, they had other ideas. They wanted to fall in love twice, the hard way. And I loved how it all came out.

For anyone who has a few extra bucks lying around and would like for them to go to a good cause, The Concussion Foundation is one such organization and can be found here: www. concussionfoundation.org

"The Concussion Legacy Foundation funds and supports concussion and CTE research worldwide while translating new research findings into education programs, policies, and initiatives to allow sports to be played more safely.

By training coaches to talk to their teams about concussions, Team Up Speak Up is teaching millions of youth athletes how to recognize and respond to concussions. The CLF Media Project trains sports media professionals and sports journalism students how to cover concussions accurately and with confidence.

Advocacy programs such as Flag Football Under 14 and Safer Soccer are changing the way sports are played to prevent concussions and CTE. Research programs like Project Enlist are serving as a catalyst for advancing our understanding of traumatic brain injury (TBI), Post-Traumatic Stress Disorder (PTSD) and CTE and in military Veterans. CLF provides guidance, comfort, care, and resources to patients and caregivers of those suffering with concussion or suspected CTE symptoms through patient and family services programs like the CLF HelpLine."

Acknowledgments

You can tell by the length of these acknowledgements that this one took a village. It truly did. And I appreciate each and every one of you. Thank you from the bottom of my heart.

Lewis – My darling boy, you have no idea how much your support and encouragement means to me. For you it's a matter of ticking off Post Its on a mirror and giving me hi-fives, for me, it's hearing I can do it, I can make my deadline, and to just push a little harder to get to where I need to be. Thank you for always having my back, kiddo x

Phil – On Monday 5th June at 8.15am my life changed forever when I stepped into the Fit Factory gym here in the town where I live. I was absolutely fucking terrified. Joining a new gym, for fat girls, is right up there with getting a pap smear. It's something we loathe that can often provide an overwhelming dose of anxiety.

Phil welcomed me into his space with a warm smile and an action plan to help combat my PCOS symptoms. He's by far the most knowledgeable trainer I've ever worked with. When I got injured he did all the right things to help me take my time so as not to make it worse, and helped me recover. More than that, three times a week he takes any amount of abuse from me, banters in fluent sarcasm, provides me with a list of movie recommendations to make me cry, and pushes me to within an inch of my sanity. I suppose he's not too bad really.

Karina – For someone whose 'Woo' strength is in the bottom five of your list, you sure as hell managed to woo me in

2023. It's been almost a year since we started our Monday morning work sessions fueled by tea, a good fry for breakfast, and a good dose of chips on the days we work through lunch as well. You've become one of my closest friends, and I don't tell you that enough. You've made my life in Larne easier, and on the weeks I don't hang out with you, I miss you. Thanks for tolerating my egg thing in the name of getting work done.

Clare – The wife. When I messaged you in a blind panic asking for you to do some dev work on this manuscript, I expected a smack upside the head. You just launched your book into the top 260 books in the Kindle Store, you spent a week fighting with your Shopify store, and you don't read contemp. But you stepped right up into the chaos, rolled up your sleeves, and got to work without so much as a squeak of protest. When the chips are down I can always count on you, that means more to me than you'll ever know.

Tracie – What a fucking ball ache this one was, eh? We've lost our entire morning routine, and this year just keeps throwing curve balls at both of us, but without our daily chats, and rants, and your continued support and encouragement, I'd be like Moira Rose in the closet. I say it at least once a week to make you all icky and cringy 'cause you don't do feelings,' but I love you so much.

Fancy – My favorite emotional support barnacle. What would I do without you? Real question that I'd rather not consider the answer to, please and thank you. Once again you stepped up to stroke my hair and tell me I'm pretty, even though you were drowning in your own life stuff at the same time. My stories are always better for your input, and my life is exponentially better for your friendship.

Amy Addison – Thanks for your unwavering cheerleading and epic friendship. It's always on days I'm feeling like I should just curl up and quit when you slide in with the most supportive tweet of my work, or picture of you reading my books and you help pull me back from the edge. Also thanks for making sure my memory of CR is accurate, and I don't fuck up my local details. Can't wait to do jello shots with you in May and buy matching Raygun shirts, because it's been too long.

Erika – We've gone from me being intimidated by your awesomeness to not being able to get enough of it. I can't believe I missed the opportunity to be friends with you sooner at the conference in Scotland 2019. Your belief in me is what gets me through my darkest days when I struggle to believe in myself. Your support isn't silent, or quiet, it's a loud-ass roar that the whole world hears, and I love you for it. A million thank yous. And I mean each and every one.

My alpha readers Amy and Katie – Y'all. I know this one was a doozy. Y'all kept saying I was writing it quickly, but it felt slow, disjointed, and a hot mess, despite the fact it was in a condensed window. Your comments and love for Raffi and Tori filled my heart with such warmth and joy. On days we don't chat, things feel quiet, I love our chaotic group chat and your ability to keep me on task when I need to be. Thank you both so much.

Megan (and the staff of The Prom Cafe in Larne) – Almost every Monday without fail, Karina and I land in on you guys at nine. Most days we leave around lunch time, but some days we're in for the long-haul and don't leave until three. You've never made us feel bad for stinking up the place (I'm usually post-gym sweaty), or for taking up space, and we always get the most delicious food and atmosphere to write our books. Thanks for not kicking us out!

Mariann, Laura (and the staff of Springsteens in Carrickfergus) – At least once a month I land in on you guys on a Sunday morning, (around an hour ahead of when I need to meet whoever it is I've planned to meet on that day.) Thankfully table 4 has always been empty, and I've never needed to throw hands at someone for taking my seat, but you always just let me sit there and do my thing, bringing me buckets of tea (and forgiving me for asking your names after like, a year of coming to Springsteens.) Thanks for everything!

My proofreader – Corinne. You've been with me from the start, and you still haven't flipped your lid at my distinct lack of improvement over dangling modifiers. I think if I started fixing them at this point you'd think I've been abducted, so it's just better for everyone if I leave them for you to fix. Forever thankful for your support and encouragement.

My editor—Editor Jess, I write these acknowledgements before you get your paws on my words so I always end up writing them with a ball of anxiety in my stomach. Just how much is she gonna make me cry this time? Did I grow, even just a wee bit, on last time? Is this going to be the MS that breaks the editor's back, and I'm out on my ear looking for a new editor?

The fear is real, girl.

And every time your edits push me a little further, a little harder, and make me laugh every single time. Working with you is one of my favorite parts of this job, and I'm forever thankful for your talents and lessons.

Even if I don't always put them into practice.

My cover designer—Kate Farlow over at *Y'all That Graphic* for bringing my boys to life on the covers.

And finally, to my ARC readers, my Facebook reader group *Margaritas, Men, and Mischief with Lasairiona*, and to each and every one of you who pick up this book: a bazillion thank yous. I truly hope you loved it enough to pick up the next one. Tell your friends! And if you're not in my group—come join us, we don't bite (unless you ask us to!).

About the Author

Lasairiona McMaster writes sassy, classy and badassy women and strong, yet vulnerable men. She challenges reader's expectations by openly dealing with mental health issues, often exploring tough-to-handle topics and 'taboos' and books with a whole lotta heart.

She can either be found enjoying a gin and lemonade by the Irish sea, or baking sweet treats in her kitchen while singing at the top of her lungs. When she's 'home' in Texas, and isn't eating fresh-popped popcorn while buying things she has absolutely no need for in Target, she can be found at Chuys eating her body weight in chips and queso and washing it down with a margarita swirl. She loves to make friends out of strangers.